A MARINER OF
ENGLAND

The wandering sailor ploughs the main
A competence in life to gain:
Undaunted braves the stormy seas,
To find at last content and ease,
In hopes when toil and danger's o'er,
To anchor on his native shore.

A MARINER OF ENGLAND

AN ACCOUNT OF THE CAREER OF WILLIAM RICHARDSON FROM CABIN BOY IN THE MERCHANT SERVICE TO WARRANT OFFICER IN THE ROYAL NAVY [1780 to 1819] AS TOLD BY HIMSELF

EDITED BY

COLONEL SPENCER CHILDERS
C.B., R.E.

LONDON
JOHN MURRAY, ALBEMARLE STREET, W.
1908

PREFACE

IN the account of his career which William Richardson gives in these pages we have, what we seldom get elsewhere, a picture at first hand and from the point of view of an ordinary seaman of life in the Navy and merchant service during the great period.

Through the courtesy of Admiral King Hall, C.V.O., and Staff-Surgeon George Bishop, R.N. (the latter of whom inherited these papers from his grandfather, who was a nephew of Richardson), I have been permitted to examine Richardson's lengthy journal, and select such parts of it as seem worthy of publication. Richardson's style is simple and straightforward, and his language has been left as it is; he tells his tale in his own way; he writes pertinently, and makes shrewd comments; he not only tells us of the handling of ships in old times under difficult and dangerous circumstances, but he also gives some extremely interesting experiences in naval warfare. We have a graphic account of Sir Richard Strachan's victory in the Bay over the French ships-of-the-line which were escaping after Trafalgar, and a telling description of the affair in the Basque Roads, where he—as a gunner—had a good deal to do with the fire-ships [though he does not take Lord Dundonald's view of Lord Gambier]. Again, in his accounts of his early voyages in the merchant service, a lurid light is thrown on the trade in slaves on the Guinea coast. Richardson does not really like the business, but he is not so much ashamed of it as one would wish him to be. We get also an account of one of the earliest attempts to construct a submarine mine in the British Navy.

Considering he had been twice the victim of the press-gang, he appears less hostile to that system than might have been expected, though he bitterly complains that pressed-men, after returning from a long voyage, were seldom allowed liberty, with the result that they were so ready to desert, and so often became their country's enemies.

It is difficult nowadays to realise the state of affairs produced by the press-gang. It is recorded in James's " Naval History " that every seaman on board the United States' frigate *Macedonian*, when she was captured, had served from five to twelve years in a British man-of-war. One of her guns was called the " Victory," because its crew had served under Lord Nelson in that ship ; another was called the " Nelson," because its gun's crew had belonged to his barge. And Sir Thomas Troubridge, when a Lord of the Admiralty, stated that our seamen went direct from Portsmouth to join the French fleet in Brest.

Of Richardson's family there are not many records : he came of a stock bred to the sea ; he believed that his father was present at the taking of Havanna, and continued to go to sea until his death. Richardson's four brothers all served in the Navy. He himself lived to a great age, dying at Portsmouth when about ninety-seven years old. Dr. Bishop records of him that "after his wife's death he took down his bedstead, and slung a hammock in his bedroom for the rest of his life."

Altogether this tough old salt was a fine specimen of those Mariners of England to whose services we owe much of our naval supremacy, and doubtless it was to seamen of Richardson's type and character that the old adage mentioned by Nelson was meant to apply:

" Aft the most honour, forward the better man."

SPENCER CHILDERS.

30, ELM PARK GARDENS,
1908.

CONTENTS

CHAPTER IV

1791–92

CALCUTTA AND THE BAY OF BENGAL

CHAPTER V

1793–95

IN THE KING'S SERVICE

CONTENTS

CHAPTER VI

1795–97

WITH SIR RALPH ABERCROMBY'S EXPEDITION TO ST. LUCIA, ETC.

CHAPTER VII

1797–99

IN H.M.S. "PROMPTE" IN THE WEST INDIES

CHAPTER VIII

1799–1802

AT MARTINIQUE IN H.M.S. "TROMP"

CHAPTER IX

1803–06

SIR RICHARD STRACHAN'S VICTORY

CHAPTER X

1808–09

WITH STOPFORD IN THE BASQUE ROADS

CONTENTS

CHAPTER XI

1809

THE WALCHEREN EXPEDITION

CHAPTER XII

1810–19

LISBON AND THE PENINSULAR WAR

THE PREFACE OF WILLIAM RICHARDSON

THE adventures of a sailor, whether in the peaceful employ of trade or fighting his country's foes, must be interesting to his friends at home, who live, as it were, safe under their vine and fig trees, which his labour or exertions contribute so much to protect and secure.

I have for many years and at different times made memorandums of the chief occurrences which have happened during my pilgrimage in this world, and together with a strong memory to help me, I now put together these pages for my friends' amusement, and which they may depend on as real facts and without any exaggeration whatever.

A Mariner of England

CHAPTER I

1768-85

A LAD IN THE MERCHANT SERVICE

Birth and early years—At Boldon School—Goes to sea with his
father—Makes several voyages in the coal trade between Shields
and London—also many to the North Sea and Baltic, and to
Archangel.

I, WILLIAM RICHARDSON, the author of this narrative,
was born in South Shields, in the county of Durham, and
baptized at the parish church there on July 22, 1768. My
father was a native of Portsoy, in Banffshire, who left his
home when young ; I have heard that he was at the taking
of the Havanna. However, be that as it may, he came to
Shields, got the command of a ship, and married there.

My mother was a native of Shields (her maiden name
was Tully), where many respectable families of that name
are living now ; my parents had seven children in the
following order, Margaret, myself, John, Robert, James,
Ann, and George, all good old English names, and my
father being in good circumstances we were all cheerful,
contented, and happy.

At an early age I was put to school, but made little
progress in learning, the reason being that my mother

would shift me from one school to another whenever I took a fancy to be displeased with my schoolmaster, so that I was in a fair way of becoming a dunce; but my father, in returning from one of his voyages, took me to task, and finding how little I had learnt, adopted the wise resolution of sending me off to a boarding school in the country, where I would be under stricter discipline, and saved from being spoiled by too much indulgence from my tender mother.

I was accordingly soon after sent off to a village named West Boldon, near five miles to the south-west of Shields, and to a schoolmaster named Emerson, a sharp hand and said to be one of the first mathematicians of the age. At my arrival he had as many boarders as he could accommodate, so I was recommended to another house, kept by one Joseph Cooper, who had already about a dozen boarders, some from Shields and others from Sunderland.

Old Cooper's family consisted of himself (a cripple), his wife, and two grown-up strapping daughters : he was a crabbed old fellow, and many a rap we got from his crutch when making a noise near the fireside in winter evenings. His elder daughter, Nanny, was of the same stamp, and kept us all under subjection, but the old lady and the younger daughter, Molly, were kinder-hearted.

I had not been long here ere my father came to see me, and brought with him a boy from London to be educated. His name was Robert Errington, and he was taken in to board at Cooper's with us. He was far from being a bashful boy, and was soon hand in glove with us all; but being a wild chap, he soon got into scrapes. He had several battles for the honour of London, because the boys called him a Cockney; but he generally came off second best, as he could not stand long before the hardy lads of this country. He would sometimes swear, which shocked us, and would go to a public-house and call for beer, and without any shame, and then he was declared to be a proper Londoner; and yet he was very good-tempered withal, and it was well the schoolmaster, or Nanny Cooper, knew nothing of his habits, or they would have soon corrected him to better manners.

I remained at Boldon School near three years, and improved much in my education, but as Mr. Emerson did not teach navigation, I was taken away to learn it at Shields; so I left Boldon—a clean, pleasant, and healthy village, but with no trade. The inhabitants were chiefly of the agricultural class, and there was neither baker, butcher, doctor, nor lawyer living in the place: the people baked their own bread, and when they wanted beef joined together and bought a bullock, killed it themselves and shared it out; part they eat fresh, a part was salted, and another part they made hung beef of, which keeps a long time; while as for grocery and things of that kind, they sent a man on horseback every Saturday to Sunderland, who brought what was wanted.

I have great reason to be thankful for the good impression of moral and religious feelings stamped on my mind at Boldon, and (together with my education) it certainly was the best and most innocent period of my life, and one on which I have often meditated with great satisfaction.

The schoolmaster at Shields that I was put to had taught most captains of the place navigation; but he was now feeble and emaciated through age and dram-drinking, so that the scholars would sometimes mutiny and turn him out of the school. I remained with him about a year, and got on with navigation as well as I could under such a master.

I had now fixed my mind on following a sailor's life (contrary to the wishes of my mother), and went a trial voyage in the *Ravensworth* with my father to London. The vessel sailed in the night, but I slept so sound I heard nothing of the bustle that was going on : judge therefore of my surprise in the morning, when I went on deck, to see the ocean around me like a sheet of glass.   It was a lovely morning, and the vessels all around nearly becalmed, with smoky Shields and Tynemouth Castle on our right hand and a number of boats rowing about ; all appeared like another world to me, and little did I then think of or know the many dangers and difficulties I should have to encounter on that dangerous element.

My pleasure was of short duration, for when I went down to the cabin to breakfast I began to feel qualmish, and could not eat, and secretly wished myself on shore again.   However, we had a fine passage to London, and when we got moored in the Pool my father hailed a wherry, which was to land me at King James's Stairs, whence I was to go up Wapping a little, and on the left hand inquire for a Mr. Horsley, who kept a spirit store there, and make myself known to him.

I had no sooner set my feet on King James's Stairs than whom should I meet with but Bob Errington, who had been my schoolfellow at Boldon, and glad we were to see each other again ; he was just going to hire a wherry to see a line-of-battleship launched somewhere on the river, but he gave that up and took me to his home, which was the very place my father had directed me to go to.   Mr. Horsley was his uncle, and in good circumstances, and Bob being a favourite of his (he having, though a comely wife, no children) 'twas said that Bob would inherit all his property ; however, suffice it to say London had spoiled Bob again.   His uncle, after this, to get him out of bad company, gave him the command of a ship and sent him to sea ; but all would not do, for with bad company and bad women he soon brought himself to a premature end.

I resided with the Horsleys until the *Ravensworth*

was ready to sail. They entreated me much to remain with them until my father returned on another voyage, but they could not prevail : I did not like London, and I longed to see my mother again.

On our passage down, and off Flamborough Head, we saw a cutter privateer in the offing and steering towards us. It being war time, we immediately cleared away for action. We had six guns, and four of them we could fight on one side. They were on the 'tween decks, so we laid the gratings over and led the braces through the holes to work them below ; besides we had an iron tiller, which we shipped in the cabin, and we had loopholes through the coamings of the hatchways to fire small arms through ; so we could fight, steer, and trim the sails below without a man on the upper deck.

Being thus prepared we waited boldly for her, and she soon came and passed so close ahead that we thought she would have carried away our jib boom; so my father hailed, and said that if they did not keep farther off he would fire into them. Their answer was " Fire and be damned ! "

Whether it was that a fleet of light colliers were coming up astern, or seeing our resolution, or thinking it not worth the trouble of attacking a light collier, I don't know, for she kept on her course towards the land and left us. She mounted ten guns and her decks were full of men. Soon after this we arrived at Shields, and glad was I to see my mother again. I remained at home a short time, and would gladly, if I could, have found an excuse from going to sea again ; but I had always said that I would be nothing but a sailor, and I could not for shame refuse when my father asked me to make another trial voyage with him. I made two, but did not mess in the cabin, as before. I was made to shift as the other boys—" to initiate me in," as my father said. Mr. Craddock, now a

Master in the Navy, was one of the boys with us at this time.

After these three voyages my father had me bound apprentice for seven years to a Captain Stephen Atkinson, who commanded (and owned with his father) the ship *Forester.* I was to have £25 for my seven years' service, and at the expiration of that time to be a freeman of Newcastle, Captain Atkinson being a freeman of that place though my father was not. The date of my indentures was January 16, 1781 ; and now, like a young bear, my troubles first began.

My master was rather short, but lusty, and of a dark complexion. He wore his long black hair hanging loose and in curls behind, as was the fashion ; he was a well-disposed man, but passionate, and had an education superior to most captains out of that place. His ship was about 350 tons burden, very old, but a good sea boat. There were near a dozen apprentices belonging to her, but some of them only for three years and high wages, men being scarce and it being war time, and one of the boys that served his apprenticeship in her with me was in 1807 a post captain,[1] and commanded a line-of-battleship in H.M. Navy.

Our ship was at this time laid up for the winter, and I went to the Trinity School at Newcastle, where I improved myself in navigation.

In the spring of this year (1781) we fitted out our ship and made a coal voyage to London ; our captain being acquainted, and often a visitor, with our family, of course I was treated well ; we then loaded with coals for Lubeck in the Baltic, but as England was at this time at war with America, France, Spain, and Holland, we durst not venture across the North Sea without a convoy. After

[1] He died at Bognor a rear-admiral in 1845, aged 73 years. His name was Samuel Jackson.

waiting some days all ready for sea, one Sunday morning, as we were cleaning ourselves to spend the day on shore with our friends, the captain and pilot came on board in a great hurry and gave orders for the ship to be unmoored immediately and proceed to sea, for the *Artois* frigate, Captain Macbride, had been seen in the offing, steering to the northward with the signal for the Baltic convoy flying at her mast-head.

All was now hurry and bustle and inward grumbling, wishing Macbride far enough for disturbing us at this time; we soon had the ship under way, got over the bar, discharged the pilot, and, the wind being fair, we steered away to the northward after the frigate with all the sail we could carry. In the middle of the night our main top-mast went over the side and kept all us hands employed until daylight; before night we came to anchor in Leith Roads, where we found the *Artois* lying with a few other vessels.

We lay here several weeks, and many other ships daily arriving, the captains of them having little or nothing to do but visit and revisit one another, the bad corrupted the good, and our captain got spoiled among them. I was at this time made cabin-boy, a situation far from being agreeable, having to do the duty of steward, butler, waiter, shoeblack, etc., besides keeping the cabin and furniture clean and in good order, and often got more kicks than halfpence, and a specimen of it was as follows.

One night after ten o'clock the captain and mate, having finished smoking their pipes, retired to bed, and I, who had been waiting, half asleep, in the steerage, was called to clear away the table and see the fire safe out in the cabin stove. This done, I retired to my hammock; but had not been long there before the cabin bell rang, and I went to know what was wanted. The captain asked me if the fire was safe out, as he smelt something burning, so I looked and told him it was, and went to my hammock again.

This was done a second time, and the third time he rang the bell so violently that I expected a squall. He got up himself, ordered me to strike a light and light a candle. We then searched all round the cabin, but could see no signs of fire until he opened the table drawer, and there it was.

In the table drawer were always put the tablecloth, knives and forks, spoons, and their pipes when done smoking. Now, one of the pipes had not been smoked out, and the fire was left burning in it, which burnt a hole in the tablecloth and made the smell. Now, the fault must have been their own in not extinguishing their pipes when done with, and again in allowing pipes to be put into such an improper place. However, I got the blame, the captain flew into a passion, knocked me down on the deck, and kicked me in a most brutal manner.

Next morning when I went into the cabin I expected a good scolding, but strange to say he never alluded to the business and was unusually kind, and I was told that was always his way after quarrelling with anybody. I remained his cabin-boy without a quarrel (except once about a cat) for fourteen months, and then got superseded by another boy, an apprentice, much to my satisfaction.

After lying here six weeks the signal was made from the *Artois* for sailing, but before we got out of the Firth we were recalled again by a report that the Dutch fleet were at sea; we sailed a second time, and were recalled in the same manner, and so apprehensive were we of a visit from them that orders were issued that when they made their appearance, our ships were to cut their cables and run up the Firth as far as we could.

[N.B.—Our Ministers must have had bad intelligence, for

the whole care of the Dutch fleet was to convoy a fleet of their own merchantmen up to the Baltic.]

At this time our homeward-bound West India fleet were compelled to go north, and put in here to avoid the French fleet that were cruising in the Channel; such a situation was poor England in at this time! All the ships now collected here numbered more than four hundred sail, and notwithstanding the great consumption of provisions drawn from the markets, to the honour of old Scotia they never rose the market price during that time.

At last, after lying here near ten weeks, a squadron, under the command of Rear-Admiral Hyde Parker, arrived to convoy us across the North Sea to the Baltic.

Thousands of people came off in boats to see these ships, particularly the three-decker, which they called the "muckle war ship."

After the squadron had watered we took our final departure, and had a pleasant passage across the North Sea, when the admiral left us to proceed on under the *Belle Poule*, and in search, with the rest of the squadron, of the Dutch Fleet which was supposed to be near. They soon met each other; the enemy consisting of eight two-deckers under the command of Admiral Zoutman. A desperate action ensued for nearly four hours, until both squadrons became unmanageable and they left off, both sides claiming the victory, but no ship taken on either side. One of the Dutch ships, a 74, sank next day on the Dogger Bank, and their fleet was prevented that year from going to the Baltic, which was a great loss to their trade. This was called the Dogger Bank action, and fought on August 5, 1781.

We arrived all well at Elsinore, and there came to anchor and to clear at the Custom House. We then laid in a stock of tea, sugar, and gin, which are very cheap here, and then proceeded alone for Lubeck; but when we got near the coast found the water so shallow that we had to anchor, and deliver out coals near four miles from Tarmoon, a place near twenty miles from Lubeck.

The coals we delivered into bilanders, which carried them to Lubeck, and we then took in sand for ballast, brought off in boats carrying a ton each, the people throwing it into the ship with their paddles; we then got under way and steered for Petersburg at the other extremity of the Baltic, and arriving at Cronstadt got the ship into the Mole to take in our cargo of iron, hemp, and tallow. Petersburg is twenty miles higher up the river, but the water is too shallow for ships of burden to load there.

Cronstadt Mole is a snug place to lie in, and large enough to hold more than four hundred sail of shipping, which lie in tiers moored to large, strong piles.

The Russians here are a hardy, dirty set of people, and wear their beards, except the soldiers. Each ship has a gang of Russians to assist in loading the ship; and although fresh beef is only at the rate of a penny a pound they could not afford to buy it, their common food being a piece of black bread, named rusk, with an onion or cucumber, and bit of salt, with which they seemed contented, especially if they can get a little train oil to rub over their bread.

There is a ketch-rigged vessel lying here as guard ship, and her Russian captain goes by the name of Tom Oazly; he takes cognisance of all offences committed in the Mole. Nothing can frighten a poor Russian more than threatening to take him to Tom Oazly; and, indeed, other people are not much less apprehensive, for he is a terror to all.

The days are very long here in summer, being near nineteen hours, and as the ships' companies work from sunrise to sunset, and then have to wet the decks to keep them from rending, and get their suppers, they have very little rest. I have often slept on a chest, being too weary to pull my clothes off.

Having taken in all our lading, we took our departure for Hull, in Yorkshire, to deliver our cargo, but soon met with stormy weather in the Baltic Sea, and were nearly driven on shore on the Island of Oland; and off Bernholm we had such a severe storm that we could not carry an inch of sail, and were compelled to let the ship drive as the winds and waves drove her; however, thank God, it did not continue long, and when it abated the wind came in our favour and we soon had the ship under a crowd of sail and passed a large Dutch ship going the same way as we were, but only setting his close-reefed topsails and foresail. It is a common saying among sailors that the Dutch, though they do not hurry themselves in carrying much sail, yet generally get on in their voyage as soon as others.

In passing between Falsterbo and Drago, on entering the Sound, we observed many wrecks on the shore, and passed between as many deals floating about as would have loaded a ship of our size. Soon after we came to anchor at Elsinore, where we found many ships, mostly English, waiting for a convoy (this being a Danish port, was neutral); and the next day arrived the Dutchman that we had passed, thinking he would have been a week in coming.

After lying here some days and collecting a good stock of tea, sugar, and gin, H.M.S. *Africa*, of 64 guns, and the *Lord Amherst*, sloop of war, arrived, and took all the English ships under their convoy. We had a tolerable passage out of the Cattegat, but on entering into the North Sea a storm came against us which dispersed the whole convoy, and each made the best of its way for shelter in Norway. We got into a port named Fleckery

[? Flekkerfiord] where we found several ships had arrived before us, but neither of the ships of war.

After lying here a few days the wind came fair, and we put to sea, contrary to the wishes of the pilot, who said this wind would not continue long; and he was right, for the next afternoon the wind shifted to the westward, and with the scud flying over our heads and the sea beginning to rise, the oldest hands on board predicted a heavy storm coming.

We soon found the effects of it. At midnight it blew a hurricane, with torrents of rain and dark as pitch: many were the cries of distress heard that night; one of the convoy foundered close to the *Africa*, who could render them no assistance. Early in the morning the gale abated suddenly, and at daybreak we found ourselves near a large brig lying on her beam ends with fore and main topmast gone, her boats gone, and not a soul to be seen on board. As it was still windy and the sea high, we were glad to keep clear of her, and seeing nothing of our commodore we bore up again for Norway, and got into a port named Eastrice [? Egersund] where we found several of the convoy, but the commodore and others got into Fleckery, a short distance off.

When the wind came fair we put to sea, but were soon driven back for the third time, and to make matters worse the weather began to set in cold and our provisions to get short, and all the little we could get from the shore in this poor country was bread like cowdung, but no beef; and we often thought of Old England, that blessed land of plenty, of which every Briton ought to know the value. There were plenty of large oysters and lobsters here, but the difficulty was how to get at them.

At last the wind came to the north-east with a clear sky, which gave hopes of its lasting, so we put to sea again, but had to leave one of our best men behind to get cured of a severe wound in the hand by the bursting of a musket in firing at seagulls. We had not got more than half way across the North Sea before the old westerly gales came on again ; the convoy soon got dispersed, and it being too far off to bear up for Norway, we continued on, taking advantage of every change of wind in our favour, until we had hardly a sail but what had been split, and seldom saw any more of the convoy.

Out of our original crew (twenty-one) eight were frost-bitten and incapable of duty, another had a fever, and the one left at Norway reduced us to eleven to work the ship in this stormy weather. Our diet was bad too, and often eaten raw, as the sea broke off all intercourse with the cook-house by washing over the ship so often, and we were nearly worn to death.

I being cabin boy, was often sent to the wheel to relieve the man there, and to assist the others in tacking and wearing the ship, and often have I expected to have some of my limbs broken, or to have been thrown over-board by the wheel when a heavy wave struck against the rudder, which made it fly round like wildfire sometimes, but then I was always ordered to let it go at the time and stand clear of it.

At last kind Providence favoured us with the wind from the north-west, and we got sight of the Yorkshire coast. We soon after got into the Humber, where we found the *Lord Amherst* sloop-of-war lying, but not another of the convoy. They had been driven more to the northward, with much loss : some had got into Shields and others into Leith Roads.

We got a pilot here, who took the ship up to Hull, where we moored her snug in the wet dock ; here we got a supply of good provisions, and sent our invalids on shore under the care of a medical gentleman, where they soon recovered. By the frost one had a toe so mortified that it had to undergo amputation.   Poor fellows! they had undergone great misery, and the only relief they got, though small, was by rubbing the parts with lamp oil.

I had by this time got so weaned from home that I thought my parents must have forgotten me, and never wrote to inform them of my arrival; but I soon had an unexpected visit from my father, whose vessel had put into the Humber by contrary winds.   He came up in his boat to see me, but could not stop long; so giving me some money and half a large cheese to carry home, departed.

In delivering our cargo we found much of the hemp damaged, and no wonder, by such weather as we had endured.   We then took in ballast, left this pleasant place, and soon after arrived at Shields after a tedious and long voyage of nine months.   The ship had hardly got into the harbour before a bundle of clothes came alongside for me, sent by my kind and affectionate mother.   We laid the ship alongside of Cookson's Quay, unbent the sails, unrove the running rigging, stowed them all safe away below, locked the hatches up, and laid her up for the remainder of the winter; and we apprentices had leave to go to our homes until wanted again, and the foremast men were discharged.

Previous to this our captain had been courting a young lady of South Shields, daughter of a Master in the Royal Navy named Roughhead, and a rough head he had; but the daughter was the reverse: she was fat, fair, and comely.   I knew her well, as she lived near us.   However, during some months of the courtship our captain had not been altogether of a sane mind; sometimes he would come on board at late hours in the night, rouse us boys up, send us aloft to scrape the masts, loose the topgallant sails, and make us furl them over and over again.   At last we took heart, and made so much noise in doing it as to disturb the people on board the other ships that lay near us, who came up out of their beds to know what was the matter, so he left this off.

Soon after this he got married to Miss Roughhead, and became altogether another man and a better, took a house in Silver Street at Newcastle and a female servant, and, as the ship was still laid up, I lived with him and assisted Betty to do the housework.

In the spring of 1783 (being blessed with peace with all our enemies, and having fitted our ship without fear of being taken by our foes) we proceeded in ballast for Wyburg, in Finland, for a cargo of deals. We had a pretty good passage until our arrival in the Gulf, when a gale came on against us, so we put into a place on the Livonian side and came to anchor.

When the gale abated we put to sea, and soon after got a Finland pilot on board, who conducted us between rocks, some above and some under water, through a most intricate channel for near fifty miles, until we arrived at Wyburg; but it was a sad job for the pilot, for in passing the guard ship we forgot to hoist our colours. The poor pilot was sent for, and got such a severe punishment with the knout that we were told he died in a few days afterwards.

We soon got in our lading of large deals, not only the ship's hold but her decks likewise full, and put to sea. In beating down the Gulf one day in hazy weather our captain took notice of the ship's dog snuffing the wind and looking to windward. "Get a cast of the lead," says he, "for I think the dog smells land." This was no sooner done than we found the ship in shallow water. She was put about instantly, and the water deepened; and thus was the ship perhaps saved by a poor dog.

We arrived safe at Newcastle, delivered our deals there, and then took in coals again for Petersburg, where we arrived, delivered our coals in Cronstadt Mole, and then began to load with iron, hemp, and tallow again. Here was Tom Oazly, with all his power; here were barbers rowing about in little boats crying out, "*Pora macula*" ("who wants to be shaved?"), and other little boats rowed by women selling their bread and milk.

After completing our lading we put to sea, and proceeded down the Gulf; but soon met with such stormy weather that we ran under the lee of the Island of Gotland and there came to anchor. Our captain went on shore to buy stock, but found the inhabitants so poor that they had only milk and a few fowls to dispose of. Every house had a large dog or two, to keep off the bears, that come from the Continent in winter when the Baltic Sea is frozen over, as it is not totally salt, the water being only brackish.

When the gale was over we got under way, and had a tolerable passage to Newcastle, having been only three months on this voyage, whereas we had been nine on the former. We delivered our cargo alongside of the quay, and then laid the ship up for the winter.

Early next year (1784) we fitted the ship out again, and made several voyages in the coal trade to London until about July, when we got a freight to load with tar at Archangel; but before we sailed we hauled our ship on the beach to examine her bottom and caulk her all over, in doing which many rotten places were found and filled up. One caulker declared that in hitting his caulking-iron it went through and fell between the timbers. This frightened our foremast men, and they left the ship; for it was said it was too late in the year to go such a voyage. However, we got manned at last, and put to sea in ballast, and soon met the Greenland ships returning home.

After this it began to blow hard, but the wind was in

our favour, and we passed round the lofty and dismal North Cape, covered with snow. It lies in the latitude of 72° 10′ N., and the sun above the horizon at twelve o'clock at night, consequently it was visible all the twenty-four hours round. We then steered along the coast of Lapland, and passed a town named Wardhuys [Vardöhuus]. It is surprising how people can live in such a cold country in winter.

When we got into the White Sea it became so hot that the air was filled with millions of mosquitoes, and when we got to Archangel it was the same. What with short, hot summers and dreary, long, cold winters, this must be a most dismal country to live in. We soon got our ballast out, and began to load; but a gang of Russian caulkers had previously come on board and caulked all the ceiling and then paid it over with clay. This was to prevent the tar which leaked out of the casks from getting to the pumps; but it was all in vain, for it did not prevent it.

The tar is brought from a great distance in the interior in large flat prams containing a thousand barrels each; sixteen hundred filled our ship, and then we left this unpleasant place for a more unpleasant passage home.

On returning round the North Cape the days were short and cold and severe, the sleet sticking to the ropes like ice.

When we reached the Highland coast of Scotland a severe gale came against us; so we bore up and ran into Lerwick, a port in Shetland, where we lay a week. It has a small town with a church, but the inhabitants are very poor, having little to dispose of except eggs and fish, which they barter for old clothes. When the gale abated we put to sea again, though the wind was against us. Being anxious to get home, as the tar leaked so much out of the barrels, we pushed on against wind and weather until we arrived at Shields, where we laid her alongside of a quay on the south side to deliver our cargo.

I never remember being so anxious in getting on shore to see my mother again, as at this time. I never met with a greater shock. When I entered the house I perceived the family were in mourning, and, inquiring the cause, was told that my poor mother had departed this life six weeks ago. I thought it impossible, and went up to her bedroom ; but she was not there. I came down again almost distracted, then sat down and wept bitterly, but I could not rest—went out, and then on board, wept in silence, and thought I should never know happiness again.

Our family after this began to separate. My father got the command of the *Favourite*, a ship of 1,000 tons, which sailed from Hull, in the Archangel trade, and we seldom saw him. My eldest sister Margaret supplied the place of a mother, and took charge of the two youngest, George and Ann.

CHAPTER II

1785-89

FROM APPRENTICE TO SECOND MATE

To Gibraltar and Arzeu (in Barbary)—Visit of a Moorish Prince—
Fracas at Cadiz—To Memel and back to Corunna—Coal voyage
to Cartagena and La Matt—At Philadelphia on July 4—Return
to Spain—Bull baiting at Santander—Promoted to be second
mate—Bordeaux to Philadelphia—Leaves the *Forester*—The
captain gets him detained in jail—Last voyage in the *Forester*—
Makes thirteen voyages between Shields and London in 1789—
Death of his sister—His family dispersed.

EARLY in the year 1785, our ship not having been laid
up, we made a voyage to London, and on our return were
ordered off to Memel, in Prussia, for a cargo of timber
to deliver at Lynn, in Norfolk. On our arrival at Memel
we delivered our ballast on the quay, where stood a high
pole, erected with a human skull with the hair on at the
top of it; on inquiry we were told that it belonged to a
beautiful lady of quality, who had perished on the rack for
the murder of her infant child.

Up to this time our captain, as was the custom, had
worn his hair in curls, and loose behind his ears; but one
of these days he came on board with his hair tied in
a queue, and looked so strange that he did not seem like
the same person; this was the first time that tails came
into fashion.

We took our timber to Lynn, delivered it there, and
returned to Shields, where we took in a cargo of coals

to carry to Marseilles in the Mediterranean; on arriving there we got the ship into the mole and moored her with her head to the quay, and in front of a row of fine lofty coffee-houses, where we could get a good breakfast of coffee and fine bread for threepence; fruit was abundant, and the finest grapes I ever saw, and everything cheap. This city is very populous, has a good trade, and a mixture of all nations here; murders are frequent, and when a dead corpse is found it is taken to the quay-side and covered with a white cloth; an old woman sits by it until she has collected enough alms for its interment.

There is a vessel lying here named the *Noah's Ark*, and when any delinquents are taken up as disorderly they are put on board her, and into a place where they must pump for a certain time, or sink.

When our coals were delivered we took in near three hundred bags of nutgalls by way of ballast, then loaded up with cotton and sarsaparilla for London, and left this pleasant place.

Early in 1786 we loaded with coals and took them to Gibraltar, where I became involved in the following scrape: after the coals were delivered we boys were sent into the hold to sweep it clean fore and aft, and one of our party, a keen, old-fashioned Scotch lad, was employed sweeping close under the cabin deck; knowing that the captain was on shore, he took the liberty to lift up the cabin scuttle, and beheld in the cabin close to him a cask of Blackstrap with a cock in it; he soon got a quart pot, filled it, and put the scuttle down again; he praised it up and said how good it was, and got the rest of us to take part of the wine with him. How long we continued at this is impossible for me to tell, but the mate not hearing any noise, as there generally is when boys are working together, called down to know what we were about, and, receiving no answer, came down himself, and there found us lying on our backs drunk, and vomiting on each other; he called the foremast men down to have a look at us, and it was fine fun for them to see how simple and foolish we looked.

On another occasion we should have got a good rope's-ending, for boys at this time in the North-country ships were cruelly used by the men, and the word and the blow generally came together; but the mate thought our crime so bad that he left it to the captain to punish us; and when the latter came on board and was informed of it, he told us it was so serious a crime that he would have us tried by the civil law, which would perhaps hang us.

I believe he only said this to frighten us, and which made us very uneasy, and had an opportunity offered to desert, we should certainly have embraced it; but the ballast coming alongside that night, together with fifty barrels of gunpowder, and some pigs of lead which we took in, we sailed for a place on the coast of Barbary named Arzeu, laying between Algiers and Oran, which eased us of our apprehensions; but I took such a disgust at wine after this that it was a long time before I could bear the taste of it.

We were told before we sailed that Arzeu was a wild place, and infested with lions and other wild animals, and never to be on shore between sunset and sunrise, as that is the time they come out in search of prey. We had a Minorca gentleman on board to manage our affairs as supercargo; his name was Taw—a good kind of man, who spoke English fluently, and understood some of the Moorish dialect; but the Jews manage the trading business for the Moors.

We arrived safe in Arzeu Bay—supposed to be the ancient Arsinaria—and came to anchor near a sandy beach, where the water was so clear that we could see the anchor at the bottom. The interior was mountainous, but, near the sea, level ground covered with brushwood, with not so much as a hut or any living being to be seen. But a day or two after our arrival we saw two animals at a distance coming swiftly along the shore towards us, and concluded they were lions; but as they came nearer we made them out to be two men on horseback, and when they came abreast of the ship they stopped.

Mr. Taw was sent on shore in the boat, and, after having some conversation with them, mounted behind one of them, and having ordered the boat to return on board, they set off at a gallop, and were soon out of sight.

We lay here near a fortnight without having any tidings from him, which made us very uneasy. But during that time we were not idle : a party of us were employed every day on shore in cutting brushwood, which grew higher than our heads ; it was for " dunnaging " the hold—that is, laying wood under the cargo to keep it from the wet in the ship's bottom. Here were the tracks of the wild beasts plainly seen, and here we met with a regularly built stone well with two troughs of hewn stone by the side of it. Three land tortoises were clinging to the sides of the well, so we got one of the boat's oars and put it down, by which we caught the three tortoises and found about four feet depth of excellent water and the well about ten feet deep : this was the only place fresh water was found on the coast, and evidently was where the animals quenched their thirst, for often during our stay we had filled the troughs and found them empty in the morning; but how the animals got at the water in the well I know not. A lion might jump in and spring out again and others perhaps by their claws.

One afternoon, after being here a fortnight, we were alarmed at hearing a noise between us and the beach, and on peeping through the bushes saw marching along a

Moorish prince with a hundred others, all well mounted on horseback, and a long train of camels and bullocks laden with wheat, beeswax, and dates, and a great many sheep with their leaders coming up in the rear; but what gave us more pleasure was to see Mr. Taw, our supercargo, among them.

They soon halted abreast of our ship, and formed a camp with their tents, placed the cattle in the centre, and in the evening made three large fires, one in the centre and others outside, to frighten off the wild beasts; yet for all that a lion got into the camp at night, but the noise the soldiers made in getting their muskets ready alarmed it, and it escaped into the woods.

The gunpowder and lead we had brought from Gibraltar were a present for this Moorish prince; and, gunpowder being scarce here, he was so well satisfied that he ordered us to be supplied with beef, mutton, and soft bread, at his own expense, as long as we remained here. He came from the interior, from a place named Masagara,[1] said to be about thirty miles off, and there the gunpowder was immediately sent. We had so much trouble in managing their bullocks and their bad manner in slaying them that we gave them up. One of them one day ran away with us, and a pair of steering sail halyards that we were dragging him with down to the boat; and yet they are not large bullocks.

We now continued loading the ship (with corn, etc.) brought by the Moors from Masagara; but some accidents happened, for if they did not reach the camp before sunset ten to one they were attacked and some of their cattle carried off by wild beasts. One evening we heard cries of distress not far from our ship, and were sure some of them were in danger. The Prince sent a party of soldiers, who shot the lion; and by the skin, which I saw the next day, it

[1] Probably Mascara.

must have been twice the size I ever saw in the menageries in England. Those farmers who bring the corn are generally armed : if they fire and don't kill the lion their life is the sacrifice, but if they don't resist, the lion will not hurt the farmer but prefer one of the cattle. Several of the Moors lost their lives during this time, not being near enough to the camp to get assistance.

One of these days our captain was introduced to the Prince by one of the Jew merchants, and was very politely received into his tent. I had likewise the pleasure of seeing him too, for like great men he was not to be seen every day. He was about five feet seven inches in height, stout made, about the age of forty, marked much with smallpox ; but was too fair to be a Moor, so we concluded that he was a Turk, especially as he was dressed in the Turkish manner. We saw only one woman during our stay here : she was covered over from head to foot with something like a dirty blanket and two holes to see through ; she looked more like a hobgoblin than a human creature.

The French brig *Tartan*, arrived here to load, and I being alongside of her one day in our boat, found an Englishman belonging to her. I asked him how he liked the French service, and he said very well, but could not at first relish their manner of living ; so saying he took us to the cooking place and showed us a stewpan with live snails crawling in it, which they were going to stew. He said at first he could not bear the sight of them, but now he liked them as well as the Frenchmen : for my part I don't see why they should not be as eatable as periwinkles.

The *Tartan* and we being now laden with wheat, dates, and beeswax, the Prince broke up his camp, and they all departed for Masagara, leaving the place as naked as when we first arrived ; so we took our departure for Gibraltar, having on board two Jew merchants as passengers and Mr. Taw as supercargo, and the decks full of sheep, deer, poultry, and some cages of turtledoves.

At Gibraltar we received orders to proceed to Cadiz, and on our arrival there were put into quarantine for six weeks, yet this did not hinder us from delivering our cargo during that time; but not one of us was allowed to land, on pain of death. When the cargo was delivered we took in the salt, and then were permitted to land. Our passengers left us with Mr. Taw; but the Jews had concealed themselves, and entreated us sincerely not to expose them, as the Spaniards are very severe on them.

Cadiz is an ancient city, walled all round, and containing forty thousand inhabitants. It is so scarce of water (which is brought from St. Maries, on the other side of the bay) that it is sold by mule-drivers about the streets, even to so small a quantity as a glassful at a time. The houses are lofty, but the streets are narrow and dirty.

We took our departure from Cadiz laden with salt bound to Königsberg, in the Baltic. On our passage we suffered much for want of water, and what little we had was muddy and full of insects, so that we had to suck it through a handkerchief. Our captain said that when we got off Dover he would get a supply; but when we got there he would not stop, as the wind was favourable, so we pushed on, and in a few days after arrived at Pillau, the only place for delivering (and twenty miles from Königsberg, which lies higher up the river) where we anchored.

We left this clean little place in ballast, and went to Memel, another bar harbour, and we had to load outside exposed to the open sea. Here we loaded with spars as long as the hold of the ship, and put to sea, being bound for Corunna, in Spain. As soon as we had got all sail set and trimmed, the next order was, as usual, "rig the lee pump"; but all we could do, bucket after bucket poured down, we could not fetch her, so at last we hoisted her up, and found her broken in two pieces. We supposed it must have been done by one of the spars hitting it in getting them in, as our pump-well was not enclosed. However, we were in a poor mess, by having now only one pump and the Bay of Biscay to cross; but as necessity is the mother of invention, we set our heads to work and put the two parts together, nailed battens round to keep them together, then wound it round with tarred canvas and rope, and on putting it down again found it answered so well that it continued so all the voyage.

In crossing the bay we had a strong gale on our beam, which caused our old vessel to ship many seas, insomuch that we had to lash ourselves to the pumps for fear of being washed overboard; and the ship, being bound up with the long spars, was not near so lively as with another cargo. However, we, thank God! arrived safe at Corunna, where we delivered our cargo and took in ballast.

This done, we lay here idle two days, and wondered that our captain did not put to sea, he being always such a stirring hand for pushing forward; but we soon found out the reason for it. It was to smuggle money; and one night a large boat came alongside with boxes containing 40,000 dollars, which were no sooner on board than we up anchor and put to sea; but had we been caught at this work, we were liable to be made convicts and transported to the Spanish mines for life.

We put into Exmouth, and the dollars were sent to Exeter (being merchants' property); and here we lay near three weeks, little to do and often on shore, where our young men found plenty of sweethearts among the

Exmouth lasses, some of whom 'twas said could earn two guineas a week by lace-making—a fine chance for a sailor!—but before a match could be made we were hurried off to sea, and arrived at Shields, where we laid the old ship up a short time in the winter.

Early in 1787 we loaded with coals for Cartagena, in the Mediterranean, and on our arrival there found a squadron of Spanish men-of-war at anchor, under the command of Admiral Lanzara. The harbour is quite open to the southward, but it is remarked that the wind never blows hard here from that quarter. The land is high on each side, and there is a rock (just above water on the left hand in coming in) without any mark or beacon to show it. The principal dockyard the Spaniards have is here. We delivered our coals, took in ballast, proceeded higher up the Straits, and came to anchor at a place called La Matt, on the open coast, there being no harbour here. The town is a little insignificant place, and Alicante was in sight to the eastward, the land very mountainous; we came here for salt.

There are, 'tis said, five salt-ponds in this place, each yielding a different sort of salt, so we loaded with the coarsest and took our departure, our captain intending to steer for Ireland or America, whichever way the wind answered best for us when we got out of the Straits. When we got out, the wind being inclined to the northward, we steered away for Philadelphia.

Soon after this we met with three Algerine frigates, which brought us to. Our captain went on board with his pass, and took with him half of a large cheese, some biscuit, and a few bottles of wine as a present. The former they accepted, but not the wine; and, our pass being correct, we were ordered to depart. After getting a few miles from them their admiral made a signal, fired a gun, and came in pursuit of us again; but by this time it was getting dark, so we pushed on, and saw no more of them.

On our passage our beef began to get short, and in order to make it hold out another mess was ordered for us for breakfast, which was oatmeal and flour boiled together like hasty pudding, and some wine poured on the top as a substitute for butter: there was much grumbling at this at first, but in a few days we got reconciled to it, and liked nothing better.

Whenever we bent a new sail we gave it a good scrubbing to wash out of it the gum (which prevents the sail from getting mildewed), and one of these days we had scrubbed a new maintopgallant sail, and in bending it to the yard aloft, being wet and heavy and four boys' weight likewise, the larboard lift broke, and overboard went poor Joe Watson. The ship fortunately was going slowly at the time, and every one ran to get the jolly-boat out to save him; but every one knows that this is not easily done in a merchantman, for the skiff is stowed inside of the longboat, and the jolly-boat on her sometimes bottom up and lumbered with other ropes; moreover, we had no tackles rove ready, and as every one was doing his utmost, and nearly got the boat ready, to our great surprise we saw poor Joe climbing over the taffarel; being able to swim, he had got hold of the beef-net towing astern, and climbed up without any hurt except a good ducking.[1]

We arrived safe in the Delaware, but it puzzled the Custom-house officers who came alongside to know where La Matt was situated, as they had never heard of such a place. We soon got up to Philadelphia, and moored ship alongside a wharf, and began to throw our salt upon it, which they took away in carts. I don't know whether the English cattle are fond of salt or not, but

[1] N.B.—No boats were carried at the stern at this time.

here we were obliged to keep them off with a good stick, they devoured it so greedily.

Philadelphia is a noble city—the streets at right angles, and built on a sloping hill near the river-side; the market-place is said to be a mile long, and all roofed over and stocked with all the necessaries of life; the people (being Quakers) are honest in their dealings, and will neither raise nor lower the price first proposed. The celebration of July 4 (the day on which they gained their independence from Great Britain) now took place, and great were the rejoicings thereat.

There is a kind of zigzag road about three or four miles long leading from the city to a place called the Schuylkil, along which the procession was to go; and first went the different tradespeople in regular order, some on sledges working at their trades, with music playing and colours flying; next followed some of the heads and members of Congress in an open temple or rotunda drawn by horses, and occasionally handing out a glass of wine to one or another, with a tall man dressed in a coat of mail riding before them. But the best sight was a little frigate, with all her sails set, drawn by thirteen horses, and so heavy that the people were obliged to keep throwing water on the axle-trees to keep them from catching fire; many people were on her decks, some giving the command, some steering, and some heaving the lead, but all this was a matter of form.

On turning each part of the road, in making her evolutions, she appeared at a distance like a ship working up a river. Hundreds of bluejackets were around her, to keep the mob off, and good order prevailed all the way until she arrived at the Schuylkil; then she fired a salute with her wooden guns, roast beef and cider were served out plentifully gratis to the people, joy and festivity was the order of the day, while the ships on the river were dressed out in the most gaudy colours and fired salutes.

But on the return of the procession in the evening the case was quite altered, for instead of merry faces and cheerful countenances the road was covered with people reeling home, some drunk in the ditches and some lying stupid with bloody heads and noses.

For the last six years, though I had got hardy and stronger, yet I had gained very little in height. My captain had measured me several times, but declared this year I had got shorter, which made me fret; but on going down the Delaware, being a warm, rainy day, I got a thorough soaking, which I suppose loosened my nerves and muscles so much that I soon after began to stretch out, and came to my natural height, which was about 5 feet $7\frac{1}{2}$ inches, and there remained.

When our salt was delivered we took in a cargo of flour and biscuit, all in barrels, for Santander, in Spain; an American brig laden with the same kind of cargo, and bound to the same port, kept company with us for a few days; but the Mother Carey's chickens (petrels) began to collect in our wake, which denoted a storm, and we soon had a terrible one, but from the westward and in our favour, accompanied with torrents of rain, thunder and lightning. The waves were mountains high, and the American brig, in danger of being pooped, brought to, while we in our old ship scudded like a duck before it under the goose wings of our foresail.

Off Cape Ortegal we spoke a ship which told us that hostilities were likely to break out between Great Britain and Spain. This made our captain hesitate whether he should proceed on or not. However, he made up his mind to push on, and we sailed along the Spanish coast on the south side of the Bay of Biscay, where the mountains were high above the clouds, and soon after arrived at Santander, where we heard to our satisfaction that the expected rupture had been amicably settled between the Courts.

St. Andero (Santander) is a safe and good harbour, with a fine quay, but not water enough for large ships to lie alongside.   Here we found two large Spanish ships bound to South America and waiting for our and the brig's cargoes, and we began to deliver. We found the Spaniards here a very bigoted people, who think it no sin to kill a heretic (as they called us), and some of us were nearly made a sacrifice. For one night, between nine and ten o'clock, four of us lads were on shore from the boat waiting for the captain: while one remained in her as boat-keeper, the other three of us were on the quay. By-and-by there came along three Spaniards, apparently tipsy, who staggered against us purposely, and then walked on. Shortly after we saw them coming back, so we agreed among ourselves if they insulted us in the same manner to resent it.

They soon drew near, and, being bent on mischief, insulted us again ; and we soon came to blows, and would have thrashed them had they not had recourse to their long knives. One of them soon had his knocked out of his hands, and it went jingling along the stones, while another was prevented from giving me a back-handed stab by our beating him off ; but a mob soon began to make its appearance, which—knowing that we should have no mercy or fair play—caused us to take to our heels in time. Being cut off from getting to the boat, we ran up a street, and from that to another, not knowing where to go for safety, and the mob after us. Fortunately we saw a vessel's masts, ran towards her, and jumped on board.

The people belonging to her, being in bed and hearing the noise on deck, jumped up in their shirts to see what was the matter, and glad were we to find they were Englishmen, belonging to the brig delivering fish from Newfoundland. They of course took our part, and, being each of us provided with a handspike, the cowardly Spaniards, who were now collected on the quay close to us, were afraid to come on board; so after some time, and it getting late, they dispersed themselves, and when we found all clear, we got to our boat again, and found the boy half asleep, knowing nothing of the business that had occurred.

Whenever we went on shore after, we each took a good oak tree-nail under our jackets; and one day, being for a turn of water at a place outside the town, we found a boat belonging to one of the Spanish ships watering there. In rolling our casks up and down the beach I thought I had seen one of them before, and, conjecturing it was the fellow who had attempted to stab me on the quay, I mentioned it to my shipmates, then challenged the fellow with it, and, though bigger than I was, offered to fight him English fashion—for there was no fear of a mob here. At first he was shy, but recollecting himself (for he could speak English), he acknowledged himself to be the person, said he was drunk at the time, was sorry for it, and wanted me to go and drink some wine with him to make it up; but, as I knew there was no good in trusting to such bigoted fellows, I made friends with him, but would have none of his wine.

One of his countrymen, a sailor, was hanged at this time for murdering his captain. It was some time before any one durst make the gallows; but one was made at last, it was supposed by the carpenter of an English merchant vessel, and for a good sum of money. I saw the culprit dragged on a sledge, bound hands and feet, to the place of execution; he was then dragged up on a scaffold and the halter put round his neck. After a few words from a priest, he was thrown off the scaffold and brought up with such a jerk that it was a wonder his head was not separated from his body. He was left hanging from noon to sunset with his face uncovered, his tongue, black and swelled, out of his mouth—a most disgusting appearance.

Five bulls were baited here one afternoon, which I saw. It was in the principal street of the town; one end was blockaded by the stalls which the bulls were in, and the other end by a number of men with long pikes. The windows of the lower rooms were left open for the picadors to jump in when too closely pursued by the bull, and the windows above for the ladies and grandees to see from. Several ropes were hanging down from the upper stories to the street for the young gentlemen to take hold of, and it was laughable to see with what dexterity they would climb up by the rope whenever the bull came near them.

The first bull that was brought out was quiet enough; but the picadors, who are dressed like harlequins for the occasion, began to attack him; yet he remained quiet until the multitude began clapping their hands and crying out "*Toro, toro.*" He then began to show courage by stamping and tearing up the ground with his fore feet, and made a run at the picadors, whose dexterity was in getting behind him, sticking a small dart like an arrow into his rump, and so bothering him before, behind, and on each side, that he hardly knew which of them to run at. When they were in danger, they jumped into the lower-story windows that were left open for that purpose.

When the bull was sufficiently baited and tired they brought out another, and it was surprising to see how tame the baited one became at the sight of the other, and he was led to his stall. The whole five were baited in this manner; but one of the picadors was caught and tossed a great height by the bull, and would soon have been gored to death had not the others come to his assistance, and drawn the bull's attention another way until he was carried off; but we heard that he died the next day.

We took in ballast here, and sailed for Shields, and, my apprenticeship having now expired, I was made second mate and had £2 5s. a month.

Early in 1788 we again loaded with coals and took them to Bordeaux, a pretty and fine place; but the people, especially the ladies of quality, daubed their faces too much with red paint. Here, on a Sunday afternoon, were rope dancing and puppet-show acting in the open squares, and play acting in the evening—serving God in the forenoon and the devil after. Here they sell their brandy in retail by weight and not measure; and (after our coals were delivered) we took in ballast and went to a place named St. Martin's, on the Isle of Rhé, near Rochelle, and loaded with salt for Philadelphia again. When we arrived in the Delaware, the Custom-house officers came alongside again as usual, and told us what fine salt that was we brought last (though coarse and black) for curing beef and pork, but this we had got now, though finer, would hardly pay its expenses; however, the cattle were as fond of it as the other, as we experienced.

Here we got a freight of Nicaragua wood for London. It looked like the rotten roots of trees, but was so valuable that every little bit was weighed like gold, and the cargo supposed to be worth £50,000. 'Tis said it would dye seven different colours, and one of them scarlet.

A circumstance now occurred which I have often regretted, and was as follows: Abreast of our ship and near at hand was a tavern kept by one Robert Tilford, a countryman of ours, who had been a long time in America; and there we went sometimes in an evening to taste his cider, and there he would boast of the advantages the American sailors enjoyed more than others, not only in having greater wages but greater privileges in trade, and he promised that he could get me a second mate's berth on board a brig bound to the Mediterranean, where I could buy nutmegs for a trifle and sell them here for a quarter of a dollar apiece, which with other emoluments would be as good as double wages.

Although I did not put implicit confidence in all he said, yet I knew it was partly true, so I thought if I could get my discharge from the old *Forester*, I would try my luck, for I thought I had been long enough in one ship ; so the first thing I did was to get my chest and bedding on shore (which was easily done, as we lay at a wharf near to his house), and then (thought I) if the captain will not discharge me, I can walk on shore and leave him, not caring for the wages that were due to me.

Therefore in the evening, when nothing was doing, I went on board and got the boys to assist me in getting up my chest and bedding ; but just as I had got them on deck, the captain came up out of his cabin, and seeing what I was at, asked me with one of his black looks what I was about ; and I muttered (for I was still in awe of him) that I was going to leave his ship to better myself. He told me that I ought to have consulted him first, and then he ordered my things to be put into his cabin ; so when he went below I slipped on shore, went to Tilford's, and told him what had happened.

" Never mind," he replied ; " you stay at my house, and you shall want for nothing." So I stopped about a week, when the captain sent a boy to tell me that if I really intended to leave him to come on board, and he would settle with me about my wages. All this time I was living, at Tilford's, like a fighting cock—bread, butter, fish, ham, tea and coffee to breakfast ; the other meals equally served up, for everything was plentiful here at this time; but this living was too good for me to last long.

So on board I went, and found him in a good humour —much better than I expected. The accounts were soon settled, but he told me it was necessary that I must go with him to the British Consul to have his sanction, which I thought reasonable enough; so along we went, I little thinking of the trap he had laid for me, for we had not gone far before two men met us. They whispered something aside to the captain, and then said "This is the right way to go." (The rascals were constables, but I did not know it.) At last we came to a large whitewashed house with iron gates, which I thought was the Consul's, and I was desired to walk in, which I did, though I did not like its inside appearance. The doors were soon fastened on me, and there I waited, expecting every minute to be sent for by the Consul.

At last a shabby-looking fellow came and asked me what I was brought in there for; and I told him, to see the British Consul, which made him smile, and to my utter astonishment he told me I was in jail. "In jail!" says I: "you are mistaken." "No, I am not," says he, and surely to my sorrow I found it too true. I made some endeavour to open the gates and get out, but they were too securely fastened for that, so with a heavy heart I was compelled to submit to my fate.

In the evening the jailer ordered every one to their sleeping apartments, and locked up for the night. I, with six rather more respectable than the others, was put into a room on the second story, with not so much as a bench or bit of straw to lie on, nor a stone for a pillow: so much for Yankee freedom! And what surprised me more was to see the others strip off their clothes. I asked them the reason of that, and they told me that if I did not do the same and stick them in the iron grates of the window, I should have them swarming with bugs in the morning; so out of necessity I was compelled to do the same, and lay down naked on the floor to sleep. Fortunately the weather was warm and the nights short.

In the morning we were let out of our den and suffered to walk in the prison yard enclosed with a high wall; our provisions were served out at eight o'clock, which consisted of only one pound of soft bread for twenty-four hours, and as much water as we could drink at the pump in the yard; and this was just enough to keep life and soul together.

Mr. Tilford sent me a dish of victuals the first two or three days I was in jail, and then that was put a stop to; and the first Sunday I was in, my shipmates came to see me and collected me a small sum of money, by which I got the jailer's servant girl to smuggle me in two or three times a few polonies, and that was stopped; in short, I was near starving, and was glad to eat some of the cabbage leaves, when I could get them, that were thrown down to the hogs in the yard; thus cooped up like a criminal, many a sigh I gave in looking through the grated window to see the people passing to and fro at their liberty.

I remained in jail until the *Forester* was ready to sail, which was thirteen long days, when two constables took me out and conducted me to the ship. We then left the wharf and proceeded down the river, but it was my fixed determination that if the ship came to anchor for the night, I would swim on shore; but no chance of that kind offered, and we proceeded on. However I was sulky and stubborn at first, but that soon wore off, and my only consolation was, that when we arrived in London I would prosecute the captain for false imprisonment; for he had discharged one man who I was told broke the articles, and he had no right to refuse the discharge of another.

We took two cabin passengers on board at Philadelphia, the one an actress named Brown, whom we put on board a small boat off Plymouth to be landed there; she left half-a-crown with the captain for me, because I was the first that saw the English land, but he never offered it to me and I never asked him for it.

The other passenger was a Quaker, a gentleman of great property in America: he was very affable with the ship's crew, and got me to make a chart of the Western Ocean, with the ship's daily course and distance on it, during the passage from America to England; this I did, and, when he was going to leave the ship in London, he sent for me, and taking a handful of money out of his pocket desired me to take what I pleased. I was simple enough to take only two shillings, thinking he would insist on my taking more; but he did not, and I ought to have known that a Quaker doesn't offer the second time.

After the ship was moored, I went on shore to employ a lawyer to get me compensation for the false imprisonment I had endured, and to allow him part of what he got for his trouble, as I had no money of my own; but to my disappointment I could get none to undertake the cause, and in the evening returned on board quite uncomfortable. The next day the captain sent for me, and told me that if I would remain by the ship he would pay me the whole of my wages; but if not he would deduct all the jail fees and constables' expenses from them; but so foolish and obstinate was I, that I refused my consent to stop in the ship, so he was as good as his word, and after all was summed up I had only about 15s. to receive, and being in want of money I was obliged to take it, and thus ended my expectations of making him pay dearly for my false imprisonment.

Thus was I situated when I parted from my old captain, after being seven years and nine months under his command, and one who wished me well, and would have helped me forward in the merchant service; and I soon had good reason to repent when too late.

I left my things on board, not knowing where to take them, and went on shore thinking I could soon get another ship; but was mistaken, for this being the fall of the year they were laying up their ships for the winter. I wandered up and down for several days from Limehouse to London Bridge, then down Tooley Street on the other side of the river and back again, inquiring as I went along for any ship that wanted hands, but always disappointed. I was ashamed to inquire after any of my friends in London, as I had brought this trouble on myself by my own folly.

Being in this melancholy situation, and half-starved, and not knowing what would be the end of it, I fortunately met a gentleman who knew me and my father; his name was Legg, and he kept a marine store in Wapping. He was surprised to see me, and said my father had sailed lately, and knew nothing of my being in London; so I thought it best to tell him all the truth, which I did, and then he took me to his house and gave me a good dinner. He then took me on board the *Mosely*, a ship commanded by my uncle Hunter (for he had married my mother's sister), and it was there proposed that I should go to Shields and meet my father; but, as the *Mosely* would not sail for some days, a passage was got for me on board the *Garland* (Captain Poscot). I then got my things from on board the *Forester* into the *Garland*, and we sailed.

On our arrival at Shields I found my father had sailed again; so I went on shore and remained for a few days. When the *Mosely* arrived I shipped before the mast on board her, and sailed in her all this winter in the coal trade to London. She was a fast-sailing ship of fifteen keels, or upwards of three hundred tons. She was long, but narrow in breadth of beam, so that when she was laden we could wash our hands over the gunnel in the sea; she had no bulwarks, and by the sea continually washing on board when it blew fresh, her decks were hardly ever dry when she was laden.

This year (1789) we made thirteen voyages to London. And this winter died my youngest sister Ann, aged ten years. Her funeral was the only one in our family that I ever remember attending, and the rest of us were distributed as follows: My father, commanding a ship abroad; my eldest sister, at home; my brother John, apprentice in the *Mary*; my brother Robert, apprentice in the *Golden Grove* with the expedition to New Holland; my brother James, in the Greenland fishery trade; my brother George, at home with his sister: so that we were pretty well separated from each other.

CHAPTER III

1790–91

GUINEA AND THE SLAVE TRADE

Joins a slaver bound for Guinea—Arrival of *The Spy* at Cape Coast Castle—Anamaboe—Character of the captain and mates—Accra—Bonny—"King Pepple"—"Breaking trade"—Preparing the ship to receive slaves—Method of purchases—Fever—Two female slaves eaten by sharks—Mutiny in a French slaver—"King Pepple" expedites the supply of slaves—*The Spy* sails from Bonny—The middle passage—Anno Bon Island—Barbarity of the captain—Arrival at Jamaica—Sale of the slaves—Return to England—Pressed into the Navy—Joins H.M.S. *London*—Paid off at Portsmouth—Joins another slaver bound for Guinea—Is wrecked at Ostend—Returns to London—Disgusted with the slave trade.

EARLY in 1790, as we were tiding up past Ratcliff Cross, we took particular notice of a fine ship fitting out there with a tier of gun ports and copper bottomed, a rare thing for a merchantman in those days. It was said she was going on a voyage of discovery, which made me think how glad I should be to join her and to see more of the world than dragging about in a collier, where there were no hopes of promotion but for owner's sons and cousins, of which there were plenty. On our return next voyage we saw this fine ship nearly ready to sail; so when we got into the Pool, and our ship moored, I made up my mind at once, and went on shore to inquire after her, and found her name was *The Spy*, the captain's name Wilson, and that he lived in Well Close Square; so to him I went, found him at home, and inquired if he had got all his men : he told me he had, but after asking a few questions told me he wanted a fourth mate, and if I would accept that berth I should have it.

This pleased me extremely, for had it been a hundred-and-fourth mate I would have accepted it ; but, instead of the ship going on discovery, I found she was going to the coast of Guinea. However, this made little difference, as I had fixed my mind on going in the ship ; so I went on board the *Mosely* to get my discharge, but knowing my uncle would not let me go without a sufficient reason, I told him I was going to join my father, which was a falsehood. " Oh, then," says he, " if that is the case you must have your discharge," so he gave me thirty shillings for the half-voyage, and I left him, after making near twenty voyages in the *Mosely*.

I took my chest and bedding on shore to a Mr. Wall (a rope maker who took in lodgers at Love Lane, in Stepney, near Bell Wharf stairs), and paid half a guinea a week for board and lodgings until *The Spy* was ready to receive her men. That very night a press broke out from all protections, and nearly stript the colliers of all their men (this was called the Spanish disturbance and only lasted for the year). Captain Wilson came to my lodgings and told me to keep close in the house until he got a ship's protection, and he would then send a coach to take me to Blackwall, where the ship would then be.

Notwithstanding this precaution, I could not rest in the house, but ventured out, and though told by people that a press gang was near, I escaped them (though afterwards I twice got pressed when I thought myself safe from them). After being on shore near a fortnight I got so tired I gave up my lodgings, got my things into a wherry at Bell Wharf stairs, and set off to join my ship at

Blackwall. In going down Deptford Reach a King's ship was fitting out there, and seeing me and my chest and bedding in the wherry, sent a boat after us; but by my taking one oar and the waterman another, we kept ahead of them until I got alongside of *The Spy*, and then they gave up the chase.

The Spy had at this time nearly all her cargo on board, consisting of brandy, muskets, swords, bars of iron, brass pots and pans, calicoes of showy colours, and other things to trade with among the blacks, and (the Captain having got a protection) the crew were smuggled on board for fear of the press, the sails were bent, and we dropped down to Gallions Reach, and anchored to take in our gunpowder.

My uncle Hunter having heard where I was, in passing us here, hailed and asked me if I would join his ship again and he would send a boat for me; I answered in the negative, and he proceeded on.

Having got our powder in, we sailed down to Gravesend, and there anchored; we received our river pay and a month's advance, the seamen having £2 5s. a month. We had a letter of marque commission to permit us to capture the Spaniards in case of war, and I was well satisfied with my situation, and to add to my comfort my father had arrived in the river and came on board to see me; he stopped the whole day and then left us, and this was the last time I ever saw him.

On May 21st, 1790, we got under way and proceeded on our voyage. From a cold severe winter I was now going to meet a hot, burning summer near the equinoctial line; from living on good fresh English beef and beer, to live on salt junk and an allowance of water with a gill of rum a day; from a land of Christians to a land of heathens, and from a cargo of black coals to a cargo of black human beings—a great contrast indeed! All this was trying to the constitution, but little to what I have endured since; yet, thank God, I have always enjoyed good health.

In crossing "the calms," a latitude in which ships are sometimes long becalmed, we got through very well, having all the light sails set that a ship carried alow and aloft; the first land we saw on the coast of Guinea being the Tooth Coast, where elephant tusks are plentiful, we came to anchor here between Cape Palmas and Cape Three Points, and bartered for a few elephants' teeth and yams.

In order not to be taken by surprise, our crew, forty-five in number, were put into two watches, and when the watch was set at night, one-third of them were quartered on the quarter-deck, another third on the forecastle, and the other third in the waist; every ten minutes or so the officer of the watch cried out, "Keep a good look-out on the forecastle there," then one from the forecastle cried out, "Keep a good look-out in the waist there," then one from the waist cried out, "Keep a good look-out abaft there," then the whole watch would cry out all together, "Aye, aye," and so loud as to be heard a good distance off, and this was to let the negroes know that we were on our guard.

In order to make our water last long (and none taken from the scuttle butt), it was headed up with a hole at the top to admit a musket barrel with its breech off, and through this we had to suck up a drink (captain and mate excepted). We found it very difficult at first, but practice soon made it easy, and in my opinion it is better than being on an allowance, for when that is gone you have to suffer till next serving, but the gun-barrel you can always have recourse to; some ships being stricter, a man after his suck had to take the barrel to the mast-head, and when another wanted a suck he had to go there for it, so no man would do that except he was thirsty.

We set sail from here to the Gold Coast, where plenty of gold dust is found, and came to anchor off Cape Coast Castle, where we landed some European plants from London for the Governor. The landing is bad here; one has to watch an opportunity to jump out of the boat on a rock when the waves get a little smooth; our doctor got swamped here, and lost his gold chain; but I rather think the negroes in saving him had got it out of his pocket.

Here is the principal factory the English have in these parts; the Castle has a lofty wall around it, and stands on rocky ground near the sea, but has no fresh water except what they save in a very large tank during the rains, and which supplies the garrison and shipping; here we got a supply, and to destroy the Guinea worms in it we put two or three spoonsful of quick-lime into each cask.

One night I was left on shore, and slept in the Castle, but in the evening I took a stroll to a negro town a little way off, and found them all full of glee and dancing before their huts, but could not help smiling at the females, who had on their best, and plenty to cover their nakedness, each having something as large as a small loaf sticking out under their garments and on their loins; it had a ridiculous appearance, but negroes are very proud in general and have their fashions.

After stopping here a few days we got under way for Anamaboe, about seven or eight leagues more to leeward, and there came to anchor. We found a great many ships lying here trading for gold dust, ivory, and slaves. A boat from a Liverpool ship came alongside, and the men were much surprised to see Mr. Cummins, our chief mate, on board (whose proper name was Thorsby). He, it appears, had lately been chief mate of the *Gregson*, Guineaman, out of Liverpool; had thrown the ship's cook into the boiling coppers, and with other crimes, had got himself put into jail at Liverpool when the ship arrived there;

but he found means to escape, changed his name, came to London, and shipped as our chief mate.

Our captain, they said, was a sharp hand, had been many years in the Guinea trade out of Liverpool, and had paid some hundreds in course of law for bad treatment to the men ; and that Mason, our second mate, was one of the same stamp, and had impudence enough to do anything, if encouraged.

Mr. Scot, our third mate, was a fine young man, but not much of a sailor ; he, like myself, had never before been in the Guinea trade to get corrupted, and, like myself, hated tyranny ; however, as yet none of us had reason to complain, the duty went on well, and I believe all were satisfied.

Anamaboe is situated on a sandy beach close to the sea, which breaks against a fort to protect the English settlers ; the land is low and cultivated, but such a surf on the beach that ships' boats cannot land. The negroes were at this time at war with the Ashantees, and generally fought their battles on the beach near the cool of the evening ; when one party fired they fell flat on the ground to load their muskets, and the others did the same ; both sides left off when it grew dark. We never saw any killed or wounded ; the reason was that they kept at too great a distance to do that.

From Anamaboe we ran farther down the coast, and came to anchor off Accra ; here the coast was bolder, with good landing, and here ships can get well supplied with pigs, goats, poultry, yams, and plenty of tropical fruit ; there are English, Danish and Dutch factories here, with their colours flying near each other. After laying in a good stock, we got under way and ran down the coast, and came to anchor outside of Bonny Bar in the Bight of Benin. The sun at this time was very hot, we being in the latitude of 4° 30′ N.

Next morning we hoisted out our pinnace and rigged her : she was a fine boat, and capable of carrying a hundred slaves ; then the chief mate and I, with a chosen boat's crew, set off for Bonny to get a pilot out of one of the English ships lying there and about five leagues from us. In going over the bar there was broken water, and we got nearly swamped ; however we had a fresh breeze in our favour and soon passed it, and after that got alongside of the *King Pepple* of Liverpool. Our chief mate went on board, and I with the rest pushed off and anchored the boat at a little distance from her; there we made a covering with the boat's sails, and slept in her that night. As we were coming in from our ship the chief mate intimated that we were now going to Bonny, and that some of us who had not been seasoned to the climate would most likely leave our bones on Bonny Point, the place where they bury European seamen ; but, poor man, he little thought then that he would be the first on board to leave his bones there !

Next morning we got the chief mate of the *King Pepple* for a pilot, the ship was got under way, and we proceeded to Bonny ; about half way, in passing Ju' Ju' Creek—a place held sacred by the negroes—we had to fire a salute to please King Pepple.

Bonny River is a noble one, spacious and deep, and wider than the Thames in Sea Reach; the land is low and covered with lofty cocoanut, palm tree, pine, plantain and banana trees. On the north side is the kingdom of Benin, and on the south Bonny, independent of each other. New Calabar can be seen here at a distance to the north-west. Plenty of palm wine is made (or rather got) here, for they have only to make an incision in the top of the tree in the evening, hang a calabash under it, and in the morning it will be full ; it is of a whitish colour, and tastes like cider.

We soon after anchored near the town of Bonny and moored the ship; we found lying here twelve English and one French ship waiting for slaves.

Next morning we were all very busy in getting the ship ready to receive King Pepple on board to " break trade," as the natives call it, but more with an intent on seeing what he can get; and whatever he takes a fancy to, it is good policy to let him have, or he might detain the ship a long time from getting her complement of slaves. Our captain being up to this, had previously stowed away all his cabin furniture of any value, and an old iron gun (a three-pounder) being brought for the purpose, was left on the deck that he might see it in going along.

After waiting some time we at last saw him coming in his largest canoe and attended by several others, and when he came near our ship he was honoured with a salute of our guns; when he got alongside we had to hoist him on board in a chair, as we do the ladies: the reason of this was that he had got a yam foot (as the sailors called it), for one of his feet was swelled like that root so that he could not walk.   Being hoisted on board, he was carried in a chair to the cabin, but did not stop long, as there was nothing there worth his notice, but requested to be carried round the deck; but seeing nothing in the way but what was for the use of the ship he at last cast his eyes on the old iron gun lying on the deck. " Ha! Captain," said he (for he could speak a little English), " what for gun lie there? " The Captain replied that it was a spare gun we did not use. " Ha! " said he again, " what fine gun he make for war canoe! " " Well," replied the captain, " if you think so you are welcome to have it," so what was intended as a gift was received as a favour.

There was another present we had brought out for him to court his favour, as is customary in " breaking trade," but this he expected only as his right: it was a blue suit of clothes edged with something like gold lace, and a cap with a plume of feathers on it; and these pleased him highly, so finding nothing more to be got, took his leave with ceremony, was lowered in the chair into his canoe, and departed under another salute of our great guns.

We now began to prepare the ship for receiving slaves, and first of all unbent all the sails and stowed them away, sent down the topgallant masts on deck and struck the topmasts; then began to build a roof over the ship to keep off the sun and rain. We first got some long spars lashed fore and aft to the lower masts, to serve as a ridge pole, and about half mast high, then lighter ones for rafters, and well lashed together, then covered with mats we got from the shore, finished the roof, and made the ship look like a great barn; and we left a hole in the roof under each top for us to get up to our chests, where they were to be kept until ready for sea and clear of the slaves.

This roof stood firm against the tornadoes, which occasionally come on here, and generally on a calm, hot day. When ships at sea see one coming, which is known by a small black cloud rising in the horizon, they immediately take in all their sails and furl them (except the foresail, which is set to get the ship before the wind) and scud before it. As the cloud gets larger it soon draws near, roaring like a hurricane, accompanied with thunder and lightning and torrents of rain; this continues generally three or four hours, then clears up, and the weather becomes finer and healthier.

The next thing to do was to clear the decks of all lumber, and a barricade was built across the main deck near the mainmast about ten feet high, with wall pieces fixed on the top to fire among the slaves if necessary and a small door to let only one man through at a time. When the slaves are on deck in the day-time the males are all kept before the barricade and females abaft it.

The 'tween-decks were entirely cleared fore and aft, and a platform fixed round against the ship's sides and hung on cranks, height about half way between the two decks : this is for the slaves to sleep on that had not room on the lower deck, and the whole deck fore and aft was divided into four rooms or partitions, each separated by strong oak palings.

The foremast and smaller room were for the Quaes, a savage kind of people, who have their teeth filed sharp at the points, and ('twas said) were cannibals.

The second room was for the Eboes, more numerous, but a harmless people, and the third room amidships was for the boys, but all abaft that was for the women. We had a deck awning over the quarterdeck, which held a deal of lumber, besides serving our people to sleep under that wished it.

During the first two months the slaves were brought to us pretty regularly, and I suppose we must have got about two hundred of both sexes, but after that they came slowly. Poor creatures ! it was pitiful to see the distress they were in on coming on board, for some of them think that we live on the ocean and wanted them for food. Some of the females fainted, and one of them went out of her mind ; we did all we could to comfort them, and by degrees they got more composed.

In the mornings, when the decks were all washed and dried, the slaves were all ordered up on the upper deck ; the men were all arranged in line along both sides of the main deck ; they were shackled together two each by the legs and then a long deck chain on each side was rove through a ring at each shackle and secured at both ends, so that the poor fellows could only sit or stand ; in the evening the deck chains were unrove and they were sent below, but still having their shackles on ; the females are never shackled, nor boys, for they assist the cook to get up wood and water and to peel the yams; when all were got below in the evenings the gratings were put over and well secured and the watch set.

In regard to victualling them, ten are put into a mess and each mess had two kits called creus, one for the victuals and the other for their water, with a little tin pannikin to drink out of; they had two meals a day, one in the forenoon consisting of boiled yams, and the other in the afternoon of boiled horse-beans and slabber sauce poured over each: this sauce is made of chunks of old Irish beef, and rotten salt fish stewed to rags, being well seasoned with cayenne pepper; the negroes are so fond of it that they pick out the little bits and share them out, but they don't like the horse-beans.

Their allowance of water was small, and they suffered much from thirst. When I have been attending the serving out their allowance, the poor creatures with their hands at their mouths in the most piteous manner would beg for " minnee wantee "—that is, " Pray give me a little water," and when I knew the captain was out of the way, I have slipped along a canful to them, and, instead of gobbling it up, they would only fill their mouths and pass it to one another as long as it lasted.

I was obliged to be very cautious in this business, for our captain began now to show himself in his proper colours, and would flog a man as soon as look at him, and assumed as much consequence as if he had been captain of a line-of-battleship: all we four mates had to attend him with hats off at the gangway in going out or coming in to the ship; he flogged a good seaman for only losing an oar out of the boat, and the poor fellow soon after died.

Some people in England think that we hunt and catch the slaves ourselves, but that is a mistaken idea, for we get them by barter as follows: their petty kings and traders get them not so much by wars (as is imagined) as by trade and treachery, and when they get a number for sale bring them to the coast and sell them. So many bars are given for each slave, and for a prime one perhaps a hundred, a bar being valued at five shillings : the reason they call them bars is, I suppose, that when ships first traded here they dealt with bars of iron.

In selling a prime slave for a hundred bars, they will have so many bars of muskets and bars of other things as make up the hundred ; and they know from experience the value of each article, but are often outwitted in the quality. For instance, the muskets are all alike, but if the flint don't strike fire well, they say it's no good and must have another, so the musket is handed below to be changed ; but the armourer with his small hammer gives the flint a tap or two, it is handed up again, and the trader finding it strikes fire well, says " Ah, he good ; he talk," not knowing that it was the same musket.

The brandy we brought out for trade was very good, but they thought it was not hot enough, and did not bite, as they called it ; therefore out of every puncheon we pumped out a third of the brandy, put in half a bucketful of cayenne pepper, then filled it up with water, and in a few days it was hot enough for Old Nick, and when they came to taste it, thinking it was from another cask they said " Ah, he bite."

There was one of their petty kings who, when he came on board, would strut along the deck as if he had been one of the greatest men in the world : he was a little fat fellow dressed in a suit of coarse blue cloth edged with something like yellow worsted, but what spoiled all was that he had no shirt, shoes or stockings on, and his naked black feet and legs being dabbed over with mud and salt water, made him a laughingstock to the sailors ; but did not put him out of conceit of himself.

My duty required me to be almost every day away from the ship, either in the pinnace or the long-boat; by a late Act of Parliament the ships were compelled to have, while on the coast, natives of the place to row their boats, so I had got a boat's crew of them. They were called "Pull-away boys," and had got names such as Jack, Tom, Will, etc.; they were a set of willing fellows, but Jack was my right-hand man, as he could speak a little English; they had their rations from the ship, and almost every day we had to go in the long-boat for a turn of water to the other side of the river, up a creek a little way, where ran a stream of fine fresh water.

Each time, just before we reached the creek we had to pass a small piece of land with a few bushes on it and surrounded with water; here they would lie on their oars, take up the bottle that held their rations of brandy, pour out a little into a piece of cocoanut-shell and then throw it towards the piece of land, and then take a little to themselves.

I asked Jack one day why they wasted the brandy in that manner, and he said Ju' Ju' was there, and if they did not give him some, ships would never come to their place again. Whoever this Ju' Ju' was I could never learn: some trees are Ju' Ju'; sharks (though they are swarming here) must not be hurt, because they are Ju' Ju'. I suppose it must have some spiritual meaning. One day in going alongside Jack missed his hold and fell between the boat and the ship; although a minute had not elapsed before he was in the boat again a shark was close at his heels. "What!" says I, "Jack, are you afraid of your Ju' Ju'?" But Jack gave only a grin, and was glad when he was on board again.

One day I took an axe into the boat with me, and went on shore near Bonny to cut a spar to make a mast for the long-boat. In going into the wood and near a small running stream I met an iguana coming waddling towards me, and thought it was a young alligator. I stood on my guard with the axe up, ready to strike if it offered to molest me, when just at the moment a negro came running up and crying out, "Ju' Ju'! Boberry Boberry coocoo!" and made me understand that the iguana was Ju' Ju'; lucky it was for me that I did not hurt it or there would have been a great bobbery, for I was informed afterwards that these iguanas are harmless animals and the negroes think it a good omen when any of them come into their huts, and they will sometimes kill a fowl and give to them.

Being so often on shore, I had many opportunities of knowing these people, and must say I always found them civil, harmless, and obliging. I never saw a quarrel or drunkard among them; they were sober and industrious, and a credit to many Europeans in their morals, except thieving (and where is the country they do not steal where there is no law to prevent them?), they are only ashamed at being caught for not being cunning to escape detection, they say they "no teffe, only takee."

One day I was sent in the pinnace to Ju' Ju' Creek (about four or five miles off) for a load of firewood, a chief living there who supplied the shipping with that article. On arriving at the place and no one near we began and loaded the boat full from a stack; but just as we were pushing off the chief came down with a party of his men, got hold of the boat's painter, and dragged her on the shore, and without further ceremony the chief jumped in and began to throw the firewood out until only a little more than half was left.

I could stand this no longer, so went to stop him, and in the struggle we both went overboard together; this cooled his courage, and we immediately pushed the boat off. The only thing I had to consider now was whether I should go on board with half a boatload or throw it on shore altogether; but on second thoughts I knew the wood was very much wanted on board, so set off with it. But I have often reflected since on my temerity in attacking an African chief on his own shore up a creek and far out of sight of the ship; they might have murdered me, and no one on board know of it or how : the pull-away boys durst not tell, and as for any of his own people we may be sure they would not.

When I got alongside the chief mate showed fine airs because the boat was not full; and not long after the chief himself came on board; when the Captain remonstrated with him about his conduct, he replied that it was true he had agreed to let us have a boatload of wood, but that the boat we sent was far too big. The chief mate went himself the next time, and to make sure took a jar of brandy with him as a bribe, but when he returned brought no more wood than I did, and some said not so much.

The only priest I ever saw here was up this creek; before his hut was a semicircle of stakes driven in the ground near ten feet high, and on their upper ends were fixed some skulls so large that I thought they might have belonged to elephants (and I suppose trophies); the priest was looking at a sick man, and, after discoursing with him a while, stooped and took up, as I supposed, a piece of earth, gave it to the sick man and departed.

Our ship's company now began to get sickly; some got the blind fever and some became delirious, and Mr. Cummins, the chief mate, among the rest : he was in a violent fever, and his last words were " water, water," but no one durst give him any; the doctor was at this time at variance with the mate. The man that attended heard the doctor say (when the mate was crying out for water), damn him, he would soon give him something that would keep him quiet, and that very night he died.

The doctor had hitherto been considered as a good kind of man, but was now found to be an artful little fellow, and carried tales to the captain, and it was thought a duel would have taken place between the mate and the doctor when the ship arrived in the West Indies, on account of these tales.

Mr. Mason now became chief mate, but was not so well qualified to carry on the duty as the other. Three more of our men departed this life, and were buried near the chief mate on Bonny Point, where the bones of many a British sailor were lying, and I had the honour of reading the funeral service over them. But our people still continued sickly, and King Pepple, whose wisdom the negroes have great confidence in (and indeed he deserves it), advised our captain to remove our ship farther from the land, which we did, and the fever soon left us. The King got great applause for this, but it was easily accounted for, because when we lay near the land we inhaled the damp vapours that hung at nights over the woods, but farther off escaped them—moreover we had a longer continuance of the sea breeze.

One evening, the slaves being kept on the upper deck longer than usual on account of some work going on in the hold, two fine prime female slaves got over the ship's quarter and slipped silently down into the water, intending to swim on shore ; the man who had the look-out there gave the alarm, and the boat alongside was instantly sent after them, but before the poor creatures had got a few yards from the ship the sharks had torn them in pieces, and not a fragment of them to be seen except the water tinged with their blood ; it was said they had been the wives of a chief living here, who had sold them to us through jealousy, such power have those fellows over their dependants. We had a slave on board who had often been alongside selling yams and fruit ; he was one day brought on board with his wife, and both sold, which seemed to give them little concern ; the cause of it was that they were caught in their canoe one night, and accused of wanting to go over to the other side and join some other tribe.

One day I had to wait on this great King on business, and found him squatted on the ground in an inner room in his double tent, eating fish and yam out of a wooden platter with his fingers, and two old female negroes attending him. He was very affable, not seeming to have a grain of pride in him ; all the goods in the tent were not worth two dollars, for, 'tis said, they hide their valuables under ground for fear of fires.[1]

There was lying here, and near us, a large French ship belonging to Nantes, which had nearly got her complement of slaves. One morning at daybreak, just as I was going to push off in our pinnace, I saw the Frenchmen running up the rigging in their shirts which made me think something extraordinary was the matter. I directly informed our captain of it, and he, taking a look with his glass, said the slaves had risen on the people to get possession of the ship ; he ordered me to get arms and ammunition into the boat as quickly as possible, and with twelve picked men we set off to their assistance.

When we got near the ship the Frenchmen in the rigging kept waving their hands to us to keep off ; but our captain, who was with us, said if we delayed till the slaves got to the magazine they would blow themselves up and the ship together ; therefore we instantly went alongside, boarded her by the main chains, and got possession of the quarterdeck among a number of females, who were making great lamentation, but offered no resistance.

The only Frenchman here was the captain, standing on

[1] I have been informed since (in 1827, by an officer lately arrived from the African Station) that King Pepple still ruled there, had got a large brick house built and furnished, and invited their commodore to dine with him.

the top of the large boilers with a pistol in each hand and in great agitation. Now our captain told us not to fire amongst the slaves without their captain's consent, except in self-defence (they being the ship's property), or we might be brought in liable to damages; but the Frenchman did not understand us nor we him, and every moment increasing the danger, as the slaves were knocking each others' irons off, we made a rush through the barricade door, formed ourselves in a line abreast, presented our muskets, and stood ready for the encounter.

Upwards of a hundred slaves were in possession of the deck, and others tumbling up from below to their assistance, some with irons off and some not, and armed with billets of wood; one had a sword, which they had got from one of the French sentinels, who with another was lying on the deck dying of his wounds.

There being no remedy but to fight, we gave them a volley, which made them retreat; and I could not but admire the courage of a fine young black, who, though his partner in irons lay dead at his feet, would not surrender, but fought with his billet of wood until a ball finished his existence. The others fought as well as they could, but what could they do against firearms? When they retreated to the forecastle and found they could get no farther, disdaining to surrender, they broke through the nettings, and every one that was able jumped overboard.

By this time boats were coming from other ships to our assistance, and seeing the slaves jumping overboard went to pick them up; but saved only one out of the whole number. Whether they died voluntarily, or were taken down by the sharks, we could not tell.

Our work was not yet done, for the slaves below were in a mutiny, knocking off their irons as fast as they could; but our captain, who had probably experienced such work before this, knew how to manage them with the least danger to us. Seeing an old sail on deck that the Frenchmen had been repairing, he ordered us to cover over the gratings with it and then knock the scuttles in close on each side of the ship to prevent the air from getting in to the 'tween-decks to the slaves; this done, we loaded our muskets with powder, but instead of shot we filled the barrels with cayenne pepper, which is plentiful here; then fired them off through the gratings into the 'tween-decks, and in a few minutes there was stench enough from the burnt pepper to almost suffocate them. This was the finishing blow; they cried out for mercy, which was granted, the sail was taken away, the scuttles opened, and the slaves let up two at a time and properly secured again.

The number of slaves shot was about fourteen; we might have shot many more, but refrained on account of what our captain had told us. So getting everything secured again, we left the ship with her captain stamping about on the quarterdeck like a madman, who never so much as asked us to have a glass of grog or wine, or even thanked us for saving his ship and their lives. On returning to our ship we saw the people very busy on board, and when we got alongside were informed that, seeing through the scuttle-holes what was going on in the French ship, our slaves had been endeavouring to force up the gratings to get on deck, but seeing us return desisted.

One day I had been up in the maintop to get something out of my chest, and in coming down the rigging again, saw a woman sitting on the quarterdeck dressed English fashion. I could hardly believe my eyes, and yet thought I knew her; but how came she here, as there are no Englishwomen in this part of the world? So I hastened on deck and was thrown all aback when I beheld her black phizgog : she was a native of this country, had been

sold as a slave on board a Bristol ship, the captain took
her to England, got her educated, and had now brought
her out again. She was telling our female slaves what a
fine country they were going to and what fine things
they would get there, which in great measure reconciled
them to their fate, for they were more contented afterwards.

We had now been nearly five months here, and had
got little more than three hundred slaves; therefore our
captain with some others went to King Pepple and told
him that if he did not get us the slaves faster they would
leave the place and go to New Calabar for them; so the
King told them he would call a palaver (that is a meeting)
with his great men, and consider best what was to be
done; so after a consultation it was agreed to have a
fair, if the captains would supply him with arms and
ammunition, which they agreed to do.

This fair, or rather unfair, was no less than a robbery,
as will be seen. The town of Bonny was soon all in a
bustle getting their war canoes ready, some of which carry
a small piece of ordnance or three-pounder lashed in their
bows, and in a few days they got them all manned and
ready.

They set off with great noise and ostentation, leaving
their wives and children making great lamentation, and
proceeded up the river, the source of which no European
knows. After getting a certain distance they landed,
and concealed themselves in the woods in the day-time,
observing at the same time for smoke, for where they
saw that, they knew inhabitants were there. Then at
night they stole along as silent as possible till near the
smoke, when they rushed on the poor inhabitants, who were
not aware of their coming, and made them all prisoners
(except old men and old women, as they would not sell).
Thus they continued their depredations night after night
for near a fortnight, and then they returned with their

canoes full of slaves to Bonny, shouting and rejoicing as if they had gained a great victory.

We soon after this got our number completed (450), near half of them females and boys, and began to make ready for sea. The first thing was to get the roof off: the mats were so rotten that we threw them overboard, being bleached and scorched by the rain and sun; then got the rafters and ridge poles down, and, all being so glad we were going to leave the place, we soon had the ship all taut and sails bent. The hold was full of yams and water and wood; under the tops were hung large branches of the palm tree full of nuts like cherries in colour. The negroes are fond of palm oil, which they rub over their skin which softens it and makes it shine; we used to fry with it instead of butter.

The ship being ready we discharged the pull-away boys and got under way, but did not salute in passing Ju' Ju' Creek, as we did in coming in, the reason being that we had got our own ends served. After passing the bar we steered to the southward for what is called the Middle Passage to the West Indies. It was pitiful to see the poor slaves with their eyes full of tears, looking to the land as long as a bit of it was to be seen; the females wept bitterly.

Our ship's company were now disposed of as follows: all hands kept at work all day and in two watches at night; Mr. Mason, chief mate, had charge of the main deck to keep the slaves in order, and five or six of the most tractable among them to assist him, who were called boatswain's mates, each with a cat-of-nine-tails to show their authority. Strange to say, they assumed more severity over their fellow slaves than any of us would do, and all this for only being allowed to go about unshackled and a little more victuals given to them occasionally.

Mr. Scot, second mate, had charge of the hold, with

a number of boys and girls under him to hand up firewood and yams, and assist the cook in peeling them ; all this they did cheerfully, without fee or reward.

My duty was to have charge of the quarterdeck and keep the log ; but at night, when the slaves were put below, we resumed our watches. Mr. Mason and Mr. Scot kept one watch, and the captain and I the other ; but he was seldom out of bed after ten o'clock, and I was left to call him if anything particular occurred. This I had soon reason to do, for one morning early in the middle watch, the ship going nine knots through the water, and no orders left to any one to look out for land, I happened to see the land ahead and the ship running right toward it. I instantly gave him a call, and told him the land was close ahead, which so alarmed him that he tumbled out of bed on the deck like a man stupefied ; however, we soon got the ship about and stood from it out of danger ; this land, we supposed, was the Island of St. Thomas, right under the equinoctial line.

A day or two after we saw the Island of Anno Bon (so named by the Portuguese because they discovered it on New Year's day). The water was so deep that we could get no soundings until we got near the town and there came to anchor. We were soon surrounded with canoes, which came from the shore with hogs, poultry, goats, and plenty of tropical fruit to barter, for they know not the use of money.

Anno Bon is a fertile island, and about thirty miles in circumference, very mountainous and fruitful beyond imagination ; it lies in the latitude of 2° S. Here our captain laid in a large stock in exchange for some of the slave goods that had not been disposed of, and signified to the ship's company that, when he had got all his stock, they might barter for theirs ; but when he had got what he wanted he ordered the ship to be got under way and deceived us all; his selfish motive being, that if they had no yams they would not pilfer his and say they were their own. A humane man would have been glad to let us have plenty after living so long on salt junk.

We left this fine island, where the natives ought to be happy if happiness exists in the world, and proceeded on our passage for the West Indies with fine pleasant weather; and I being on the quarterdeck all day had a good opportunity of seing the conduct of the females, and must say few could conduct themselves better in their situation, which made me think that all mankind were alike in human nature and only education or custom made the difference. They were fond of dancing, which was encouraged to keep them cheerful and healthy; they would sometimes form a circle, dress one of the party out in old handkerchiefs and ribbons, given them by the sailors, place her in the centre and dance around her, singing and clapping their hands in unison with a tune which was very pretty, and at the end of each verse cried out " O deri Jah."

They could make a song on anything, and take off any person they pleased: those they did not like ended with " Adigma, Cookoo," but those they liked with " Adama, Cookoo," and it generally ended with a hearty laugh. One of our men was stationed with a cat to keep them in order, but he never used it except when running round and round the quarterdeck, and then he would give the hindmost one a light touch, which made the others laugh and her run faster: this was to keep their health and spirits, and it did so, for I cannot recollect a single female dying on the passage.

One of these days our captain behaved in a most barbarous manner to one of them. He had generally two or three to wait on him at dinner, and one day a knife was missing; a search was made, and a female slave was found to have taken it; he immediately had her seized up by both hands to the main rigging, then stripping off his upper garment he began to flog the poor creature over her naked back with a cat-of-nine-tails until he was tired; he then stopped to rest awhile, and began again, and I doubt if he would have left off until he nearly killed the poor creature, had it not been for the cries and lamentations of the other female slaves, who stood near, the poor creature having fainted.

By this time our captain's timepiece was far ahead of the ship's log, and he thought we were near Barbados, and muttered out hints that the log had not been kept properly; so in the evening we hove the ship to, to wait for daylight, but when daylight appeared no land was in sight, and we ran before the wind all that day at ten miles an hour, and in the evening hove to again, which made him think we had passed the island; however, next morning we got sight of it, and it answered pretty fair with the ship's reckoning, and soon after came to anchor in Carlisle Bay.

We stopped only a short time here, for our orders were to proceed to Montego Bay in Jamaica to sell the slaves; so got under way again and went to that place, where we moored ship. On the following Sunday I was sent on shore with a hundred of our healthiest male slaves to give them an airing, but more with the intent of letting the planters see what fine slaves we had got. The poor fellows were glad to have their feet on shore again, and followed me about the town like a flock of sheep after the shepherd, and met with several negroes whom they had known on the coast of Guinea. At the farther end of the town there was a pond of fresh water, and as soon as they saw it they gave a shout which startled me, until I saw them run into it and, having their shackles off, begin to plunge and jump and shout, quite delighted, and tumbling one over the other like a set of wild men ; after they had got a good washing, we went down to the boat and then on board, not one missing.

I was much pleased with this excursion, as it gave the poor fellows so much pleasure ; and soon after they were all sent on shore and sold in the following manner. They are all put into a large dark room, and the planters have each as many tallies as they want slaves in number. They are then admitted into the dark room, where they cannot see to pick and choose, and each ties his tallies to the neck of the slaves that he gets among ; they are then brought out, and each planter knows who are his by the tallies ; they sold at the rate of £44 each, currency.

Having got clear of the slaves, our captain now began to get clear of those of the ship's company that he did not like, and Mr. Mason, Mr. Scot and several seamen were discharged. Mr. Mason, we supposed, was discharged for striking a slave with his fist : the slave died, and was opened by the doctor on the quarterdeck, where a black spot was found on the liver which the doctor said caused his death. Mr. Scot was a fine young man, though not much of a sailor, but I never knew him to displease the captain in any respect, and I was left the only mate on board to carry on all the duty while the captain lived on shore.

The first thing to be done was to give the ship a good cleaning all through and prepare her for receiving a cargo of sugar and rum. We loaded then with sugar, rum and mahogany, and got under way near about the middle of March 1791, bound to London.

Off Beachy Head we were brought to by the *Nemesis* frigate (Capt. Ball), who pressed all our men except four Germans (sugar bakers whom the captain had shipped in London to do the drudgery of the ship). Some of the poor fellows shed tears on being pressed after so long a voyage and so near home. The frigate sent an officer and a party of her men to take us into the Downs, and bore up with us, where we both came to anchor.

Next day an officer came on board with our men to get their clothes and notes for their wages; and our captain had the impudence to deduct from each man £3 for the loss of the two female slaves that got overboard and were destroyed by the sharks at Bonny (p. 56). But such a base demand caused them to reject it, as it was not their fault, and the officer supporting them, he was obliged to give it up and give full wages; but this shows what a fraudulent fellow he was.

The frigate took her people from us, and we got ticket men from Deal (called so by having tickets to keep them from being pressed), and when we got to Gravesend our captain left us and went to London, leaving the pilot and me in charge of the ship. Two days after we got to London and moored in Church Hole; here I sent one of the Germans on shore to inquire at my former lodgings how all my friends were, and on his return he told me my father had been dead some time, from a severe cold he caught. This affected me very much : he was a man generally beloved by all who knew him, and more attentive to others' welfare than his own, which sometimes impaired his circumstances ; but I hope his soul, please God, is now happy in heaven.

Two days after our arrival, as I was busy in getting a derrick up to get out the cargo, a galley came alongside, and the officer told me to get my things ready to put into her and go along with him. I told him I had charge of the ship, and he must be answerable for what happened. He said he knew that, but I must go; so I got my things into the galley or press-boat, and in rowing to the *Enterprise* receiving-ship, lying off Tower Stairs, they let me know that the doctor of our ship had informed against me by telling them that I was only acting as chief mate, and had no protection, which was true.

But what surprised me most was, that the doctor and I had been good friends, until I recollected that in coming up the river he wanted the four Germans to clean the cabin out, but as at that time we were foul of a ship, and very busy, I could not spare them. This, I suppose, hurt his little consequence (for he was very malicious), and caused him to inform against me; or perhaps the captain, now finding the ship safe and that he could do without me, might have urged the doctor to do it.

However, I was young and had the world before me, did not fret much, and was willing to go to any part of the world. Next day my uncle Hunter, hearing of the ship's arrival, searched me out and found me a pressed man on board the *Enterprise*; he tried all he could with the regulating captain to get me clear, but could not, and the owners' clerk came on board and paid me my wages. The captain had charged me largely for slops, but as I had kept no check against him I put up with it. The owners' clerk was much of a gentleman, and advised me to leave part of my pay with the owners, as it might soon be spent on board a man-of-war, so I left with him £10 and got his note for my security.

After being confined several nights in the *Enterprise's* hold with many other pressed men, and nothing but our chests to sleep on, we were put on board a tender (but little tenderness was there), and carried down to Gallions and there put on board the *Otter* (Capt. Parker), who took us to the Downs and there put us on board the *Marlborough*, of 74 guns; and next day we were put on board the *Nemesis* frigate, where I got among my old shipmates again; thus we had knocking about enough with our chests and bedding.

My shipmates, who thought I had been a fortunate fellow, were greatly surprised at seeing me again. We proceeded to Spithead, where I with some others were sent on board the *London*, of 98 guns (Capt. Westcot), and bearing the flag of Rear-Admiral Goodall.

It was on June 4 (the birthday of George III.) that I went on board, and was stationed in the maintop. Her lofty masts and square yards appeared wonderful to me, and I wondered how they were able to manage them; but I soon got accustomed to that, for we had plenty of exercise with them and the great guns almost daily. The fleet here at this time consisted of thirty-six sail of the line, with the proportion of frigates, etc., and moored in two lines abreast of each other, all under the command of Lord Hood, blue at the main, on board the *Victory*, and this was what was called the Russian disturbance.

Although the usage was good in general on board the *London*, yet I did not altogether like their manner of discipline, for soon after I got on board we had to cat the anchor, and in running along with the foul, boatswains' mates were placed on each side, who kept thrashing away with their rattans on our backs, making no difference between those that pulled hard and those that did not.

One day a man fell overboard when not a boat was alongside; he could not swim, and went down twice, but came up again. I had heard that if a man goes down the third time he rises no more, therefore without waiting to pull my clothes off I jumped overboard and caught hold of him, but before I could recover myself he had got on my back and clung to me like a leech; I tried to shake him off, to hold him by one arm and swim with the other, but could not. A heavy rope was thrown, which I caught hold of, but there was so much slack I let it go again: it is strange that no one threw a grating or a stool overboard to us; and in this manner we kept drifting astern, it blowing fresh and a rough swell on, and I very nearly suffocated; and in this near fatal affair we should certainly have both been drowned had not a dockyard launch coming along taken us up. To mend the matter, when we got on board I did not receive the least pity, for the man I had saved had a tail the size of a short pipe-stem; and an old boatswain's mate swore that it was no wonder the man fell overboard— "only look at his tail!" said he; "was it not enough to drag him overboard?" and set them all a-laughing.

A singular affair happened about this time; a midshipman belonging to the *Saturn*, having the evening watch, did not hear the Admiral's gun fire at nine o'clock. When the first lieutenant, Mr. Shield (commonly called Billy Shield), came on deck and asked the midshipman why he had not reported the gun being fired, he replied that he had not heard it; some words ensued, when Billy ordered a girt-line to be rove, and the midshipman was hoisted up by it to the masthead.

This aroused the midshipmen of the fleet, and circular letters were written by them to each other and to Mr. Leonard, the midshipman who had been hoisted up, to bring Billy Shield to a court-martial for tyranny, which made a great stir at the time. Lord Hood, being informed of this, had the midshipmen before a court-martial to prove that Mr. Moore, midshipman of our ship, was the ringleader of the circular letters; and he, poor fellow (a fine young man of good character, who had been several years in the service), was sentenced to a month's imprisonment in the Marshalsea, to be severely reprimanded, and admonished to be more circumspect for the future.

The first three months I had been here, no seamen got liberty on shore except those that had entered into the service (and I had not); but it being now reported that the fleet would soon be paid off, liberty was given to all, so I with near fifty more got leave for forty-eight hours, as they did not care now whether we deserted or not. This was the first time I had ever been at Portsmouth, and the first place that brought us up was, of course, a public-house; but as I was not partial to strong liquors I went to see the town, and in the evening met one of my brother top-men, who (knowing his failings) begged me to take care of his watch until the morning. Next morning I met him again, and with a woeful countenance he told me he had lost his watch. I asked him where, but he could give no account of it whatever. "Now," says I, "this is the result of drinking too much, and you ought to know better and be more careful." He promised he would for the future, so I gave him his watch, which surprised him greatly!

Soon after this we sailed for Plymouth, where the ship was paid off with many others—this was September 24— and I received £4 10s. for four months' duty at the rate of three and ninepence per day as Paddy called it (that is three farthings and ninepence a day); we subscribed two shillings apiece to buy Mr. Cooper, the boatswain, a silver call with chain and plate, with a suitable inscription on it for his kindness to the ship's company, and a silver pint pot for his wife; then several of us went on board the *Quebec* frigate for a passage to Portsmouth, she being ordered for that purpose, and soon after landed there.

I had three of my messmates with me, all bound for London, so we agreed to walk it at our leisure and have a good view of the country; so after dinner we set off, and in the evening we got to Horndean, where we stopped for the night. Here we found several people in smock frocks at the inn, whom we took for farmers' men until a weary soldier came in and called for a pint of beer. One of the smock-frock gentlemen soon began to ask him questions, some of which he answered and some he would not, when to our surprise the smock-frocker pulled off his frock and discovered himself to be a serjeant, and the others that were with him were of his party. Fortunately the poor soldier had a furlough, which cleared him, but we could not help thinking how easy a poor fellow might get trepanned when he was least expecting it : these soldiers had been stationed here to take deserters either from the army or navy.

We set out next morning on our journey quite cheerful, and passed through Petersfield ; it was a beautiful day, and we intended to bring up at the first public-house we met with for refreshment, but alas, we could not meet with any, for we had got on a long heath and could not see the end of it ; moreover, we were very tired and our feet sore, so that when we came near any water we stood in it to cool them. We were so fatigued that I expected we should have to sleep on the heath that night, but fortunately a cart came along, in which the driver gave us a lift to near Godalming for a shilling apiece, and there we came to anchor for the night, but our feet were so sore that we had to go upstairs to our beds on our hands and knees.

Next morning after breakfast we gave up all thoughts of walking to London, and agreed to take the coach ; but the landlord told us it did not stop there—we must go four miles farther, to Guildford ; so finding we must go, we made a shift to hobble on, but better than I expected. When the coach arrived we mounted, and were landed in the Borough. My messmates and I took leave of each other on London Bridge, and I crawled along with my sore feet to my former lodgings in Stepney, where I found Mr. Wall and his family all well and glad to see me.

Some visitors were at the house at the time, and we kept it up in singing songs and telling stories till next morning. One of them was a pretty girl, and sang delightfully, she soon got my heart in tow, and had I had the needful, we should soon have been spliced together ; but my money was nearly gone, and though I had £10 to get from the owners of *The Spy*, yet I considered that I must provide myself with clothing for another voyage, and it might be some time before I could get a ship ; and I was right.

Next day I went to the owners' house and got my £10, and bought such things as I stood in need of; then returned to my lodgings and enjoyed myself till my money began to get short again, when I went to look out for a ship. Day after day I went up one side of the river, crossed London Bridge to save a penny, and down the other side and back again, but without success, for most of the ships, the Greenlandmen, Baltic and West Indiamen, were laid up and their crews discharged, besides the great influx of seamen lately paid off from the Fleet : hundreds of them, poor fellows, were starving, and begging through the streets for employment, some without a shoe to their feet.

For my part, though I had a good lodging to go to, yet I was much distressed in mind because I was beginning to get in debt to them. I thought to myself that I would rather be at sea in the hardest storm I ever knew than on the land in my present situation.

I continued several weeks here like a fish out of water, until one day I happened to go to a Limehouse dock, where I saw a large ship in the dock getting her bottom coppered, before fitting out for the coast of Guinea.

Although I had said I never would join such a barbarous trade again, I was now obliged by necessity to it, for poverty compelled me. So I inquired her name, which was *The Surprise*, and found that Mr. Calvert was the owner and lived in the Minories, so I went immediately and waited on him, and asked for a second mate's berth.

He told me I was too young for that situation on board so large a ship ; moreover, he had got all his mates except a fourth, which I might have, and which I accepted; so I went on board and assisted in rigging her while in dock, but had only two shillings a day and no provision. I gave up my board and lodgings to save me from getting further in debt, and made several good meals at a cook-shop ahead of the ship for only threepence—viz., a basin of good leg-of-beef soup for twopence, and a pennyworth of bread, and was satisfied.

The owners of ships, though floating in wealth, were very hard on poor sailors at this time, not shipping them till the last minute, and then giving them low wages. As soon as the ship was ready we got her out of dock; then Captain Hanson, with the three other mates and ship's company, came on board, and then the ship was victualled. We soon got the cargo in, went down to Gravesend, came to anchor, and cleared the ship.

On my former voyage to Guinea the men had £2 5s. a month, but then men were more scarce, being the Russian disturbance, and now our men had only £1 10s.; and when I received my river pay and a month's advance I sent £1 10s. to my landlord, to whom I owed it, by a friend who never gave it to him; and we sailed from Gravesend on December 21, 1791, being bound first to Ostend to take in spirituous liquors for trade, as part of the cargo. We hoped to enjoy a good Christmas at Ostend, but were sadly disappointed, for when we drew near the coast it blew so strong from the north-west, which made so much swell on the bar, that the pilot we had brought from London, was afraid to run the ship into the harbour, though the wind was fair for it; so we hauled on a wind to keep her off; but the gale increasing, we drove nearer the land, and on the 24th there was danger of the ship going on shore that night; so to save our lives the captain thought it best, as the harbour was under our lee, to run her in haphazard.

So everything being prepared, with one of the anchors hung under the bowsprit to bring her more on an even keel, we bore away under close-reefed fore and main top-sails, while the lofty waves and broken water all along shore looked dismal, and gave poor hopes of saving our lives. There are two wooden piers running out from Ostend, seaward—the easternmost is farthest out ; and, though top high water, she soon struck on the bar, but the roaring wind and waves forced her along, and the next stroke she gave unshipped our rudder ; but still the wind and waves drove her along, until the want of the rudder caused her to sheer to port, and, having by this time entered the mouth of the harbour, she ran against the easternmost pier with such force that she stove in her larboard side and soon went to the bottom : this was about the dusk of the evening, Christmas Eve.

Fortunately it was not so deep but that the gunwale was even with the water's edge, and the pier broke the force of the waves that approached us (we being inside of it), yet our situation was a deplorable one, as we had to remain in this manner all night in a strong gale of wind from the north-west, accompanied at times by snow and sleet, without anything to eat or drink ; so we kept moving about to keep the blood in circulation as well as we could, and, as St. Paul said, we wished for the day.   If ever blood came from men's fingers by the cold, as I have heard say, it came from mine at this time ; but whether from the bitter cold, as it was, or from the handling the new hard ropes, I cannot say.

Next day (Christmas Day) a boat got off to us from the shore and brought us a hard Dutch cheese and some gin, but no bread or water, which, however, they soon after got, and we refreshed ourselves a little ; and, as the wind fell, we got a cable out ahead and another astern fastened to the pier, and hove them well taut to prevent the ship from drifting into deeper water.

We had now another disagreeable job to go through, and that was in delivering the wet cargo in this cold weather; and as each vessel went from us laden, and consequently lightening the ship, we kept heaving the ship nearer to the pier, where the water was shallower, and at last got her so near that we got at the broken part of her hull and patched it up with tarpaulin and plank, so as to keep her afloat, and then we got her into the basin.

The ship being unfit for us to live on board, the captain sent us all on shore to lodge at the "Ship and Sheers," a tavern kept by one Spencer, an Irishman. Soon after, Mr. Calvert, the owner, came over from London in his yacht, and finding the ship too much damaged to pursue the voyage by repair she might get here, discharged all hands, but promised to provide a passage for us all to London.

Thus ended a broken and uncomfortable voyage amidst dangers and hardships, and being in poverty, and no wages to receive, next morning we officers waited on Mr. Calvert to see what he could do for us.

He had another ship fitting out for the same voyage, and offered us the same situations; but I would not accept mine, as the spring was drawing near, when they fit the ships out, and then I thought I could get one going on a better voyage than in a slaver. I took to my old lodgings again, where I was kindly received, notwithstanding my poverty and debt to them, as I found they had not received the thirty shillings I sent to them from Gravesend.

CHAPTER IV

1791–92

CALCUTTA AND THE BAY OF BENGAL

Sails for India in *Prince of Kaunitz*—Crossing the line—Arrival in Madras Roads—The Hooghly and Diamond Harbour—Calcutta —Joins the *Nonsuch*—Native Customs—Suttee—The Englishman in India—Joins the *Active*—Ball practice from Fort William— Rats as food—Loss of a day by misreckoning—To Balisore Roads in the *Hope* brig—Returns to Calcutta—War declared between Great Britain and France (1793)—The *Bien Aimé* seized in the Hooghly—Joins the *Elizabeth*—She founders in the Bay of Bengal—Thirteen in a leaky boat—"Ship ahoy"— Landed at Fulta—Taken by the press gang in Calcutta—On board H.M.S. *Woodcot*—Fails to escape—Transferred to H.M.S. *Minerva*—End of thirteen years in the merchant service.

AFTER this (in 1792), trade yet slack in the shipping way, I one day saw the *True Briton* lying off Tower Stairs, and thought to myself if the captain would give me a passage to Ostend again, I would go there and try my luck; so on board I went, and told the captain what I wanted and that I was willing to work my passage there, and he consented, and I soon got my things on board; sailed the next morning, arrived at Ostend after a fine passage, and then I waited on Mr. Spencer, who had promised me the second mate's berth on board of one of the Ostend Indiamen.

He seemed glad to see me, and renewed his promises; and I again boarded and lodged with him, but now on my own account (as before Captain Hanson had paid our expenses). I waited here several days, and finding no prospect of a berth (although the ships were fitting out) I became very uneasy; so one day I waited on Captain Tennant of the *Prince of Kaunitz* (in which Spencer had promised me the second mate's berth), and found that he had got all his mates long ago; but he offered me a quartermaster's situation if I would accept it, which I did, being heartily tired of waiting so long for a ship; so I went on board her to my duty, and volunteered to sleep on board her at night while she lay in the basin, having a shilling each night for it, beside my other pay going on.

The *Prince of Kaunitz* was a fine ship of about 800 tons, built at Bombay of teakwood, her masts and yards of the same, and belonged to Mr. Gregory, a Scotchman, and a Monsieur Banche, a member of the French National Convention: as she was to sail under Genoa colours, a captain of that nation was on board *pro tempore*; the rest were Captain Tennant, a Scotchman and commander; Mr. Palmer, chief mate, an Englishman and half-pay lieutenant in the British Navy; all the other mates were Scotchmen—the second too a half-pay lieutenant; but such a crew as I never would wish to sail with again, they being a mixture of English, Scotch, Genoese, Italians, French, Flemings, and Prussians. When the ship was partly laden we hauled her out of the basin and moored her to the westernmost pier to take in the remainder, and, when ready for sailing, we received each two months' advance of pay, thus with my fourteen dollars, river pay and night watching I had a pretty good sum; so after paying what I owed to Spencer, and getting myself a good rig-out, and remitting two guineas to my landlord at London (which I had the pleasure of hearing he received), I was perfectly contented and clear of debt.

We sailed from Ostend about the 1st of June, being rather in a hurry, as the French Republicans were expected in daily, and proceeded towards the British Channel, bound to Madras and Calcutta, and we had on board several ladies and gentlemen from England as passengers.

We had all along fine weather, and in crossing the line Neptune as usual with his lady Amphitrite paid us a visit; shaving with a notched piece of hoop-iron began, and the water flying about in all directions; but it proved fatal to a good and worthy gentleman passenger named Roberts, who had his wife on board with him: he had in the fun tried to throw a bucket of water on another person, but his foot slipped, he slid to leeward, and struck his knee against an eyebolt, which cut it open, and he being a corpulent man, a mortification came on, which caused his death a few days afterwards.

Hitherto we had been pretty comfortable on board, but now a circumstance occurred which upset it all, and fell hard on us that were innocent. The third mate, Mr. Mills, had been employed with a party of men almost daily in doing something in the ship's hold; and one day at dinner-time, the hatchway being left open, he went down to get something, and there saw a hogshead of porter spilled and the porter running into a bucket. This he reported to the captain, who was very angry, and ordered a search to be made, when they found a hamper broken open and several small jars of brandy taken out of it—it being the private venture of Mr. Nickols, the second mate. Likewise some cheeses had been taken out of boxes, where they had been preserved in bran.

The captain ordered the hands to be piped up and sent to the quarterdeck, where he mentioned what had been done, and promised that if any person would let him know of one or more of the thieves he would give them a month's pay and their name should be concealed; but if not he would keep all hands employed all day at work, and only their watch at night to rest, and would keep us on short allowance of other kinds and other things to make us uncomfortable. And he was as good as his word, for no one gave information (as the thieves themselves would not, and the innocent knew not who they were), and the consequence was we suffered so much —but more from the short allowance of water—that our lives were a misery to us.

He put himself and passengers on the same allowance, as a show; but as they were living mostly on mutton and poultry, and had plenty of wine and porter, they could not suffer much, whilst we, broiling in the hot sun, working hard, and living on hard salt junk, required three times as much water to serve us, and to make our pittance last, had to suck it through a quill in the cork of the bottle. I often thought that, if it pleased God I should ever get near a spring of fresh water again, I would live and die by it.

Being thirsty, we dared not eat much of our salt provision, and often when seeing the half-picked bones of mutton and poultry brought out of the cabin and given to the captain's dog, I longed to have them, but was ashamed to ask for them. I have often wondered since how I had patience to endure such sufferings.

I don't wonder that mutinies happen on board ships, but do wonder they don't happen oftener, where men are driven to such extremities, that they don't care whether they live or die: well might Lord Collingwood say that when a mutiny took place on board a ship it must be the fault of the captain or officers!

Mrs. Gordon, a lady passenger on board going out to join her husband, who held a high position in India, had brought out a cask of spirits to give some to the ship's company on Saturday nights (to drink to "sweethearts and wives," and in rough weather), but the captain put a stop to it. She was very kind to me, and often when she heard me at the con cry out "Steady!" and knew the wind was fair—and fortunately it happened so nearly the whole passage—she would send by Mrs. Hayes (her waiting-woman) a glass of grog for me. (This Mrs. Hayes came over a passenger in the *True Briton* with me to Ostend to go out with Mrs. Gordon to India.) But when put on short allowance of water she would get a glass of wine smuggled up to me out of the quarter galley. Though this was only as a fly-bite in regard to my thirst, yet it was more precious than gold, and I shall ever remember with gratitude her goodness.

We might easily have touched at the Cape of Good Hope and replenished our water, but the captain would not, and we saw no land on the passage except Tristan d'Acunha, a mere rock, until we got off Ceylon: the fragrance of which we smelt before we saw the land. Soon after we came to anchor in Madras Roads, after a passage of only three months and seven days, being the shortest ever known, and fortunate for us as we had only three days' water left. Perhaps the captain thought there was plenty of wine and porter in the ship in case of emergency; however, he ran a great risk, and beside, he being proud and haughty, showed how obstinate he was.

As soon as we came to anchor a catamaran came alongside, with two natives in her quite naked. As they were coming in at the gangway, the captain's lady and Mrs. Gordon, who had been walking arm-in-arm together, on seeing them come in, gave a shriek and ran into the cabin; when they were told they were two men, it was with difficulty they would believe it. These catamarans are only three logs of wood fastened together, some managed by one man, but others are large enough to bring off ships' anchors.

The *Perseverance,* an English 36-gun frigate, was lying here, and some of our people wrote a letter to her captain, stating that if he would send a boat with an officer in her they would enter into his ship. But of this our captain had got notice, and had described our crew as a bad and dishonest set to him, so that he would have nothing to do with them, and our captain was so ex-asperated that he soon had an opportunity to show it.

Our carpenter's mate, a namesake and messmate of mine, and as sober and quiet a man as I ever sailed with, was in the early part of the evening putting away the tools he had been working with, when the third mate, Mr. Mills, told him to do something which was out of his line of business, and to which he made some objections. The mate reported him to the captain, and the captain ordered him up to be punished. As soon as Willy, as we called him, heard this, he got his axe out of the tool chest, ran forward, and did not stop till he got to the jibboom end, and there he declared he would cut the first man in two that dared to take hold of him.

We were all aloft at this time, furling the sails; and seeing what was going on, set up a loud laugh, which provoked the captain more, who had been bawling out for us quartermasters to come down to seize poor Willy. Knowing this, we were in no hurry to come down; but the first that did was Bill Martin, who had no sooner set his feet on the deck than he received a blow from the fist of the captain, which set his face all in a gore of blood; then several of the people were selected out and got a severe flogging before he was pacified. The carpenter's mate still held out, and was firm in his resolution; but the captain, who had by this time got cooler, and thought, perhaps, he had got satisfaction

6

enough in flogging the others, got Mr. Bogree, the carpenter, to tell him to come in and he should not be hurt; and Willy, knowing Mr. Bogree would not deceive him, came in, and hostilities ceased.

Mr. Palmer, our first mate, left us here, but I don't know what for: he was rather too fond of grog, and I have seen him sitting sleeping on a chair on the quarter-deck in his watch at night giving the word of command with as loud a voice as if he had been awake at the time; however, he was a smart officer.

We lay here a week or more, and received a supply of good water, and then we got under way for Bengal, and, having got about forty or fifty miles up the Ganges, we came to anchor for the night.

From here we got under way, and soon after came to anchor off Diamond Harbour, where the India ships take in their cargo. Here Mr. Gordon came alongside from Calcutta for his lady in one of the finest budgerows in the country, which we supposed belonged to the Governor of India: she was sixty feet long, with seats on each side for each man to sit on and use their paddles (they were natives); she had a fine pavilion in her stern large enough to contain twenty people, well furnished and gilded all over; she was really a grand vessel. He took his lady and Mrs. Hayes, her waiting-woman, into her, and set off for Calcutta, and not long after I heard that Mrs. Hayes got a rich husband there.

From here we proceeded up the river with a rapid flood tide and fair wind; we passed through the beautiful Garden Reach, where the Company have their gardens on the left, and passed on the right a house like a palace, said to have been built by Warren Hastings, Esq., lately Governor of India; we soon after came to anchor abreast of Calcutta, and moored the ship near the old Fort Ghaut.

Here I had the job of making slings for a fine Arabian horse which the ship was to take to England, being a present from Lord Cornwallis, Governor General of India, for the Prince of Wales, and the passage for it was said to be a thousand pounds. Our cargo at this time had been delivered, and part of another (consisting of cases of sugar) taken in ; and during this time, unknown to me, some of our people had sent a petition to the Governor requesting their discharge as being British subjects and not wishing to sail any longer under foreign colours ; but probably the petition would not have been granted, had it not been for a lady who came out as one of our passengers, whose uncle here was judge or some other high officer in that line. To him she had told of the hardships and sufferings we had undergone by the captain, and he so used his influence that the Governor sent an order to our captain to discharge all British seamen from his ship that wished for it.

In consequence of this order we were all called aft on the quarter-deck, and there the captain promised fine things if we would remain by the ship ; but if not, though he had an order to discharge us, he had no order to pay us our wages ; therefore he gave us the choice. But this revived our old grievances, and with one consent we all left the ship, except one (the poulterer) who was no seaman, and left our hard earned wages behind.

Mr. Nickols, now chief mate, endeavoured much to persuade me to stay, and said if I did it would prove to my advantage ; but I could not agree to sail again with a proud haughty tyrant, and well I did not, for the ship was lost on her return near Ostend.

There were thirteen of us who left the *Prince of Kaunitz*, and we immediately entered on board a large country ship mounting thirty guns, and commanded by a Captain Canning. Her name was the *Nonsuch*. She was ready for sea, and only waiting for a cargo of opium to trade among the Malays, a savage and treacherous people, who come out with their prows full of men, and, if opportunity offers, will board a ship, murder the crew, and then plunder her. Some instances of the kind had lately happened, and for this reason the *Nonsuch* was well armed, and, being a dangerous voyage, higher wages were given.

We waited here three months for the opium, and having little or nothing to do, went often on shore to see Calcutta and its environs, and to learn the manners and customs of the natives. We found them a mixture of Hindoos, Gentoos, Mahometans, and idolaters. At the corners of the streets were placed idols of such hideous forms as would puzzle Old Nick to tell what they represented. There are several castes or sects among the people, and the Brahmins are their priests, but attend to secular concerns likewise. One caste has the custom of burning the living widow with her deceased husband, and our carpenter told us he had seen it done. We asked him if she cried out much, but he could not tell, for immediately the torch was put to the pile it was instantly in a blaze, and the Brahmins made so much noise at the time that it was impossible to hear her.

The widows are not absolutely compelled to be burnt, but if they refuse they are abandoned by their friends and looked upon as outcasts : such power has priestcraft over weak minds ! It was reported here at this time that the Governor, wishing to persuade a widow not to be burnt, desired her to hold her finger over a candle and consider the pain ; she did so, and so long that the Governor desired her to take it away.

With another caste, when their sick are past hopes of recovery they are taken at low water to the river's side, and there washed away when the flood comes to reach them. I have been near a man in that situation, and saw his lips move as if in prayer ; he was perfectly resigned to his situation, and the flood tide washed him away.

These people are terribly afraid of losing their caste, which may easily be done, by eating or drinking out of any utensil a European has made use of, or eating victuals out of any utensil a European has touched, or touching the bone of an animal cooked by a European. Sometimes a mischievous sailor will throw a beef-bone into a dinghee when alongside; instantly the dingheewaller (waterman) will jump overboard, and, hanging by the dinghee's side, beg in the most piteous manner for the sailor to throw it out again, nor will he enter in until it is done.

But some may regain their caste again. In the market-place at Calcutta there is a swing, the height near fifteen feet, and when a devotee wishes to recover his caste two hooks at one end of the beam are hooked into his loins; then certain people pull the other end of the beam down with ropes, which raises the devotee from the ground. They run round and round for fifteen or twenty minutes amidst the acclamations of the people, and if he bears it well he regains his caste again; if not, he is a lost man, debarred from the society of his friends, and his only resource is to become a Halachore, and get his living among the Europeans by doing anything they require of him (a people, they say, who will " eat hog, eat dog, eat ebery ting, fight ebery ting, and fear neither God nor debil ").

The females are small in stature and delicate, wear long black hair, clubbed up behind, and of a dark copper colour; they stain their teeth red with betel root, which they chew, and think it makes them look pretty; they smell strong of cocoanut oil, and wear bangles or large rings on their wrists and legs, and some have rings to their noses of such kind of metal, from brass to gold, as they can afford to buy; they are clean in their persons, and come to maturity sooner than Europeans, and many are grand-mothers at thirty years of age.

After waiting three months for the opium none was to be got: it had been a bad harvest. So orders came on board to send the guns and ammunition on shore and prepare to take in a cargo of rice for Madras. This disappointed us much, as it was only like a coal voyage to London, and the wages would be less; so we made up our minds to leave the ship, and asked for our river pay. But the captain, although a very good man, told us he would give us none except we would go the voyage. However, we left the ship, and fifty rupees of pay behind, intending to employ a lawyer to get it for us.

There are plenty of ships to be got here, and another good thing was that they always advanced four months' pay before the ship sailed, and it was easy to get credit on shore to that amount. So off we went, and took board and lodgings for half a rupee a day at one Francisco's, an Italian, and a good sort of a man. It was in the Radak Bazaar, and near the Black Hole, where 146 Englishmen were confined one night, and, whence in the morning only twenty-three came out alive, the rest having died of suffocation (there is a monument now over the place, enclosed with iron railings).

Calcutta swarms with mosquitoes at night, so we slept on the housetop, it being flat, to avoid them. Everything here is very cheap, as there are no taxes. The following articles cost as follows: a dozen ducks or fowls, 1 rupee; a side of dried bacon, 1 rupee; a maund (or 80 lb.) of soft sugar, 1 rupee; four pairs of country shoes, 1 rupee; two chip hats, covered with silk, 1 rupee; 1,000 cheroots of tobacco, 1 rupee; good tea, from 4d. to 6d. a lb.; bread and beef in proportion; and as for clothing, a sailor might rig himself out in light clothes for a six-months' voyage for 7 or 8 rupees: a rupee might be valued at this time at 2s. 3d. The natives work for a penny a day, but their diet costs little, being nearly all rice.

The English gentry live high, and nearly burn their livers up with curry ; in going only a few yards they must have their palanquin, where they loll along their whole length in it at their ease ; they keep a number of Hindoo servants at very little expense, but each will do only his own work ; if he is a water fetcher he will do nothing else. The houses of the English are lofty and grand, and occupy one part of the city ; the natives' on the other part are merely hovels, and their shops mean but well stocked ; the doors secured at night with two or three padlocks on a staple little thicker than a straw, but few robberies are committed here. I have often passed through their bazaars in the day and seen heaps of gold mohurs and rupees lying on the ground before a money-changer's door, and only a lazy Gentoo half asleep watching it. I have often thought what a fine chance there was for some of the light-fingered London gentry if they were here.

Calcutta is a hundred miles from the sea in a straight line, but a hundred and fifty by water. I never felt the heat in the West Indies or coast of Guinea so much as I have here. Many die here by the stroke of the sun, or by sleeping on the saltpetre ground in the night. One of my shipmates lost the use of a hand for several weeks by letting his hand over the bedside and touching the ground in his sleep. One morning I saw a stout man lying on the ground apparently asleep, but when examined he was quite dead.

There is a fine new church lately built here for the orthodox, and it is pretty well attended on the Sabbath, as the Governor is there then. One day my attention was drawn to a stone-built hut in the churchyard, and the door being open I went in, and found it near filled with a great monster standing on its legs, though dead. Being dark inside, I could not make out what kind of beast it was, but on inquiry was told that it had been a favourite elephant belonging to the East India Company many years, and when past labour through old age was permitted to go about the town a-begging. It was quite harmless, and would take a piece of bread or fruit from the hands of a child and then make its salaam. It lived to a great age, and when it died was skinned and the body buried. A stone model of it was made, and the skin put on it, which now is nearly as hard as iron.

Nearly two miles below Calcutta stands Fort William, the largest and strongest in all India, near the river's side, which supplies it with water. It has all the resources of defence within itself and walls, with dwelling-houses for the garrison, and a large market place. On the opposite side of the river which they call the Sulkee side, is a small row of houses for the natives, a large one for the education of soldiers' children, and some distance higher up a good ship yard.

Being now tired of the shore, eight of us shipped on board the brig *Active* (Captain Cummings). Her former crew had been twenty lascars, but the captain thought eight Englishmen would suit him better. We received four months' advance, being sixty-four rupees. Our cargo was rice, and bound to Pondicherry.

Having settled our affairs with our landlord, we repaired on board the *Active*; got her under way, but came to anchor off Fort William to wait for the captain, who was on shore. As we were leaning over the rails chatting to one another it was a mercy we were not shot, for several came whizzing a little above our heads, which we thought was the noise from the Brahminy kites. The dog was the first that had the sagacity to know what it was—gave a moan and jumped down the hatchway, but not hurt. This made us laugh, until we found it no laughing matter, for the shot began to hit the masts, and then we, like the dog, bundled down below.

The cause was as thus : the soldiers at Fort William were exercising and firing at a mark ; but we could not see them, as they were inside of the rampart, nor they us. Every shot that was fired too high came over the rampart to us—and there were a good many of them—and it was a mercy that none of us were hurt.

Our captain came on board next morning, and we got the vessel under way ; but the south-west monsoons were against us, and we had to tide it down all the way from Calcutta to the sea, which caused us a good deal of labour, as we had often to let go the anchor to prevent her getting aground ; this took us near a week, and, being so busy, the log-book was neglected, and we lost a day, which caused us to miss our port. The south-west monsoons continue from April to October, and blow strong, with clouds and rain ; the north-east ones blow from October to April, being six months each, but the latter have finer weather and gentle winds. But the tides are so rapid here, that ships in some places cannot ride against them ; the *Fort William*, a country ship of a thousand tons, drove with both anchors ahead, hooked an Indiaman's mooring off Diamond Harbour, and drove with them all until the tide slacked.

At the mouth of the Ganges, being a fine morning, we saw near a dozen alligators basking on the water, and when we got past the sandheads into Balisore Roads we stood on a wind to the south-south-east for the opposite side of the Bay of Bengal, where the wind blows contrary, for it takes a long time for a laden merchantman to beat up a long shore against the south-west monsoons. Having got to the southward of Sumatra we found the wind come in our favour, with fine weather, and then steered under all sail to the south-west. We caught several dolphins : one I hung up at the windlass bits in the night, hoping to have a good dinner from it next day; but the brig was swarming with rats, and next morning nothing was left but the bones.

These vermin were so bold that they cared but little for us, and would even get up to the tops in search of food; however, we made a trap, and caught many. One of our people (a Yorkshireman) used to skin, grill, and eat them, and they tasted as well as a rabbit. Had I known as much then as since, I would have had many a good meal of them, for our diet on board here was nothing but rice, doll,[1] and ghee and water—food that was not fit for an Englishman to live on—and we suffered much by it. The doll is like split peas, and one pound of it is put to ten pounds of rice, said to prevent the latter from hurting the eyesight; the ghee is buffalo's butter, to help it down, and is something like pork-slush, and such is called the country allowance; but all ships are not so.

The vessel was swarming with ants, cockroaches, centipedes, and scorpions; we could not move a cask after a wet day, or an old sail, without some of the latter crawling out. One night at the helm I was bitten or stung near the wrist, which became very painful and swelled; the only remedy was rubbing it with lamp-oil, as others had done, and in a few days it got well.

Our captain took a kind of lunar observation now and then, which never agreed with the longitude by the log, and he supposed it to be by not having assistance enough, as only he and I could handle a quadrant; but I rather suppose it was that we had lost a day and did not know it, so we must have taken the declination of the sun and moon wrong each time, and no wonder the reckoning did not agree.

After steering, as we thought, far enough to the southwest, we kept more to the west to make the land; and when we got sight of the Coromandel coast we saw

[1] Dhall.

Pondicherry so far on our weather-bow that the captain gave up all hopes of beating up to it against the wind and current, so we bore away for Madras Roads, and next day came to anchor there.

A boat soon came alongside, and we asked them why all the ships had their colours flying, and they said because it was Easter Sunday. We said they must be mistaken, as it was Saturday; but they insisted they were right, and so they were, and now we found that we had lost a day— a circumstance I never heard of before except in circumnavigating the world.

An English transport with troops on board anchored ahead of us, and we soon after saw a great many pieces of salt pork thrown overboard, and come floating towards us. We soon jumped into our boat and picked them up: some were rusty and some not, and wondering why they threw such good meat overboard we thought an infection might be among it, therefore threw the worst overboard, but could not bear to part with the best, so took our chance and ate them; had we known that the pork was thrown overboard because the pickle had leaked out of the cask when surveyed on board the transport, we should have kept the whole and been glad of it. Had those troops been living on rice, doll, and ghee, as we were, they would have jumped mast-high for such good meat!

From here we ran farther down the coast to the northeast, and came to anchor off Bimlipatam, to deliver our cargo.

When the rice was delivered we loaded with salt, and arrived safe with it at Calcutta after a voyage of three months, and there left her; and as we had received four months' advance, we gained a month's pay. The captain never asked for it, perhaps thinking it needless, or that we had sufficiently earned it—and so we had.

About this time news arrived (June 1793) of war being

declared between Great Britain and France; and the *Bien Aimé*, a French Indiaman, with some other vessels of that nation lying here, were taken possession of, and their crews sent as prisoners to Fort William; and a Danish 32-gun frigate being here for sale, a Captain Elliot bought her. Her name was *Elizabeth*, and was to remain under Danish colours on account of the war, as that nation was at peace with France.

A Mr. Bee, a Dane, who spoke English well, and a nephew of the governor of a Danish factory up the river, was entered as chief mate and captain of the colours, and I second mate and gunner. Her masts, yards, and sails being too large for a merchantman, we got them all reduced, and began to load with wheat and sugar for Ganjam. Captain Elliot sent on board to me a good chest of clothing of the best quality, and orders for Mr. Bee to pay my mess (as we had our victuals together, and I no money), and he would settle it with him afterwards; for the mates of country ships have to victual themselves in harbour and at their own expense, but at sea mess with the captain at his expense.

Sea-cunnies, or quartermasters, are appointed to large ships (four, six or eight, according to her size) to steer, heave the lead, and stow the hold; they are generally European seamen. The serang, tindals, or lascars (of whom we had eighty) do the rest of the duty, and have a separate place to cook for themselves, and for their water, lest any of us should touch it and they lose their caste.

Having got the *Elizabeth* ready for sea, Captain Elliot came on board, and we got under way; in going down the river and about half ebb tide we got aground on a mud-bank and lay there until next flood, when she floated off again, apparently without any hurt, and soon after got out of the Ganges and stood out to sea to beat up to Ganjam against the south-west monsoons. On the second night of our being at sea, and under single reefed topsails and a rough head sea, about one in the morning and my watch, one of the lascars came and said to me, "Bote pawny neechee hae," that was, "There is much water below"; so I followed him down to the 'tween-decks, and sure enough there was much water on the leeside; but seeing it come in very much at the hawseholes when the ship pitched, I ordered the people to cram gunny bags into them to stop it; but as fast as they poked them in they were washed back again and the people often with them.

Thinking it somewhat extraordinary, I ran on deck, went and informed Captain Elliot of it, and asked his consent to get the ship before the wind until we got the hawseholes stopped, which he consented to; but the ship was by this time so much down by the head that she would not answer her helm, and appeared going down head-foremost.

Captain Elliot, being on deck at this time, ran to the pumps and sounded the well, but found so much line wet that he dropped it and ran to get the boats clear. We had only two on board, a skiff and a jolly-boat; the longboat had been left behind to be repaired. By this time the alarm of the ship's sinking having spread, the passengers and others came running up in their shirts, and a dismal scene it was to see the distress every one was in.

As Captain Elliot and others were getting the jolly-boat ready (which was nearest at hand and on the main deck), I ran to the skiff which was stowed before her, and got her lashings cast off, expecting the lascars would come to assist me and save their lives; but instead of that they gave themselves up to despair, and clinging to the weather rigging, some were crying out to Allah and some to Jos to save them.

Meantime the captain with Mr. Bee and passengers had

got the jolly-boat to the gunwale, which was then under water, and pushing off, and seeing I had no one to assist me with the skiff and not a moment to lose, I made to the jolly-boat instantly, and had just time to get hold of her stern and get in. By this time the ship's lee foreyard arm was so low that the forebrace nearly took us down, and would if not cut away. The last thing we touched of her was a push from the lee foreyard arm, and down she went headforemost with all the sails set as before, as we had no time to take them in—if that had been any service.

There were thirteen of us in the boat, and only two oars and a broken one by which I steered her. We were in much confusion in getting clear of the ship for fear of her suction, as not a thowl was to be found to row against; but, as necessity is the mother of invention, the people found their handkerchiefs would do by making grummets of them, and they answered well, and we rowed along before the wind and waves, some of which dashed into us at times. A Danish officer (passenger), who had been long in India, came swimming after us, and got alongside; but he was not permitted to come in as the boat was so deep—particularly by an Irish officer, who pushed his hands off whenever he attempted to catch hold of the boat, and the poor fellow swam back again. Mr. Bee was assisting the captain in getting the boat ready, but when pushing off he was missing, and we saw no more of him. In the boat were many live ducks, which we ought to have preserved, as we had no provision or fresh water, but in the confusion they were all thrown overboard.

Being in this distressed situation in a dark night on the wide ocean, a leaky boat and no compass to steer by (and in fear of the boat filling every minute), every one that was not rowing was ordered to sit close down in the boat's bottom and bale out the water with their hats and caps.

At one time it was proposed by the Irish officer that the boat should be kept broadside to the sea, which would soon have swamped her ; and when he found that would not do, he proposed that part should get overboard, and hang at arm's length to the gunnel to lighten her, but as he did not like to show the example that was dropped.

We continued in this manner between hope and despair until daylight, and then found that the plug had been out all this time ; and when we came to see each other it was really laughable, notwithstanding our danger, for there had been a good deal of the ducks' dung in the boat, which mixing with the water, had washed over all those sitting in the boat's bottom and drenched them so completely that we could hardly know one from the other.

About eight o'clock the wind abated a little, and soon after we had the pleasure of seeing a ship coming our way, but a little to leeward ; so we rowed might and main with our two oars and held the broken one up with a handkerchief to it ; but they saw us not and went past. Fortunately soon after a man was going to the masthead, and looking on the weather quarter, beheld us ; we soon saw the ship put about and come towards us, and, blessed be God ! we all got safe on board.

The captain and officers were very kind and relieved our necessities, but as the ship was outward bound the captain promised that if we met any vessel bound to Bengal he would put us on board her, and that very afternoon we spoke a large sloop laden with rice, which had sprung a leak and was returning again to Calcutta. As we had no luggage to encumber us, we were soon put on board, and were a great help to her small crew in pumping ; the wind was fair, and we bowled along in the old sloop until we got into Balisore Roads, but there not being daylight to see our way between the buoys to enter the Ganges we had to anchor for the night.

The old sloop pitched and rolled, so that it made her leak more ; and for fear she might go down before daylight, we hoisted the boat out (the only one she had) and dropped her astern with a good strong rope to hold her and to be ready in case of emergency.

As soon as daylight appeared, to see the buoys, we got under way, and in entering the channel between the buoys, the sea was so rough that by a jerk of the boat's rope it fairly dragged her stem out, and she was soon out of sight astern and full of water, and her stem dragging after us. Fortunately we had a fresh gale and young flood tide in our favour, and we went rapidly along, pumping and sailing, until we reached Diamond Harbour, and there we ran her on shore plump on the mud.

Mr. Thompson, the postmaster (for letters were sent to and from Calcutta by boats at this time), sent one of his boats, and we landed and got a good breakfast with him of curried rice, fowl, etc., and he lent us a boat and crew to take us to Fulta, a place ten miles higher up the river, where we landed and repaired to a Dutch tavern to enjoy ourselves ; here we got a good dinner and finished the day in drinking wine, singing songs and smoking cheroots, and were so merry that we forgot all our troubles.

A boat was hired here, which took us next day as high as Garden Reach, but the tide making down, we landed and walked along the river side to Calcutta. Here I repaired to my old lodgings, where I was received kindly, but with sorrow for my misfortunes. Antonio, who was mate of the *Active* when I was in her, was there, and kindly gave me two rupees.

The next day, as I was sitting near the door, and it open, and smoking a cheroot while brooding over my hard fate, a guard of soldiers came along, and the serjeant seeing me, came and said that I was to go along with him. I asked him what for : that I was no deserter from an Indiaman, which I supposed he was looking after. He replied that his orders were to take every English seaman he could meet with, and at this time he had upwards of twenty that he had taken, and one of them was the chief mate of a country ship which I knew, and said it was best to submit, as the serjeant must obey his orders.

The reason of this pressing, a thing seldom known here, was that the *Woodcot* Indiaman was lying here in want of seamen, having on board stores and ammunition and 150 artillerymen to sail for Pondicherry, a French place our army was besieging; so we were all taken to Fort William and put into prison for the night, and after that sent on board the *Woodcot*, and put under the charge of Mr. Cole, a Master's mate of the *Minerva* frigate, who had been here with a prize and was returning to his ship again in the *Woodcot*.

Shipwreck and loss of all our clothes is distressing enough, but to be pressed into the bargain is really shocking; and I began to despond even to tears at my hard fate.

Hope, now, was my only comfort, for I knew the ship must anchor several times before she got to sea, as the south-west monsoons were against us; so I made up my mind, should an opportunity offer while at anchor in the night, to swim on shore in defiance of tigers, alligators, or anything else, and run my chance; and the following evening after leaving Calcutta, we came to anchor a few miles above Fulta, where we had been so merry the other day. After the watch was set, the people being much fatigued with hard duty all day, soon fell asleep, but the artillerymen were stationed all round the ship as sentinels.

Although I was fatigued as much as others, my mind would not allow me to go to sleep, for I kept watching and hoping some of the sentinels would soon go into a doze; and at last one of them on the poop began nodding, and lay with his head over the rails as if asleep. Now is the time, thinks I; so passing silently along the quarter-deck to the poop and taffrail, I was in the act of getting over to slip down the boat's painter into the water when the sentinel awoke and asked what I was doing there. I had just presence of mind to answer that I was going to bail the boat out. He said I should not go there without leave of the officer of the watch, who was sitting asleep in a chair on the quarterdeck; and he, hearing the noise, awoke and said, "Damn the boat! never mind her," and went to sleep again; so I thought it best to retreat in time, went forward and then below, where I slept on a chest lid until the morning.

We got under way from here, and the next place we came to anchor at was Cudgeree, where they make the pots. Here we lay farther from the land than before, but a country brig laden with rice came alongside to deliver. Her captain and crew were all natives, and I began to hope I might conceal myself in her hold; so when the hatches were taken off, none was more ready than I to jump down and begin to sling the bags of rice as they were hoisted up, and thus I continued until it was all out; then I stole forward to the fore-peak, lay down and covered myself with some mats lying there, hoping every minute the brig would put off and I escape, for the wind and tide were running strong up the river; but while I was thinking of this the black captain came into the hold and began taking up the mats and shaking the loose rice together, and discovered me, but I have thought since the black rascal had watched me.

He seemed much surprised, and I, being prepared, got up and told him I had been mate of a ship at Calcutta; how they had pressed me, and brought me away against my inclination. Seeing he hesitated, I offered him my watch to say nothing, but he would not take it, and going silently away I was in hopes that all was right; but very soon after I heard the rough voice of Mr. Edgar Hay, the chief mate of the *Woodcot*, hailing us to know who was there, so I answered it was me, and that I was waiting for an empty bag to put the loose rice into. "Damn the loose rice!" said he; "if you don't make haste and jump on board you will lose your passage" (God grant it! thought I—nothing would please me better); but he had no suspicion of my intentions, and this was the last prospect I had of escaping.

The French Indiaman captured at Calcutta, lately named the *Bien Aimé*, having joined us here—she having the Governor, Lord Cornwallis, and suite on board—and bound to Pondicherry, and with the *Triton* Indiaman, we set sail together from this place, and after beating up three weeks against the south-west monsoons we arrived in Madras Roads, where we found lying H.M. frigate *Minerva*, of thirty-eight guns (Captain Whitby), and bearing the flag of Rear-Admiral Cornwallis (white at mizzen), brother to the Governor. The *Minerva*, with two other Indiamen, had just returned from Pondicherry, that place having surrendered to the British arms on August 23 of the present year (1793).

We pressed men (to the number of twenty-three) were sent on board the *Minerva*, and being arranged along the quarter deck, were examined by the admiral and captain. I told them I had been only three years at sea and had no clothes but the shabby ones on my back, and tried all I could to get clear; but it would not do, and out of twenty-three only three of us were kept; the other twenty were sent on shore at Madras to shift as well as they could. And thus ended my services of near thirteen years in the merchants' employ, a period of poverty, hardships, dangers, and disappointments such as few, I believe, have experienced during that time.

CHAPTER V

1793-95

IN THE KING'S SERVICE

Begins life again as a bluejacket—Joins H.M.S. *Minerva*—Learns to make his clothes—Lord Cornwallis leaves India—Drill and marching exercise—Diego Garcia—Turtle catching—Swearing put down—Sails for England—Chased by the *Intrepid*—Pass four French frigates in the Channel—Sir Edward Palliser's action with them—Admiral Cornwallis and the ladies—Drafted into the *Prompte* (May, 1794)—To the Moray Firth—The Duke of Richmond and the Marquis of Huntley—In dock at Sheerness—Flushing and Leith Roads—Promoted to quartermaster—" Pass him along "—Louis XVIII. on board the *Prompte*—Captain Leveson-Gower to command—Meets his brother James—All five brothers in the Navy—Appointed Acting Gunner (September 1795)—Returns home—Finds Shields sadly changed.

THE *Minerva* was a fine large frigate, with a poop lately erected on her for the convenience of the admiral and captain, and mounting 48 guns. I was stationed to do any duty in the maintop; all my clothes were on my back, and with an old silver watch and one rupee, which constituted my all, I had now, as it were, the world to begin again; and a poor prospect I had before me. I had no bed, neither did I care for any, for my bones had got so hardened since I came to sea that I could sleep as comfortable on a chest lid or on the deck as on the best bed in the ship; and having only one shirt, I went without when I had to wash and dry it.

The *Bien Aimé* was bought into H.M.'s Service, and

Lieutenant King (since Sir Richard King) was appointed to her as master and commander; she was officered and manned totally from the *Minerva* and the *Minerva's* crew (filled up by pressing out of the East Indiamen as they arrived from Europe), and a great many able seamen we got out of them.

Soon after this Lord Cornwallis came on board, and we got under way; he was brother to our admiral, and we proceeded to Pondicherry. A day or two after we came to anchor off that place, and his lordship went on shore to view the works: it was at one time in contemplation to blow them up, but that was not done. He returned on board again, we got under way, returned to Madras Roads, and landed his lordship again.

One of these evenings, as I was sitting on the coamings of the after-hatchway pondering my hard fate, Mr. Robinson, our first lieutenant, a worthy and good man, observed me, and sent for me to his cabin; and then, taking a sheet from off his bed, gave it to me and told me to get some clothes made from it, and said that when his dabash (a gentoo agent) came on board he would give me a good rig-out of clothing; but the ship sailed before he came, and so disappointed us. However, I got a light jacket and two pairs of trousers made from the sheet, and was very thankful for his kindness to me, a stranger.

There were no slops at this time on board the *Minerva*; the purser at stated periods served out to the ship's company so many yards of dungaree as were required to each man for jackets, shirts and trousers, with needles and thread for them; and my messmates, being a set of good fellows and accustomed to the work, soon taught me to cut out and make them, by which means I soon got a good rig-out and a new straw hat, which I made by their instructions; as for shoes and stockings, they were not worn by sailors in this hot country.

Shortly after this Lord Cornwallis embarked on board the *Swallow* packet for a passage to England, and we, with the *Bien Aimé*, got under way and convoyed her clear of the Mauritius, where the French had several ships of force lying. We then proceeded to the Island of Diego Garcia, one of the Mauritius Islands, and having been told that a French frigate and brig were lying there, and as it was thought there might be an occasion for landing, 150 of our crew were picked out to be trained to the use of small arms, and I was one of the number. Nothing could be more diverting than to see the blunders we made at the first beginning : we were arranged in two lines along the quarterdeck, with the captain and fugleman in our front, and the booms full of people laughing and grinning at us ; some put their muskets on the wrong shoulder, some let the butt fall on their next neighbour's toes, some could not stand with their backs straight up, and were threatened in having a cross-bar lashed to it, and some had their shoulders chalked by the captain, that they might know the right from the left, which only bothered them the more ; in short, there was nothing but blunders for a week or two, and then we began to mend.

This exercise was performed twice every day, and for our encouragement when over we were marched, with drum and fife playing before us, round the quarterdeck gangway and forecastle, and in the evening had an extra pint of grog each ; but the awkward squad had to stand on one side with their muskets presented to us as we marched past them, and not allowed extra grog. We improved so in the course of a few weeks that it was said we fired a better volley than the marines.

When we arrived off Diego Garcia we hoisted French colours, and, though the wind was against us, worked the ship into the harbour and there came to anchor. We saw no frigate, but discovered a brig lying at the upper end of the harbour, and immediately sent our boats manned and armed to take possession of her, which they soon did, as the crew and few inhabitants, who are turtle catchers, fled into the woods for safety.

This is a noted place for catching turtle, and we found a pen with two hundred in it. The island is low and very woody, and the harbour a good-sized one; and, as we were in want of fresh water, we digged holes deep enough for each cask bung deep, and, putting them down in the evening, we found them full in the morning; but it was rather brackish, and only served for cooking. Our people caught several wild pigs here, which were good eating. In the course of their rambles several lascars who were hidden in the woods, hearing our people speak English, came and delivered themselves up to them: they said they had been wrecked here in an English ship belonging to Bombay several months ago, and, being afraid to deliver themselves up to the French for fear they would have sent them to the Mauritius and sold them for slaves, they had hid themselves in the woods, and lived on cocoanuts and what else they could find there; so we took them all on board, and, when we arrived at Bombay, discharged them, to their great satisfaction.

Having nothing more to do to draw our attention here, we loaded the brig with turtles, and got near fifty on board the *Minerva* and the *Bien Aimé*, being as many as we could conveniently stow on the main deck between the guns; then, setting fire to the poor Frenchmen's huts (which happened to be on Guy Fawkes' day, November 5th, 1793), we got under way, and stood out to sea.

We shaped our course for one day, and each day lived like aldermen on turtle soup: every evening for near six weeks, a turtle was hung up to the skids by its two hind fins and the head cut off to let it bleed; and although each one was large enough to serve a day for our crew of three hundred men, scarcely half a pint of blood came from it. Next morning it was cut up and put into coppers, and when boiled, served out to all hands with two or three bucketsful of eggs into the bargain.

About midway on our passage we parted company one dark night with the *Bien Aimé* and brig, and when we got on the Malabar coast came to anchor off Tilicherry, where our admiral went on shore, but soon returned again with intelligence of a large frigate and a brig having passed that way, steering to the northward ; and as we made sure they must be enemies, we got under way immediately and steered our course after them. On the following night, as we were going along with a fine breeze from the east, and a fore topmast steering sail set, we saw a large frigate and a brig pass us to windward, but on the other tack ; and instead of putting our ship about to follow her, Captain Whitby ordered the hammocks to be piped up and the drummer to beat to quarters, and then gave his chief attention to us at the quarterdeck guns, in seeing that we primed them in a proper manner. Although I was a young man-of-war's man, I had my thoughts, and was surprised that he did not put the ship about and stand after the enemy.

At last the old admiral came up in his nightdress, and asked what direction the enemy was in ; and I, being nearest to him, said she was going from us on the other tack. He immediately sent for Captain Whitby, who was then on the forecastle, and, when he came, told him to haul down the steering sail, put the ship about, then steer after the enemy, and he would have sufficient time to get the guns ready ; so accordingly this was done, or we should not have met each other till we had got to the Antipodes.

We came up with them early in the morning, our people all eager for battle ; but when daylight appeared, (which was waited for, knowing they could not escape our superior sailing), we were much disappointed in seeing them hoist Portuguese colours ; so we sent a boat to board the frigate, and found they were from Goa, and bound to another port in the Portuguese settlements on this coast ; so we let them proceed, but could not help laughing to see their seamen going aloft dressed with stuffed clothes, cocked hats, and some with boots on.

The *Minerva* was under good discipline, and, had we had an experienced captain to carry on the duty, should have been more comfortable ; but he was too young—had come out with the admiral on this station a midshipman, and in the course of three or four years had got made a post captain, when only nineteen years of age ; he could work the ship very well, and that was all. Not a word was to be spoken in wearing or tacking the ship except from the commanding officer ; everything was done as silently as possible, and the boatswain's pipe just loud enough to be heard, the admiral not allowing the side to be piped for him or any other officer ; they were not to be whistled in like dogs.

Not an oath was allowed to be spoken, but as there were so many new pressed men in the ship it was almost impossible to avoid it, and when any was heard to swear their names were put on a list, and at seven next morning were punished, though not severely, few getting more than seven or eight lashes'; yet it was galling, and how I escaped God only knows, for my name had been put on the list several times, and I suppose it must have been through the kindness of my good friend Mr. Robinson, the first lieutenant.

Though the punishment was light, it displeased the men very much, who had not had time to divest themselves of this new crime they had been so long accustomed to, and was nearly attended with serious consequence. Every evening, weather permitting, it was customary for the people to have a dance, and one of these evenings the lanthorns were lighted as usual, and hung on each side of the launch, which was stowed in those days on the main deck under the booms, and the fiddler on the topsail sheet bits began to play away on his violin; but nobody came to dance.

By-and-by the gunners' wads began to fly about in all directions, the lights were extinguished, the lanthorns knocked to pieces, and a wad rolled into the admiral's cabin as he walked there. The old boy soon saw that something was the matter and sent for Captain Whitby; but when Captain Whitby came he pretended that he knew nothing was the matter with the ship's company. The admiral's steward came into the cabin at the time, and being asked if he knew what was the matter with the people, replied that he heard the men say that there was too much dancing at the gangway in the morning to keep them dancing in the evening; so the admiral, seeing through it immediately, instead of using severe means (as many a tyrant would have done, and perhaps caused a real mutiny), adopted a better way, and that was in cautioning Captain Whitby not to use the cat on such light occasions, and never to flog a man again without his permission.

When the people heard of this they were greatly satisfied, and did their duty more cheerfully and better, and not a man was flogged after this but one, and he richly deserved it—it was for striking an officer when on shore on duty. But in all my experience at sea I have found seamen grateful for good usage, and yet they like to see subordination kept up, as they know the duty could not be carried on without it; but whenever I hear of a mutiny in a ship, I am much of the opinion of Admiral Lord Collingwood, who said it must assuredly be the fault of the captain or his officers.

Our ship being leaky, we went to Bombay and there

docked her, and during this time the *Bien Aimé* and prize arrived ; but the turtle had all lately died from the cold weather at nights. The prize was immediately sold, and I received three rupees and a quarter for my share.

My little prize money was soon expended, together with my watch, which I sold to pay my part of the expenses of the mess ; and the most of it went for gin, though I was averse to ardent spirits. But some of them were as wild as March hares, and among them a little Welshman named Emmet, whom we had sometimes to lay on a chest and tie his hands and feet to the handles till he was sober. One day when he was on shore on liberty, and of course tipsy, in passing a shop in Bombay he saw a large glass globe hanging in it, with gold fish swimming and live birds in it ; he stopped and stared at it with astonishment, and muttered to himself, "What, birds swimming and fish flying !—impossible " ; and in order to be satisfied, he threw a stone which hit the globe and knocked it all to pieces about the shop.

He was soon arrested and sent to jail, and a report was sent on board next morning that one of our people was there. An officer was sent to see who it was, and there found poor Tom Emmet very much cast-down in the mouth. He was released and brought on board, but the globe was to be paid for ; therefore the ship's company subscribed eight hundred rupees (a great sum for the value of the globe), and paid the owner for it !

One day a Gentoo, who spoke a little English, came on board, and said he was from Dongaree, and sent by one of our men for his leg, as he could not return on board without it. This demand seemed so strange that they took no notice of it at first, but the Gentoo in his bad English insisted that he was right, and, after a deal of puzzling, one of the people recollected that Bandy (the ship's cook) was on shore, and inquiring among his messmates, found that one of them who had been on shore with Bandy, and slept in the same house, had brought away Bandy's wooden leg by way of frolic—and no wonder the man could not return without his leg, which was soon sent to him, and he returned on board.

The *Minerva*, having got her leak stopped, and new coppered, was brought out of dock, and the *Bien Aimé* went in ; but she was found so rotten that they broke her up, after being only a few months in the service (she mounted 20 guns). We then began to rig the *Minerva* with all speed ; and I could easily have deserted here, but we had such accounts from England that the war could not last six months, as almost all Europe were at war against the French Republic, that I fixed my mind on returning to England in the *Minerva*, in order, when paid off, to visit my remaining friends and relations, then bid them a long farewell, return to Calcutta, and there remain until I could do something to better my situation.

The *Minerva* being rigged and stored, we sailed from Bombay on January 12, 1794, none of us knowing (except the Admiral) where we were bound for, for he always kept the ship's destination a secret to himself. Some said we could not be bound for England, as we had left several casks of water behind on the Bunder Head, and that no ship had come out to relieve us ; however, when we got a little distance out we shaped a homeward-bound course, which made us rejoice.

Near the entrance of the British Channel we came up with and passed two homeward-bound Indiamen, but as they hoisted Dutch colours we did not stop to examine them, as we were then at peace with that nation ; but we heard afterwards that they were French, and were captured soon afterwards and carried into Plymouth by one of our frigates.

In proceeding up Channel we were chased a whole day

by a line-of-battle ship, which in the dusk got within hail of us; we were all ready to fight her, as our Admiral hoped to succeed by manœuvring, though she was of such superior force. They hailed to know from whence we came, and our reply was "His Britannic Majesty's ship *Minerva*"; they then asked if it was not the *Minerva* out of Havre de Grace, and were very suspicious of us; we answered that it was H.M. Ship *Minerva*, Rear-Admiral Cornwallis, from India, and this satisfied them; they shortened sail, hove to, and their captain came on board to pay his respects, and we found her to be the *Intrepid* (64 guns). One of their boat's crew, an Irishman, when alongside was hardly satisfied that we were English, for, said he, what right had we to have a poop, being only a frigate? One of our wags told him it was to keep our prize-money in, and Pat believed him!

Next morning we saw four frigates ahead standing across our bows, little thinking they were enemies; fortunately a fog came on, and we passed them. Next morning we saw four more, who would not let us escape. The first that came up was the *Arethusa*, Sir Edward Pellew (since Lord Exmouth), who, seeing our flag, brought to and came on board, and told us the other three frigates were the *Flora*, *Concord*, and *Melampus*, all under the command of Sir John Borlase Warren. When he was told we had passed four English frigates yesterday (he very near committed himself for swearing), he said, with an oath, that there were not four British frigates together in the Channel but themselves, therefore the others must be French; so hastening to his ship he gave us a salute, then bore down to his Commodore, gave him news, and off they all set in search of the other four frigates, and the next day, being April 23, 1794, they overtook them. A smart action ensued, and ended with the capture of the *Pomone* (44 guns), the *Engageant*

(56 guns), and *Babet* (28 guns); the other escaped, having run on shore on the French coast, being chased by the *Concord*, Sir Richard Strachan.

That same day we came to anchor at St. Helens, after a fine passage from Bombay of three months and seventeen days; but instead of finding the war over, found it only beginning—a sad drawback to many of our hopes. Next morning, the Channel Fleet, under Lord Howe, weighed from Spithead and anchored here, previous to the glorious battle of June 1, and we got under way went to Spithead, and there moored ship.

As the Admiral was dressing to go on shore, he saw out of the cabin windows two wherries pulling up to the ship full of girls; he came out much agitated, and sending for Captain Whitby, desired him not to allow any such creatures to come near the ship, so they were hailed to keep off; but as soon as the Admiral got on shore they were permitted to come on board, and the ship was soon full of them.

It was very strange that the Admiral—a religious and good man—could not bear the sight of a female; and yet he had been very much among them in his youthful days, and called a wild fellow. It was reported on board here as a fact that he once went on shore to dine with the Governor at Madras, and, as some ladies began to take their seats at the table while he was there, he arose, took up his hat, and left the company, to the astonishment of them all, and came on board!

I now began to weigh matters and ponder on my situation, and found that since I had left England the balance was much against me: then I had a chest of clothes and bedding, and my liberty; now I have little clothing, no shoes or stockings, and no liberty, and much decayed in my condition; my gums were swelled over my teeth by the scurvy so that I could not chew my victuals without them being covered with blood. I and several others ought to have been sent to the hospital, but instead of that were not allowed to set our feet on the land!

The Admiral struck his flag and went to London; the *Minerva* went into Portsmouth Harbour to be paid off; and after being a week in there (the ship stripped and nearly cleared of her stores), without having a moment's liberty on shore, after being so long abroad in unhealthy climates, thirty-seven of us were drafted on board the *Royal William* at Spithead, and the same day drafted again into the *Prompte*, a frigate of twenty-eight guns (Captain Taylor), and ready for sea. Here was encouragement for seamen to fight for their king and country! A coolie in India was better off! This took place on May 2, 1794. However, by getting good, fresh provisions the scurvy began to abate, thank God! and my gums broke away bit by bit at a time, and without any pain as the new ones came.

"There is a tide in the affairs of men which, taken at the flood, leads on to fortune," so says some poet; so I suppose I have taken the tide soon after high water, for it has been on the ebb with me this long time past. However, I hope now it is on the rise, for as soon as I joined the *Prompte* I was made a captain, but it was captain of the maintop—a great rise certainly, but with only the same pay as I had before. This puts me in mind of a cabin-keeper in Portsmouth Dockyard named Bowyer, who (through Parliament interest) got made captain of a seventy-four gun ship. When it was mentioned to Mr. Diddams, the master shipwright, he would not believe it, and said it must be a mistake, until it was cleared up to him and told it was the *Alexander* (74 guns), a lazarette, lying on the Mother Bank. But Bowyer's captainship, though not so high as mine, was much more profitable, he having £100 per annum, while mine, with ten times more duty to perform and much more danger, was only £14 12s. 6d. per annum.

When we first got on board the *Prompte* from the *Royal William*, one of our men named Dick Pottiford, in throwing his bag down on the deck, heard something in it knock hard. "Oh," says he, "somebody has been playing a trick with me, I suppose"; and on opening it discovered a cobbler's lapstone and other tools. "Ah!" says Dick again, "I wish I could find out who has played me this trick," and on searching further found several letters, and then Dick found he had brought some one's bag from the *Royal William* instead of his own; so in order to find out whom the letters belonged to, they were read over, which caused great diversion, as they were copies of love-letters and full of sweet words, as "my darling," "my angel," and wishing he had wings like a dove to fly to his dearest love. We thought he must be some dashing fellow, by the tenor of his letters, when, in the midst of our merriment, who should come on board but the very identical chap himself to inquire after his bag! Instead of being the dashing fellow we thought, he turned out quite the reverse, being a little, shabby, dirty-looking fellow, and ordinarily rigged out in slops and a purser's cap on his head. His bag was given to him, and Dick went on board the *Royal William* and found his own, so all was well; but the words "my angel" and "O my darling" were quizzing words long kept up in the *Prompte* afterwards.

We soon received here our pay for the *Minerva* and an advance for the *Prompte*, and fitted ourselves well out with warm clothing and shoes and stockings—things we had long been strangers to, and of which we had hitherto felt the want, the weather being cold at times. Our first trip was to Weymouth, where we took under our convoy several transports with French prisoners on board, and came to Spithead. We soon sailed again to the Nore, and convoyed a Baltic fleet across the North Sea; then proceeded to Fort George in Scotland, in the Moray Firth, and came to anchor and moored ship near to where the Battle of Culloden was fought.

In the middle of the night I was awoke by a great noise on the quarterdeck, and wondered what the deuce could be the matter there, so I got up, went to have a peep, and to my surprise saw several Highland gentlemen and ladies dancing in their Highland dresses to the music of our little band, consisting of a clarionet, a violin, and a pipe and tabor; they danced away with all their might, now and then shouting out "He-hou." Upon inquiry we found they were the Marquis of Huntly, with his sister, the Duke of Richmond (her husband), and some others in high life, and they kept it up merrily until daylight.

In saluting them with our great guns, the Duchess took the match out of the man's hand and fired off the guns on one side herself: she was a cheerful, active, little woman, and could draw and sheath a sword behind her back as quick and well as many could do in their front.

After waiting here a few days we put to sea, having under our convoy several transports with Highland troops on board, under the command of the Marquis of Huntly. A great many boats, full of the friends and relations of the troops, came off from the shore and followed us out of the harbour, our little band playing up all the time "Farewell to Lochaber." Many tears were shed, and particularly by the Duchess, who wept bitterly. All this was very affecting, and very few of those brave soldiers ever returned to their country again, being most of them slain on the Continent.

The Marquis was a fine-looking and cheerful young

man, and—when the weather permitted—he frequently left the transport he was in and came on board our ship. He, with Mr. Mansel, our second lieutenant (a son of General Mansel), and the Duke of Richmond, amused themselves in running up the rigging to the mast-head; and one of these times it was hinted to me to make the Marquis pay his footing, so one day, as he was sitting on the cross-trees and looking around at the shipping, I took up a piece of spun-yarn and muttered out something about people being tied there who had not paid their footing. " I understand you," said he; and coming down into the top he said something in a whisper to the Duke, who was there, and who gave us half a guinea to drink their healths.

When we arrived in Yarmouth Roads, and came to anchor, the Marquis went on shore in one of our boats, and on his return, in coming along the pier (it being dark), came close to a man standing there and watching his boat. "Come, my brave fellow," said the Marquis, "will you come along with me?" The poor fellow, a Swede, not understanding a word of English, foolishly enough went into the boat with him and was brought on board, and the Marquis returned to the transport quite forgetting the affair. Next day the man was seen standing on the forecastle, and no one knew who he was, so he was sent for on the quarterdeck, and being asked who he was, replied to every question, "Orla hou," which perhaps was " I don't understand you." To end the matter he was put on the ship's books by the name of " Orla Hou " and stationed on the forecastle; and when I left the *Prompte*, near five years after, he was still in the ship and one of the best seamen on board, and had learnt to speak English as well as any one.

Although our ship had as fine a bottom for sailing as any ship in the service, yet we could hardly ever get her to sail better than the transports, and often tried her trim, and thought she sailed best about twenty inches by the stern, and she often in stays missed and ran so fast astern in staying, which made our men say that she sailed fastest stern foremost, and being long and narrow made her rather crank, so our captain got permission from the Admiralty to go to Sheerness and there dock her.

In examining her bottom there in dock we found nothing the matter with it, so we got her masts and yards reduced and changed our long nine-pounder guns for sixes. We were hulked on board the *Boreas* frigate all the time and not any liberty whatever to go on shore, which caused several of our best men to desert. All this time we not only fitted out our own ship, but likewise assisted in fitting out the *Dædalus* frigate and *Jupiter* 50-gun ship.

Our captain was none of the brightest men in the world, although he had been a midshipman with Captain Cook the circumnavigator. Whenever the hands were turned up for punishment he generally made a speech, the chief of which was that we should have our allowance of victuals (which God knows was little enough), and when the war was over we would get our pay and discharge and then go and see our wives and families, and so on. "Damn him," the sailors would say, "don't we know that as well as himself?"

Our first lieutenant, F. G. Bond, was a smart officer, likewise a gentleman and a sailor. It was reported that he had been one of the handsomest officers in the British navy, but—having got himself blown up in an engagement with gunpowder—his face was so indented with scars that the sailors nicknamed him "Gunny-bag Face," after the name of rough coarse bags used in India to stow rice and sugar in.

All the rest of our officers were very well in regard of usage, though our captain was one of the most timorous men I ever knew, but Mr. Bond carried on all the duty. After having got all ready for sea we went to the Nore and took twelve transports under our convoy for Flushing: we met a severe storm on the passage, which dispersed us all, and we arrived at Flushing without them; however, they all arrived safe soon after. We found lying here the *Sheerness* (44 guns), bearing the flag of Rear-Admiral Harvey, and the *Albion* (54 guns), likewise seven or eight Dutch two-deckers. The French Republican army were so near that we heard the report of their guns; and about this time I was promoted and made a quartermaster.

We sailed from here for the Leith Station, and encountered severe stormy weather in the North Sea; when we arrived in Leith Roads, Christmas being at hand, we took the ship to Inverkeithing, a snugger place, struck yards and topmasts, and hoisted the boats in, so that nothing might hinder us from keeping up Christmas merrily; plenty of Scotch whisky was smuggled into the ship, which made us half mad not being used to it; our captain with the gun-room and warrant officers dined together, so Christmas Day was kept as it should on board a ship, and that was by being merry and cheerful.

Early this year (1795) we received an express from the Admiralty ordering us to detain all Dutch ships on this coast; and as a Dutch frigate was lying at this time in Leith Roads, the order was given to unmoor immediately and get under way, although the cables were frozen so thick with ice that we could hardly heave them through the hawseholes. We got the ship under way and, the wind being fair, soon after had her anchored in Leith Roads with springs on our cables close to the Dutch frigate—the *Circe* (28 guns, Capt. Halket) being here anchored on the other side of her.

We sent a boat on board the Dutch frigate to let them know that we had orders to detain them, and they complied with our request, and we kept them with only a small supply of provisions lest they should endeavour to escape in the night. Their officers and ours visited and revisited each other during nearly six weeks that we lay here.

During all the time we had been in the *Prompte* we had no liberty given to go on shore, and several of our best men had deserted from the boats. One day an officer was sent to press out of a merchantman just arrived in the Roads, and as soon as the officer stepped on board the boat's crew shoved off, set their sails, and ran up the Firth, the wind being fair, as far as they could get, then landed and travelled to Greenock. Advertisement of their description was soon sent all over the country, and, just as they were getting on board a ship bound to America, they were apprehended and brought back and put into irons to wait until a sufficient number of captains arrived here to form a court-martial. However, as there was no prospect of that, they, after a few weeks' confinement, were flogged on board the *Prompte*. So strict a guard was kept at night that a man could not go to the head without being challenged by the sentries with " who comes there ? " (and I have been told since by a follower of the captain's that when he left this ship and joined the *Andromeda* he kept up the same discipline there); so one day, when the captain went on shore, the girls of the town had made their minds up to have a little fun on the occasion with him, and when he came near enough they ranged themselves into a line, and one of them cries out " who comes there ? " another replies " William Taylor " (the Captain's name) ; " Pass him along," says another, and then they set up a hearty laugh, which so humbled him that there was no more " passing " the people to the head of his ship afterwards.

At last an order arrived from the Admiralty for us to take the Dutch frigate and moor her under the batteries at Queen's Ferry, which we did, unbent her sails and struck her yards and topmasts, and there left her, as hostilities had commenced between us and the Dutch. Her name was the *Zephyr*, and she mounted thirty-six guns, but when bought into His Majesty's service was named the *Euryalus*. I got for her as my share of prize money £4 0s. 9d.

We left Leith Roads in the spring of 1795 in company with the *Circe* and *Albicore*, and arrived at the Nore, where, soon after, we took on board three tons and three-quarters of money (said to amount to three millions sterling) for the use of the British army on the Continent. We took on board likewise the brother of the late French King (Louis XVI.), who has since become Louis XVIII., but he now went by the name of the Count de Lisle of Rouen; he was a fine-looking, dark man, and much reserved. His only companion was a Swiss gentleman. We took the whole to Cuxhaven and landed them there; but I could not help thinking that the freight was too precious to be entrusted to a small frigate like ours. What a grand prize we should have been to Johnny Crappo had we met with a superior force of his at the time !

We left Cuxhaven in company with the *Albion* (74 guns, Capt. Savage), and went off the Texel, where we hoisted French colours and the *Albion* Dutch. We were admirably adapted to deceive the enemy, as our ship was French built, and the *Albion* had no poop, which made her have a foreign look. The wind being off the land, we soon saw a number of vessels under way and steering toward us, thinking that we had come to convoy them to their destined ports; so confident were they that we were friends that, in passing under our stern as we were lying to, some of them hailed and told us the name of the French ports they were bound to, and we soon had possession of nineteen, all neutrals, laden with corn for France! We took them to the Nore; but just at this time the bounty for capturing neutrals in carrying corn to France was taken off, so we got nothing for them, except one which was found to have saltpetre stowed under her corn, and that condemned her.

We then sailed from the Nore, and arrived in the Downs, where our captain left us (he being appointed to the *Andromeda*), and was succeeded by the Hon. Edward Leveson-Gower, from the *Petrel* sloop-of-war, who brought several of his followers with him. To my surprise and joy, who should be among them but my brother James, then a Master's mate, whom I had not seen or heard of for six years, and of course we were glad to meet each other again. From him I learnt that my brother John was in the *Assurance*, Robert in the *Seahorse*, and George in the *Espiègle*; so that we were all five in H.M. Royal Navy.

We left the Downs and arrived at Spithead, where ten of us at a time were allowed twenty-four hours' liberty on shore, Captain Leveson-Gower having said that his ship should never be called a prison ship. I had the luck to be among the first ten, and glad was I to get my foot on English ground again, *being the first time since I left it to go to the East Indies!* When we left the ship in the liberty boat some of our officers seemed to signify that they did not expect to see us again, and among the rest our old rip of a boatswain, who had been a deserter himself; but they were all mistaken, for we returned to our proper time (and so did the others that went after us), for we thought it would be very ungrateful now to desert, when we had got a captain who would give us liberty.

I think it only fair and just, that when seamen are pressed in coming home from a long voyage, they should be allowed a few weeks' liberty on shore to spend their money among their friends and relations; when that was gone, they would soon be tired of the shore, return more contented to their ships, and by such means there would not be half so much desertion.

We left Spithead (with four transports under our convoy) for Guernsey, and when arrived there, as our ship sailed little better by reducing her masts and yards, etc., we got her into the harbour and lashed her alongside of one of the piers to scrub her bottom as the tide fell. By this means we scrubbed off several bunches of mussels, and got all finished by low water. Sentinels were placed along the pier to prevent any of our people from getting into the town; but our officers had not considered that the end of the pier was dry at low water, and our people soon availed themselves of that opportunity, and when the ship floated again there was hardly any one on board to warp her into the roads again.

The captain was of course very angry, so he, with some more officers, went into the town, and found most of them half-seas-over in gin-shops, and the sentinels on the pier not much better. It was laughable to see them staggering along and hastening on board when they heard the captain was after them; they all came on board except one, who by accident fell into the water and was drowned, and the ship was soon anchored in the roads. As our captain knew what sailors were, none were punished, but it is a great pity that sailors should be so fond of strong drink; it is the only thing that disgraces them.

We left Guernsey with the same four transports, and found our ship to sail a little better. On our arrival at Spithead, Mr. Taw, our gunner, got an appointment to a higher rate, and Captain Leveson-Gower, who had been very kind to me, ordered me to take charge of the gunner's stores, and said he would soon get me a gunner's warrant; but I begged him to excuse me, as I knew little of gunnery, and, indeed, I had never been so much as in a gunner's crew. But he was a man that would not be contradicted, and he ordered me to go to the gunner's cabin and take charge of the stores immediately, and next day he got me an acting-warrant from Sir Peter Parker, the Commander-in-Chief on this station (dated September 3, 1795); moreover, I was sent on shore to pass my examination before the passing gunners and a mathematical master: very inconsiderate was this for me to be sent to pass without any preparation! However, I was fortunately relieved from my anxiety by meeting one of the passing gunners, who informed me that they could not pass any one who had not been four years in H.M. Service; and as at this time I had only been about two years and a half, I returned on board and continued acting-gunner, and when at leisure began to study the art of gunnery from books my brother James bought for me. I soon improved much, and my brother officers taught me how to keep my books and make up my accounts of stores.

We sailed from Spithead, and then steered for Shields, to the great joy of my brother, myself, and other North-countrymen on board, and soon after anchored outside of the bar. My brother and I went on shore, but found Shields not that merry place we had hitherto known it; every one looked gloomy and sad on account of nearly all the young men being pressed and taken away, and not a soul knew us that we met in the street, except a woman who had been a servant in our family, and had nursed us; she, poor creature, though sad as any one, rejoiced to see us again.

We called at a public-house kept by a relation of ours,

a female, and asked if they knew where any of Captain Richardson's sons were? " Ah," she replied with a sigh, " I believe they are all pressed into the Navy." We then visited our two uncles, Tulby and Hunter, who were much surprised at seeing us again at Shields, and I met with my old shipmate Tom Robinson, who after leaving the East Indies had come home to his fond mother, who, no doubt, was surprised and glad to see him again, and that he had not been taken by the tigers.

CHAPTER VI

1795–97

WITH SIR RALPH ABERCROMBY'S EXPEDITION TO ST. LUCIA, ETC.

H.M.S. *Prompte* joins Admiral Christian's fleet—Convoys Sir Ralph Abercromby's force to the West Indies—Fleet dispersed by storm near Torbay—Sets sail again from Spithead—Gale in the Channel—Abercromby's *sang froid*—Fleet driven back to Spithead—Admiral Christian blamed—Fleet sails under Admiral Cornwallis—" Blue Billy " court-martialled—Captain Leveson-Gower's ill-luck—Admiral Christian again in command—Abercromby lands at St. Lucia—Assault on Wegee—Surrender of St. Lucia (May 1796)—Demerara—Sir John Jervis's victory (February 14, 1797)—*Prompte* joins convoy from St. Kitts—Refractory West Indiamen—Arrival at Spithead—Trial of the Nore mutineers—Different fate of two of them—Marriage with Miss Sarah Thompson.

A NUMBER of transports were in Shields Harbour waiting for troops, and as soon as they were embarked we got under way and steered our course for Spithead, where we arrived safe, and joined a large expedition getting ready for the West Indies. The troops, to the number of ten thousand, were to be commanded by General Abercromby, and the fleet by Rear-Admiral Christian. But first of all we were sent over to Guernsey to bring wine for the Admiral, and on our return were nearly lost in a storm off the Caskets; but by carrying a press of sail on the ship we just weathered the lights, and, thank God, were saved.

At our return we found the troops embarked and the fleet ready, which consisted of the following:

Prince George (Rear-Admiral Christian) .	98 guns
Impregnable	„ „
Commerce de Marseille	120 „
Irresistible	74 „
Colossus	„ „
Alfred	„ „
Ardent	64 „
Lion	„ „
Trident	„ „
Undaunted	„ „ frigate
Prompte	28 repeater
Babet	„ „
Albicore	18 „
Ulysses	44 guns, a trooper
Terror	8 „ a bomb
Vesuve	a large gun brig

On November 11, 1795, we left Spithead with a fine breeze from the eastward, having many other ships under convoy beside the transports; but next day, before we had got near Torbay, the wind shifted to the westward, and towards evening increased to a storm, with torrents of rain. In the dark we were all in the greatest danger of running into each other by being on different tacks. A three-decker nearly ran us down, her bower anchor having torn away part of our quarter gallery. Some foundered, others were driven on shore, and many more would have been lost this boisterous night had not Providence abated the wind suddenly after midnight. In the morning the fleet bore away for Spithead to repair their damages.

Next morning we were ordered to put to sea with our ship to look after the missing convoy, and on looking into Portland Roads saw several of their wrecks on the beach, and were told that the shore had been covered with the bodies of dead sailors and soldiers, and two hundred of them they already had buried; so from this account we concluded that these wrecks were the missing ships we had been in search of. We returned again to Spithead.

It was December 9 before we got ready and proceeded to sea again, the fleet consisting of 380 sail altogether; but the *Prince George* was left behind, having been knocked up by the late storm, and so was the *Commerce de Marseille*, the largest ship that had ever been seen in England. She had been so filled with stores and laden so deep that she was shaken almost to pieces. She soon after went to Plymouth, and was there broken up.

The flag was now on board the *Glory*, of 98 guns, and the *Alcmene*, frigate, had also joined us. We sailed down Channel with a fair wind for four or five days, and got into the Western Ocean, when the wind shifted against us, and began to blow great guns, and continued so day after day. Some of the convoy were frequently making signals of distress, and the answer was to bear up for the nearest British port. One night, it being as dark as pitch and the sea running mountains high, and our ship lying to under a storm mizzen stay-sail, the *Vesuve* (a large gun-brig, lying to under a close-reefed main topsail) drove slap up against our weather quarter, which alarmed every one exceedingly. One minute she was higher than our mast-heads, and the next we thought she would have fallen on us; and we expected nothing else than both of us would soon knock each other to pieces and go to the bottom. However, by throwing her main topsail aback she dropped astern without any other damage than leaving her bower anchor sticking in our quarter near the water's edge, and when it dropped out by the rolling of the ship the water came in so fast that many thought she was sinking. All the pumps were set to work, and Mr. Walker, the carpenter, and his crew with active exertions cut away the ceiling in the master's cabin and got at the leak, which they stopped for the present in a temporary manner.

One of our "mids" named King, a fine young man, on his first trip to sea, was terribly alarmed, and wanted a pistol to shoot himself; being asked the reason, he said he was afraid of drowning, but by shooting himself he would be out of pain in an instant.

Our ship was so leaky in her upper works that we had seldom a dry bed to lie on, and frequently shipping a great deal of water, the decks were never dry; one of these nights a heavy sea struck the flagship and stove in several of her middle deck ports, and so much water got in that they thought the ship would have foundered; so they were obliged to bear away before the wind to save her. At one time Admiral Christian sent a messenger down to General Abercromby, who slept in the gun-room, requesting him to come up to his cabin, as the ship was in danger; but the old veteran sent for answer that he was as ready to die where he was as in the Admiral's cabin.

That same night we did not escape scot-free, for a heavy sea broke on board, which stove in the bulwark on the weather side of the forecastle, sprang our bowsprit, carried away the mainstay, and drew some of the main rigging channel-bolts out, and almost shook the little *Prompte* to pieces. All hands were called, and set to work in securing the bowsprit and mainmast by preventure shrouds, stays, etc.; and by great exertions all was secured.

When daylight appeared, to our great surprise there was not a ship in sight. Our station was on the Admiral's weather quarter, and as we had seen no night signals we could not think what had become of them, not knowing at the time the danger the flagship had been in; so our captain, supposing they had borne up, we did the same, and at ten in the forenoon got sight of them to leeward, and lying to in a scattered manner, and by the time we joined it nearly fell to a calm.

Here we found the *Alfred* and *Undaunted* totally dismasted; the *Ulysses* lost all her topmasts, and many of the convoy having suffered more or less; so they were ordered to make the best of their way to the nearest British port; the *Albicore* was ordered to see and attend the *Alfred* and *Undaunted* safe into Plymouth, and our number of shipping reduced considerably, so that we often wished and often looked to see the signal up on board the *Glory* for the remainder of us to bear up for a British port.

At last (on Sunday, January 25, 1796) the wished-for signal was made, after we had been tossed about almost in continual storms for forty-seven days; and out of our 360 sail there were not now above fifty of us together. Away we steered with a strong westerly gale (and fair for us) to Spithead, and were only three days in returning.

Next morning we all got to Spithead and moored our ship, and by the ship being so continually wet the green grass was growing on her sides and on her decks under the gun-carriages; and well it was for us that we returned, for the storms continued for near a month afterwards, and long after this they went by the name of "Christian's gales," alluding to the name of the Admiral.

Various were the reports in England about our second time being driven back: some said it was a judgment from God, for sending so many brave men to the West Indies to die, as the yellow fever was raging there so horribly at this time; others said it was a judgment against the nation for going to war with France, which we had no right to do; and others blamed Admiral Christian, and said that he was an unlucky man.

It is astonishing, to think what ignorant people will invent: now the Admiral was a good, brave and persevering officer, and could not prevent foul winds and stormy weather, and the King was so pleased with his good conduct that he knighted him for it.

After the fleet had repaired their damages and collected here again, they sailed under the command of my old shipmate Vice-Admiral Cornwallis; but we were not ready to go with them, and they had not gone far before the Admiral's ship, the *Royal Sovereign*, got foul of another ship, and damaged her stern and cutwater so much, that he returned to Spithead in her and let the fleet proceed on under the command of the senior captain. For this Blue Billy (as the sailors called him) was brought to a court martial for not shifting his flag to one of the other line-of-battle ships, but, being a great man, was acquitted.

In February 1796, as we lay at Cowes waiting to collect another convoy for the West Indies, our captain (the Hon. Edward Leveson-Gower) was promoted to the *Active*, a larger frigate, and left us. Although little more than nineteen years old when posted into our ship, he was as smart an officer and a sailor as ever I sailed with: perhaps he had learnt much from his father, who was an Admiral; though short-sighted, he could make out a signal from the Commander-in-Chief with his flags sooner than any of the signalmen. But he was afterwards very unfortunate. He soon after lost his frigate, the *Active*, in the river St. Lawrence; he then got the *Pomona*, a very large frigate taken lately from the French, and got her on shore near Guernsey, and damaged so much that with difficulty they got her to Portsmouth, and there she was broken up; but being of a great family and much interest, he soon got appointed again to a new frigate named the *Shannon*, and soon after lost her on the coast of France near Boulogne!

Commander George Eyre, of the *Albicore* sloop-of-war, was posted into our ship, and succeeded Captain Leveson-

Gower; also at this time Mr. Walker, our carpenter, was appointed to a higher rate, and on leaving the ship requested my brother James and me to take a parting supper with him on shore at Cowes. Though I could not be spared at the time, my brother James went; but in the morning, before he could get on board, we were all under way and proceeding for the Needles, and he was left behind. I was very sorry for this, especially as he lost such a good opportunity of getting made a lieutenant in the West Indies, where so many death vacancies were occurring at this time; but, however, I hope it was all for the best.

We were hurried to sea sooner than we expected, and sailed through the Needles the same day (being March 20, 1796). Our fleet, consisting of—

The Thunderer (Rear-Admiral Christian, Capt. Bowen)	74 guns.
Invincible (Capt. Cayley)	74 ,,
Grampus	50 ,,
Astrea	32 ,,
Prompte (Capt. George Eyre)	28 ,,
Albicore	18 ,,
Terror (bomb)	8 ,,

and about fifty sail of merchantmen, proceeded to the westward with fine and pleasant weather. To the westward of Madeira the *Albicore* was sent in chase of two strange ships, which she captured and brought into the fleet. One was a French privateer of 16 guns, and named the *Alexander*, the other a large Portuguese Brazilman, her prize; the latter we sent to Madeira, but the privateer we took with us to the West Indies, and there sold her. Her crew were a complete set of democrats, who could not suppress their indignation at seeing the officers' servants doing any menial office for them; they said, "why did not the officers do it themselves?"

We arrived at Barbados on May 1, and made the

9

passage in six days less than the time of our last attempt, when we had to return again. We had such fine weather that a jolly-boat might have gone all the way with us. Here we watered our ships, and then, after seeing the convoy safe into Fort Royal, Martinique, we stood across for St. Lucia, where our army, under General Abercromby, were landing to besiege the place. In passing Pigeon Island the enemy fired several shots at us, but without taking any effect, and we soon after came to anchor in Choc Bay, where a division of the army had landed.

At the entrance of the Cul de Sac, or Carenage Harbour, there stands a sugar-loaf-shaped hill (on the left hand in going in) fortified at the top. As it was necessary to take it before the island could be conquered, the Twenty-first Regiment volunteered for that purpose. So, the night being very dark, about ten o'clock they began their march, and soon the firing commenced on both sides, and continued all night; but in the morning we had the mortification to see the French colours still flying on the hill which was named the Wegee [Vigie]. But this demands an explanation, for it was not the fault of the men, as they were competent enough to take it; the cause was, that when the regiment got up unobserved by the enemy, near the top of the hill, their guide lost his way, somebody unknown ordered the retreat to be beat, and the enemy, catching the alarm, opened his fire on the British as they retreated down the hill, and destroyed near a half of them. However, the rest, on reaching the foot of the hill, made a stand, set the town on fire, and musketry was popping off at different places all the night long. A strict inquiry was made next day to know who had ordered the retreat to be beat, but the villain could not be found out.

We assisted the army with seamen from the fleet, and

made a strong battery on a high commanding piece of ground, a valley lying between us and the enemy. We might easily enough have shot one another with musketry, but that was not allowed to be done—for what reason I don't know. Instead, in order to deceive the enemy and make him believe we were more numerous than we were, we kept landing each day many seamen from the fleet, and at night brought them off again. One day when I was on shore on duty among the rest, a cart came along with wounded men, and I could not but admire the fortitude of one of them, whose leg was shot off, in seeing him hold up the stump and crying out, " Hurrah, my boys ! I shall now get to old England again, and see my mother !"

The island surrendered on May 29, 1796 ; and I, being soon after sent up the Carenage on duty, landed, and went to the top of the Wegee (where there was such slaughter among the 21st Regiment) ; and was surprised and much disappointed in seeing it such an insignificant place—a serjeant's guard might have taken it. The rampart was a parcel of loose stones without cement, and a dry ditch, and all their artillery was an iron gun of the size of an 18-pounder, a few swivels mounted on stocks, and a mortar dismounted. Thousands of the enemy's troops, mostly blacks, were at this time on the Wegee waiting for their destination ; they were very civil, and those that could speak English told us they were much in want of bread.[1]

[1] " On the 26th April [1796] Rear-Admiral Christian, with a squadron and transports, aboard of which was a large body of troops under the command of Lieut.-General Abercromby, stood across from Barbados [to St. Lucia]. After considerable opposition from the batteries, the first division of the troops made good its landing on the 28th April. On the 29th the whole expedition advanced to the attack of Morne Chabot, which was assaulted and taken with the loss of thirteen officers and men killed, and about sixty wounded and missing. An

The Governor, the General, and other chief officers were brought on board our ship. The former was a rough old fellow, could speak English, and had been captain of a French line-of-battle ship in Louis XVI.'s time. The general was a smart young fellow, and had his wife (a creole) and child with him. His aide-de-camp was a fine young fellow, an American, and was wounded on the knee; he said he got it from the sword of an English serjeant who lay wounded on the ground.

Our captain took none of them into his cabin, but ordered them screened berths under the quarterdeck, which hurt their feelings much. The reason for this was, that when he was taken in the *Speedy* brig at the beginning of the war the French not only used him ill, but likewise robbed him of his clothes.

We took the French officers to Barbados, and as we lay there, in Carlisle Bay, watering the ship, the *Bittern*, a fine new sloop-of-war, was chased in by two French ships of force. We immediately made the signal for the watering party to make haste on board and leave the casks on shore, and soon had the *Prompte* under way, and proceeded to sea in company with the *Bittern* in quest of the enemy. We got to the windward of Barbados—where the French privateers generally cruise to catch our outward-bound ships which come this way— and cruised ten days without seeing anything of them.

attempt to dislodge the republicans from a fort [the Vigie] on the 3rd May failed after a loss of nearly similar amount, and another attempt on the 17th was equally frustrated, with casualties to the extent of 180 men and officers; but at length, on the 24th, the enemy demanded terms, and on the 26th 2,000 men laid down their arms and surrendered the island. Both services exerted themselves on this occasion with their usual promptitude and gallantry, and the sailors astonished their land associates with their ready resources to establish batteries on almost inaccessible eminences. The British loss in the entire conquest was about 500 or 600 men put *hors de combat.*"—Cust's *Annals of the Wars.*

On the eleventh day in the forenoon we found ourselves in a fog, among a fleet of outward-bound West Indiamen, and when it cleared away we saw the *Proselyte* frigate (Capt. Loring), convoying them. So we bore up to return to Barbados along with them; but in the afternoon we saw the two rascals to the northward of us watching the fleet, and instantly hauled out wind and stood towards them. They boldly lay-to to receive us until they saw the *Bittern* coming—which, by the way, she was very slack in doing—and then they filled their sails and ran off, and in the dark we lost sight of them; but at break of day next morning we saw them again, and only a short distance off, and continued the chase after them all this day, and many manœuvres they performed to escape us. But it was very strange that the *Bittern*, which before could sail around us, could now hardly keep up with us.

We had now passed Barbados and Martinique, and in the evening were to windward of St. Lucia, when the enemy's two ships parted: one ran away before the wind and was chased by the *Bittern*, the other hauled close on a wind and was chased by us. Whenever we got near him (he being prepared) he would helm up instantly, set his steering-sails and run before the wind, and before we could do the same get some distance from us; and then when we came near again he would down steering-sails and haul on a wind again. At last, finding that we had got up to his manœuvres, and were likely to catch him, on the following morning he bore up, set all the sail he could carry, threw his guns, carriages, and spars overboard; and then he outsailed us. So our captain, finding it no use to pursue him any longer, especially as we had run to leeward so far out of our station, reluctantly gave up the pursuit.

Thus ended a chase of forty-two hours, and during that time we passed Barbados, Martinique, St. Lucia, St. Vincent, and ended off Grenada; and we heard after this that they got safe into Guadeloupe. However, it was fortunate for the convoy that we met them in time to chase these fellows off, for the old *Proselyte* was a Dutch-built frigate, and such a bad sailer—even much worse than ourselves—that we may be sure she could not have prevented some of them from being taken.

We returned again to Barbados, completed our water, and then went to Demerara, where we heard of the gallant victory obtained by Sir John Jervis over the Spanish fleet on February 14, and fired a salute on the occasion.

The river at Demerara is much wider than the Thames, and full of tall trees, and the tropical fruits so abundant that on the side opposite to the town we could load the jolly-boat for nothing with bananas, plantains, shaddocks, oranges, etc.; thousands of parrots in flocks used to fly over the ships in the morning and return again to their abode in the evening, and this place would be like a paradise were it not so hot and unhealthy.

Here we found about twenty sail of British merchant ships laden and waiting for us to convoy them to St. Kitts, there to join the grand convoy collecting there for England. But when we arrived at St. Kitts we found they had sailed for England, and as it would be late before another convoy would collect, the merchants and captains joined in a petition to our captain to proceed on and endeavour to come up with the grand convoy; and, the Governor sanctioning it, we turned to with cheerful hearts in getting the ship watered and ready, in hopes of soon being in Old England again and getting refreshed after being so long in this starvation country.

We got our ship under way and ran down to Old Roads to water—the worst place for watering, I believe, in the West Indies. The people were up to their middle in filling the casks in a stream that runs down a mountain into the sea, and then up to their necks on the rocks among the surf in rafting them off. However, this was done as quickly as possible, and then we got under way with our convoy, hoping that we might not overtake the others, for fear their commodore should take our twenty sail under his convoy and send us back; and what we feared nearly came to pass, for when we had got so far north as the banks of Newfoundland we came in sight of each other, and our signal was made to close with them.

This convoy was under the charge of Captain Miller, in the *Vanguard* (74 guns), with the *St. Tomaso* (74 guns), taken at Trinidad (Captain Wood), and the *Alarm* (32 guns, Captain Fellowes). So our captain went on board the *Vanguard* to receive his orders, and at his return the people were watching his countenance as he came alongide; for when he was displeased they said he always made a long face, and it was soon whispered about that we should be sent back again, as they knew it by the captain's face, and they were right. Now Captain George Eyre, though rather long-featured, was as well made and handsome a man as any in the service, but disappointments will alter any one's countenance.

Next morning, when he went on board to the Commodore again to receive his instructions, he took with him a copy of the defects of the ship, and likewise a report that much of our copper was rubbed off. But all would not do: the Commodore told him we might go to Halifax and get it put to rights. But Captain Fellowes, who had always been very friendly with our captain, helped him out, and told the Commodore that the *Alarm* was in such a bad state, and leaky, that he did not know but he might be obliged soon to run for the nearest port; and how inconvenient it would be not to have a frigate in the convoy. So the Commodore, weighing things together, consented to keep us with him.

All hands were now watching the captain's countenance at his return, and it was whispered about in a very short time that we should not be sent back, but should go home after all ; and sure enough they were right. And when the Commodore bore up and made sail we followed him, steering nearly before the wind, and a short time after the signal was made for the convoy to close nearer ; but not being obeyed, our ship, as whipper-in, was signalled to enforce it ; and in threading our way through, to get to the outwardmost ships, we nearly ran foul of a West Indiaman, through their obstinacy in not porting their helm a little. Our captain, though a good man, was rather hasty, and he hailed with " Damn you, sir, why don't you put your helm a-port ? " and the other's answer was, " Damn you, sir, I am going my right course." This rather astonished our captain, and some sharp words ensued between them. Our captain then told him that this was H.M. *Prompte*. " I know nothing about *Promptes*," replied he ; " I know the Commodore, and that is enough for me ; and as for my ship's name, it is the *Maria*, of Liverpool, and I don't care who knows it."

Our captain then told him to heave to, and seeing he would not, we sheered close up alongside of him, beat to quarters, and got the guns ready to sink him ; but the mate of the ship, fearing the consequence, ran to the wheel and brought the ship to. We then sent a lieutenant in the jolly-boat to bring her captain on board ; but he, judging their intent, ran to the cookhouse, seized the cook's axe, and swore he would split the first man's head in two who dared to take hold of him. So our captain seeing this—for we were close alongside of him—told the lieutenant to wait for more assistance, so we hoisted out the pinnace and sent her with a party of marines in her, and then he surrendered himself.

He was a dark-looking, daring fellow, and not the least

humbled, and we supposed had got his quantum of grog, being just after dinner-time; so our captain asked him how he dared to make use of such language to him. "Why," he replied, "did you not begin first?" so finding nothing but impertinence was to be got from him, he was put under a sentinel's charge, and we bore up both ships together to speak the Commodore.

They both went together on board the *Vanguard*, and our captain stated his complaint, and the other said that he did not know at the time that the *Prompte* was a King's ship; so the case being difficult to settle, the Commodore reprimanded the captain of the West India-man, and told him he was liable to a penalty of £500 for disobedience of orders, and being cautioned for the future, was sent on board his ship again.

Another affair of a different nature happened soon after this, which was that of a Scotch brig which sailed so badly that she, being always astern, detained the whole fleet very much. One day, she being far astern, our signal was made to tow her up to the fleet, and when we got a good hawser made fast to her bows, we set steering-sails alow and aloft and dragged her bows under; she lost the use of her helm, and nothing but the tow rope kept end on. They were so alarmed on board her that they hailed us to cast her off, and would have done that themselves, but could not get at the tow rope for the rush of water over her forecastle. When we got her ahead of the fleet we cast her off, but she had got such a twisting that she wanted no more towing during the passage.

We arrived at Spithead once more, thank God, on July 12, 1797, and were steering for the *Royal William* to cheer her, as ships do on arriving from a foreign station; but met a boat with a lieutenant, who told us we were not to cheer at all. Being asked the reason, he replied that there had been too much cheering already, alluding to the late meeting where the seamen had been standing out for a necessary supply of victuals and wages[1]; this was the first account we had heard of it, and fortunately by this time it had ended.

Many of our people were bad with the scurvy, and if you only made a dent with your finger on the flesh it would remain a considerable time before it filled up again. From a small pimple that broke out on a man's thigh (and which the doctor could not stop) it increased until all the flesh on the thigh was consumed, and this was by the scurvy; but being now in the land of plenty the rest of them soon recovered.

At this time they were holding a court martial on some of the mutineers of the Nore in Portsmouth Harbour; and our captain was surprised to receive a letter from one of them requesting a good character, which I suppose not a man in the ship would have done. When he was boatswain's mate in our ship he went by the name of Devereux, a daring, wicked fellow, whom I have heard say would never be easy until he went to the yard-arm. Now he was in a fair way for it; for he had deserted from us at the siege of St. Lucia, shipped on board a merchantman, returned to England, was pressed in the Downs, and I think was put on board the *Montague*.

When the mutiny broke out he became one of the delegates, and behaved so badly that he was picked out among some others to be tried by a court martial; and now his sentence was that he was to be hanged, and this took place a day or two afterwards at Spithead on board the *St. Tomaso*, the same ship that came home with us in the convoy.

Another shipmate of mine when in the *Minerva* (but not so bad a character) was likewise to be tried as a mutineer, and by the same court martial; his name was Davies, and

---

[1] The Mutiny at the Nore.

he had acted as captain to the noted Parker, admiral of the mutineers.   When in irons previous to his trial he wrote a well-worded and penitential letter to another of the *Minerva's* crew named Pinch, a seaman on board the *St. Fiorenzo*, which was then cruising off Weymouth with the King and Queen on board, beseeching him never to rebel against his country, and to take warning by the ignominious death he was going to suffer.   This letter was shown to an officer on board and from him to Sir Harry Neale, the captain, and from Sir Harry to the King; and the consequence was that his life was spared.   He was sentenced to be kept two years in the Marshalsea, and was sent there; but although the walls are so high that it was thought not possible for any one to escape over them, Davies and another got over and made their escape, and got on board an Indiaman at Gravesend.   But the police having got some scent of them, left London and went down to Gravesend to take them; but Davies and his partner no doubt had kept a sharp look-out, saw them coming, and as the police came alongside they jumped into a boat on the other side, pushed off and landed. They soon got into the country and made their escape from the police, but what became of them afterwards I have never heard.

Our ship was ordered into Portsmouth Harbour to be docked and repaired, and during that time I got united in the holy bonds of matrimony with a Miss Sarah Thompson, at Kingston Church, on July 23, 1797.   She was a daughter of Mr. John Thompson, a master stone-mason of Portsea; I had been acquainted with her previous to my last sailing to the West Indies, and she had promised to wait for my return, which she did.   I have every reason to be satisfied with my choice, and her kind care and affection for my welfare, and I hope I shall be grateful for it.

CHAPTER VII

1797–99

IN H.M.S. "PROMPTE" IN THE WEST INDIES

Confirmed in appointment as gunner in *Prompte*—Sails with convoy to St. Domingo—Death and burial of the captain—Chase of two Spanish privateers—Failure of the attack on them—" The Happy *Prompte*"—Bahamas—Nassau—Blackbeard's tree—Capture of French schooner—She founders—In a hurricane near Bermuda—Reach New Providence—Refit the ship—News of the Battle of the Nile—Fracas with privateersmen on shore—Chase of Spanish convoy in the Gulf of Mexico—Capture of a Spanish store ship off Cuba—Returns to Jamaica (March 1799).

I HAD now been more than four years in H.M. service, and therefore passed my examination for a gunner, and got confirmed to my own ship the *Prompte*; and, it being the time of the fair at Portsea and Portsdown Hill, I enjoyed more pleasure and comfort than ever I had done since I first came to sea. But it was not of long duration, for our ship was only three weeks in dock, and then we hurried on to get her ready for sea.

She was new coppered, and our captain had been advised to have her hold so stowed that she might sail nearly on an even keel, and the advantage was so much in her favour that we never met a ship that could beat us afterwards; indeed, we ought to have known that nearly all French-built ships sailed best on an even keel.

We sailed from St. Helen's on October 4, having

nineteen sail of West Indiamen under our convoy bound for Jamaica, and several of us left our hearts behind. When the Masters of the merchantmen came on board to receive their instructions I was agreeably surprised to see among them an old schoolfellow of mine when at Bolden, and who had boarded in the same house with me; his name was Brown, one of North Shields, and he now commands a large ship named the *Empress of Russia*. Of course we were glad to see each other again, and when we arrived at Cape Nicla Mole[1] in St. Domingo I paid him a visit on board his ship. He was now flourishing like a young bay-tree. He bought a prize vessel that was up for sale, and was in a fair way for making his fortune. A few days after he caught the yellow fever and died !

We had a pleasant passage out, and on November 25 joined a squadron under the command of Vice-Admiral Parker cruising off Cape François, St. Domingo, and delivered wine and other things on board his ship the *Queen* (78 guns). We then took our departure, and soon after arrived with the convoy at Cape Nicla Mole.[1]

. The enemies' brigands were at this time in possession of the high lands around the Mole, and the yellow fever was carrying off thousands of our sailors and soldiers, so we lay here only a few days to victual and water, then went to join the squadron off Cape François under Admiral Parker, but found he had gone to Jamaica, and the squadron was now under the command of Richard Rodney Bligh, a Rear-Admiral on board the *Brunswick* (74 guns).

We were soon ordered to the Mole again, and then to Port au Prince, where we found the *Hindostan* (54 guns) lying as guard ship, and the brigands along shore had their posts within gunshot of ours. Why they did not

[1] St. Nicolas Mole.

fight I don't know, but I believe there was a treaty going on at this time about our evacuating the island. From here we went to Negril Bay, on the Island of Jamaica, where the grand convoy bound to England were to collect, and here we careened our ship to stop a dangerous leak which had broken out near the magazine and spoilt some of our gunpowder.

On January 23, 1798, the grand convoy appeared in the offing, so we got under way and joined them; then all bore away together for the Leeward Passage, and to see them safe past the Havanna, where the Spaniards had a squadron of line-of-battle ships. Ours consisted as follows :

Queen (Admiral Parker, Vice of the red, Capt. Dobson)	98	guns.
Hannibal (Capt. E. T. Smith)	74	„
Carnatic (Capt. Bowen)	74	„
Valiant	74	„
Thunderer (Capt. Hardy)	74	„
Trent (Capt. R. T. Otway)	36	„
Renown (Capt. Rolles)	36	„
Ceres	32	„
Aquillon (Capt. Boys)	32	„
Prompte	28	„

A signal was made for a trial of sailing, and the *Prompte* being the fastest the Admiral despatched us ahead to cruise off Cape Antonio until he came that way, and we soon left the fleet astern and out of sight. As soon as we got off the Cape we captured a large Spanish schooner laden with sugar, and sent her to Jamaica, but just as she got in sight of Port Royal Harbour she was captured again by a French privateer.

We cruised off Cape Antonio two or three days, and seeing nothing of our fleet we supposed they must have passed us in the night, so made the best of our way for the Havanna, where we joined them; but the merchantmen had left them and proceeded on to England under convoy of the *Maidstone* and *Ambuscade* frigates.

On June 2, and after having the command of our ship only twenty-six days, departed this life our noble captain of a dysentery, and, being too well beloved on board to give him a watery grave, we ran the ship under French colours into Cumberland Harbour, and there came to anchor near a fine sandy beach on the weather side, where some fishermen were drying their nets. Here we landed the remains of our noble captain, and deposited them in a grave made by our men and gave them military honours ; a large sheet of copper, with his name, age, and noble character, was fixed to a post at the head of his grave, and with a sigh we left the place and returned on board without being molested by the Spaniards.

Mr. Young, our first lieutenant, now took command of the ship, but he was little better than an old woman. Mr. Ross, the second lieutenant, was the mainspring of all our actions : he was a smart officer, and really a good hearty fellow.

We left Cumberland Harbour, and were beating up towards Cape Maize, when we saw a French privateer to windward and coming down along shore to get into St. Jagos ; however, we stood in and cut her off from getting in there, and when he found he could not escape he ran her bump on shore amongst the rocks, and the high surf soon dashed her to pieces. Many of them must have lost their lives, for we saw only about twenty that had got on firm land, and they, having hoisted the Republican colours, marched away along shore for St. Jagos.

A little after this, and early in the morning, we discovered two more privateers, but a long way off to windward and near the shore ; and soon after they must have run into some creek or small harbour, for we lost sight of them all at once. It being nearly a calm, our boats were hoisted out, manned, and armed, and with our dinners with us we set off in search of them, Mr. Ross and I in the launch, Mr. Alexander (midshipman) in the pinnace, and Mr. King (midshipman) in the cutter, amounting together to thirty-seven, all volunteers.

We rowed along shore a long way under a hot, burning sun and calm weather, and looked into every opening in the land, but saw nothing of them. In the afternoon we came to anchor with the launch's grap-line, and the other two boats hanging astern by us, and we went to dinner, a small current going to the westward and against us. As soon as dinner was over we prepared to weigh, but the grap-line had hooked a rock, and we could not get it up; one of our men made an attempt to go down and clear it, but before he got halfway to the bottom he came up again and said the current was too strong for him. The lieutenant then gave orders to cut the cable and heave it.

Now, naval stores were scarce at this time in the West Indies, and a grap-line being such a useful thing I felt sorry to part with it, as we had not another in the ship, so I volunteered to go down and clear it; and overboard I went, got hold of the cable and went down by it hand over hand, and was soon at the bottom and cleared it from a rock it had hooked (there was four fathoms and a half of water where we lay). I was soon at the top of the water again, indeed much sooner than I expected, and nothing the worse. Luckily for me there were no sharks in the way, and which I had never given a thought about or I should not have run such a hazard (and perhaps the other man that tried, and who was a good diver, had thought of this, which made him return so soon); as for the current, it was not worth mentioning. The grap-line was saved, and thanks to Providence, no harm done.

We now rowed along shore again and looked into every opening as before, but saw nothing of the two rascals, so Lieutenant Ross and I began to cut up bullets for slugs, intending to land and shoot something to take on board with us. But there was another projecting point of land ahead, and it was proposed that we should row up to that point and look in, and if we did not see them there to give up the chase.

In rounding this point, all of a sudden a narrow harbour opened to us, and there, to our joy, we beheld the two privateers we had been all day searching for. One of them, which mounted fourteen or sixteen guns, and full of men, mostly black fellows, was moored with her broadside towards the entrance of the harbour ; the other lay near a clump of trees, but they had got her guns on shore and made a battery behind some broken rocks, which we could not see, neither did we know of at the time, so, giving three hearty cheers, we rowed towards the one full of men, intending to board her sword in hand. She opened her fire at us with her guns, but all her shot went over our heads and hurt no one ; but when we got abreast of their masked battery they opened such a fire of round and grape shot that they made the water ripple around us like a hailstorm, and had they been good marksmen few of us would have lived to tell the tale. We were now obliged to stop and attack the battery with our carronade and musketry, but they being hid behind the rocks, we could not do so much execution as we wished, and at last the transom of our launch " started " (by firing the carronade so often), and we were compelled to retreat with the boat nearly half full of water.

It now became dark ; one of our boats we had sent away with a man who had been shot through the arm, and we had lost sight of the other in the dark, so were in a pretty predicament with a boat half full of water on the dark ocean, our ship out of sight, and miles from us. With the carronade in the bow to lighten her abaft, and those that could be spared bailing out the water as fast as possible, our situation was truly miserable; however, we kept up our spirits and rowed along in the direction we thought best to meet our ship, it being quite dark. Meanwhile, she having caught the land breeze came along rapidly towards us, and near midnight we had the pleasure of seeing her light at the masthead, and soon after got on board both hungry, tired, and weary.

Next morning we got off the harbour with the ship, and found it named on the chart Escondido, or in English "hidden harbour," and we intended running in with the ship, having a hundred volunteers ready to land, but as we approached it the water shoaled so, and they having dragged the privateers a long way up, we put about, and in stays fired a couple of broadsides at a great number of people among the rocks, which soon dispersed them all except one daring fellow, who stood his ground and seemed to bid us defiance.

A few months after this we had a prisoner on board who had belonged to one of these privateers, and knew our ship again, she having black sides and a red stripe around her, and who told us that they had between thirty and forty killed and wounded in that affair, and when he was told that we had only one man wounded he shrunk up his shoulders and gave such a look, as much as to say that was a great lie.

When I came to reflect on this affair, even if they had not got any battery erected to annoy us, yet I think it was rather a rash affair to attempt to cut out two large privateers, full manned, with only thirty-seven of us, and how we escaped so well as we did seems to be miraculous.

We now returned to Cape Nicla Mole to victual and

water, and get another captain; another lieutenant from the *Queen* was appointed our commander, whose name was John Mathias Spread, and, like the other, proved to be a good fellow. Our second worthy lieutenant, Mr. Ross, left us to be flag lieutenant in the *Queen*, and we got a Mr. Barford, a lieutenant from the *Tourterel*, another active young fellow, in his room. The *Prompte* at this time was so comfortable from the good usage the men got, that they would go through fire and water to please their officers, and she got the name of the "happy *Prompte*."

In the latter end of August 1708 we convoyed two homeward-bound merchantmen from New Providence clear of the trades, then stood towards Bermuda to get some naval stores we were in need of, and at this time we had a great many of our men on the sick list.

One of these mornings we saw a large schooner far off on our weather bow, going as we were, so to prevent suspicion we hung a black hammock cloth from the taffrail to the mizzen shrouds, to make it appear like a round house, and hung another over the guns to hide them; our flying jibboom was in, and mizzen topgallant-mast on deck (as it was now one of the hurricane months), and the ship appeared very much like a merchantman.

The French at this time captured American vessels, and the captain of the schooner, with the vanity of a Frenchman, thinking we were one, kept edging down to frighten us, until he got nearly within gunshot, when we threw off our disguise, showed our guns, hoisted English colours, ran close alongside and told him to surrender and come on board. Nothing could equal the surprise of the Frenchmen, for so they proved to be; they abused their captain, and chopped away the boat's lashings with an axe instead of casting them loose when the captain came on board. She was called the *Courier du Cap* or Cape Packet, laden with sugar and coffee from St. Domingo, and bound to

Bordeaux; a French lady and some Republican soldier officers were on board her (as passengers), who with all the crew except two were brought on board our ship.

Our captain had intended to send me on board her as prize master, but Lieutenant Barford wishing to go, the captain of course gave him the preference, which proved fortunate for me, as will be seen presently; so he took possession of the prize, and with a party of our men set sail to accompany us to Bermuda. At this time we expected soon to have sight of Bermuda, but in the evening of September 23 the weather began to have a gloomy appearance, with strong squalls from different quarters of the horizon, and at ten o'clock at night we furled all our square sails and lay to under our main staysail for the prize to come up, expecting a hurricane to come on soon. At midnight the prize got near us, but with more sail set than was prudent. I had charge of the watch, and observed to some of our officers that if they did not get her under a snugger sail something not very pleasant would happen to her; and sure enough, in the morning at break of day we saw her with a signal of distress flying.

We bore down and spoke her, and they told us she had sprung a leak; and as at this time it blew a strong gale from the E.S.E. and the sea ran high, we hailed and told them to get her before the wind, and follow us towards New Providence, which they did. As the gale was getting stronger and the sea rising higher, we got our topgallant masts down on deck and made everything as secure as possible. At ten the prize (still in company) cut or carried away her mainmast, and we were now scudding under bare poles. Between three and four in the afternoon the prize went down, and was no more seen.

We hove-to immediately under the storm mizzen stay-sail, with faint hopes that we might save some of her people; but not an article of her was to be seen, and we lamented the fate of Lieutenant Barford and our brave shipmates, whom we had sailed so long together with, little thinking we should so soon nearly share the same fate.

As I was entrusted with charge of a watch, it became my turn to dine with the captain, and at four o'clock, the ship still lying-to under the storm mizzen stay-sail, the sea mountains high, and the wind roaring so loud that we thought we had reached the height of the hurricane, all at once it came with almost double force, blew the stay-sail to atoms, laid the ship down on her beam ends, and threw us all at dinner (table and all) slap down against the lee side of the cabin.

We crawled up as fast as we could, and got on deck, where all were in consternation. The captain ordered the helm to be put hard-a-weather to get her before the wind, and the fore storm staysail hoisted to assist her; but it blew away into rags before half-way up, and then the fore-sail was loosed, which blew away in the same manner; the mizzen-mast was then cut away, and a heavy sea having struck the ship at the time on the weather bow, threw her head off, and thanks to kind Providence, we got her before the wind, which soon brought her upright again, and away she flew as if she would never stop again.

Everything now depended on good steering, for if she had once broached-to, it would soon have been all over with us. So, finding our lives all at stake, I off with my uniform coat (the only one I had), threw it over the stump of the mizzen mast, took charge of the helm, and continued steering her until near four the next morning, when the hurricane subsided. Although so long, it appeared to me like a common two hours' spell only, my attention being taken off from everything else by the danger.

In the middle of the night the ship was in great danger of foundering; the sea was so high that it pooped us several times, stove in the dead lights, washed down the cabin bulkhead, and made a sweep right forward along the gun deck, carrying everything before it, and sometimes the ship lay so buried under water that we thought she never would have arisen again. The maintopmast blew away like a twig, though no sail set on it; so much water had got into the hold that the carpenter reported it near breast high in his store-room, and the ship, it was thought, was sinking.

As most of the water below was in the forepart of the ship, Mr. Barnes, our first lieutenant, a smart fellow, with some others, got six of the foremost guns thrown overboard. Every one (prisoners and all) exerted every nerve in working at the pumps and bailing the water out of the spirit-room with buckets, and continued so until four next morning, when the hurricane suddenly abated, thank God, having continued most violent for near twelve hours.

Any stranger seeing the poor *Prompte* at daylight on the morning of September 25, 1798, would have pitied our distress. She was lying with her starboard gun-ports nearly in the water, as the ballast and casks in the hold had shifted over to that side; the mainyard was swinging about in all directions by the braces and lifts being torn away; the mizzen and maintopmasts gone, and all the sails (though they had been well furled) blown away from the yards, and even the staysails in the foretop and jib, and the staysail stowed at the bowsprit end were gone. It is almost incredible that the wind should have such power, but it is actually true.

The people were jaded nearly to death, and the cry was for water to drink; but there was none handy to be got—for the scuttle butt, which stood on the quarterdeck at the fore-part of the mainmast, had been washed overboard, and even the binnacle and compasses had shared the same fate. So the first thing we began at was to get a cask of water up out of the fore-hold ; but to our disappointment we found the upper tier, which had been empty, full of shingle, ballast, and salt water, and a weary job it was to clear away and get at the ground tier, and when there found all the water in the casks spoiled by being badly bunged, or perhaps by the force of the shingle ballast, scrubbing over the bungs and making them leak. The only resource we now had was to haul up the cable from off the ground tier in the main hold, and there we found only five butts of drinkable water.

These were really fatiguing trials, but necessity drove us on for self-preservation ; and when we had some refreshment, we began with a sickly and still fatigued crew to get the ship righted, and found in the after-hold pease casks, flour casks, etc., knocked to pieces and mixed pell-mell together. We next bent another set of sails, got up another maintopmast and yard, and bent the maintopsail. We then shaped our course for New Providence ; but God only knows when we would have got there, for we were steering right down for the coast of Florida. We had run a greater distance to the westward during the hurricane than we were aware of, and, the binnacle and compasses having been washed overboard, we knew not what course we had steered, having throughout the storm been under the necessity of keeping the ship right before the wind, whichever way it blew.

Fortunately we met an American vessel, who gave us the true longitude ; so we hauled our wind on the larboard tack, and soon after saw the " hole in the wall " on the Island of Abico, and next day arrived at New Providence and moored the ship head and stern in the harbour.

What was very remarkable was that, although the

hurricane scoured the American shore as far as Halifax, and did great damage, the American vessel we had spoke to had not felt it, though not far from us, neither had they felt it at New Providence; but they had expected it by the dismal appearance of the sky, which often foretells their coming.

Our ship being in such a disorderly state from what she had suffered lately, we got everything out of her on shore, gave her a thorough good cleaning inside, and stowed everything afresh. We got masts and yards from some large Spanish prize ships lying up the harbour, while canvas (for sails) and rope (for rigging) were purchased from the merchants' stores. The gunpowder was put on shore to be dried and aired, and we got six single-fortified 12-pounders from a lot that was lying on shore. Nobody knew whose property they were, being merchant guns, but supposed them to have belonged to some ship wrecked here long ago. We made great exertions in getting ready again, and employed people from the shore to assist; and when all was done we got vouchers made out and signed by the captain—I for airing and drying the gunpowder and painting the guns and carriages (which the Board of Ordnance allows pay for when the gunners do it themselves); the carpenter for making masts and yards and a new bowsprit (the old one having been found sprung); and the boatswain for getting the new sails made, etc. These vouchers we took to the agents, Munro & Forbes, to get cash for; but they said they must first send them to England to be approved, and when so they would cash them. So we trusted them with the vouchers; but, for my part, I have not heard or received a penny for them since.

Here we first heard of Nelson's glorious victory—the battle of the Nile—and fired a salute on the occasion. In the evening we illuminated the ship, and our noble and only lieutenant, Mr. Barnes, made a large bowl of famous punch, and we drank the health of the gallant Nelson with six more guns; then the health of our noble captain, who was on shore dining with the Governor, with four guns; and then that of the officers and crew of the *Prompte*, and let off sky-rockets and blue lights many, and concluded the night with mirth and cheerfulness.

One day, when Mr. Belcher, our carpenter, and I were on shore on duty, we saw more than a hundred privateers-men coming along, with drums beating and colours flying, to get volunteers; and, as they were passing, we saw one of our men, named Eagle, among them, whom they had enticed to desert. We immediately claimed him, and a row ensued, the captain swearing he would not part with him, as he had given Eagle the bounty. I don't know how this affair would have ended, as we were obstinate on both sides, had not our barge landed—fortunately for us—at the time. Her crew were a set of strong, athletic fellows, and, hearing of the hobble we were in, came immediately to our assistance, and soon took Eagle from the privateersmen and carried him on board.

This caused great animosity between the privateers' people (who carried on a great sway here) and us, and soon after caused another quarrel when the barge was on shore. Our brave fellows came on board conquerors, and brought a sword they had taken from one of the captains of the privateers. However, it was returned to him next morning; and they were more submissive after this; the reason they had been so impudent being that no pressing was submitted to on this island; but when we caught them at sea after this, we paid them off for it.

We left New Providence some time in December, and convoyed two homeward-bound merchantmen clear of the trades, then went on a visit to Blackbeard's wells on Crooked Island; then went down the old Bahama Channel and came to anchor off the Island of Anguilla, careened the ship and stopped a leak that had broke out near the bread-room, then went off the Havanna, and chased a brig in there so close that they fired at us from the Moro Castle. A large frigate was lying there ready for sea, and, as we observed them hoisting on board their stream anchor, we expected they were coming to pay us a visit, so we lay-to for her until the evening, and not seeing her come, filled again and stood away along shore towards the Matanzas.

Early next morning (being January 29, 1799) we saw a large fleet to windward coming down along shore towards us, bound to the Havanna. We soon made them out to be Spaniards, and as their convoy appeared strong (being two frigates, an armed ship, a xebec, and another very large like a line-of-battle ship) our captain thought best to get a little more into the offing and watch the opportunity to cut some of them off, and in standing off one of the frigates gave chase after us, and when we had got as far as we thought proper we hove-to to engage them.

But before he came within gunshot he hove-to likewise; so we, seeing he had no intention to fight, put our ship about and stood towards him, which he seeing put about also and made all sail toward his convoy. As we neared he made a great many signals to them, which caused them all to put about and run away as fast as they could back to the Matanzas again, where they had sailed from that morning.

We now conjectured that the big ship could not be a line-of-battle ship, therefore we carried all the sail we could, and were coming up with the deep-laden merchantmen very fast who were left by their ship-of-war to their own fate. About ten, as the sea breeze freshened, we found our foretopmast sprung, and so bad that it was nearly going over the sides. This was a very trying affair. If we waited to get up another they might all escape, and as the mast was sprung only a little about the cap it was thought best to reef it, and no sooner said than done.

With the exception of the foresail, all the head-sails were clewed up in a twinkling, the topmast lowered until the wound was under the cap and then secured ; the rigging was soon sheepshanked and set up taut, the foretop-sail double-reefed, and soon after all the head-sails set, and the little *Prompte* was pursuing them as fast as ever. If they had had courage to attack us during the business we should have been obliged to run before the wind from them ; but we heard afterwards that their excuse was that their ship was mostly manned with Indians, whom they could not trust in battle. This might be partly true in their having some Indians on board ; but as they were four to one they ought to have made some endeavour to save their convoy instead of abandoning them to their fate.

We came up with them again very fast, and in the afternoon got among their merchantmen, where we could have taken as many of them as we could man ; but Mr. Pell (our pilot) and some others persuaded our captain that the large ship was a galleon, and if we took her she would be of more value than all the rest, and he being of the same opinion, and forgetting the old proverb that a bird in the hand is worth two in the bush, let the merchantmen escape, who as soon as they found that we did not stop to take possession of them bore away before the wind for the Havanna under all the sail they could crowd, no doubt as happy as birds escaping out of a cage.

All our endeavours were now exerted to get up to the others before they could get into the Matanzas, especially

as it was getting late ; and about sunset they all got into
the harbour except the large ship, who, being in such confusion, missed stays, and before they could get into order
we were within gunshot of her, and finding no chance of her
getting into the harbour bore away before the wind. But
finding we would soon be alongside of her, they ran her on
shore on a steep, rocky coast, where they got on shore
from the bowsprit and jibboom which hung over the land,
and, except three, all escaped.

We hove our ship to instantly, and with our three boats,
the lieutenant in one, Mr. Oldham the master's mate in
another, and I in the third, boarded her immediately.
The first thing we did was throwing all her sails, which
were still set flat, aback, hoping they would force her off ;
but she would not start, but only slewed round with her
starboard side to the shore. We then had recourse to
a large anchor stowed abaft the main chains ; but being
too heavy for our boats to carry, we got a hawser out of
one of the hawse-holes, passed the end aft and bent it to
the anchor, and then cut the latter away. We then took
the hawser to her capstan and hove on it with all our
might. But she would not start, for, as we found afterwards,
a piece of rock stuck in her bottom and held her fast.

We now found that she was not a galleon, but a Spanish
King's store ship, named the *Cargadora*, laden with cedar
and mahogany timber for building ships at the Havanna.
Though not a galleon, her cargo would have been of great
value had we got her to Jamaica, where ship timber was
so scarce at this time that ships were repaired with
mahogany for want of oak.

As there appeared no chance of getting her off, Mr.
Barnes, our lieutenant, left her under my care with two
boats' crews, and went on board the *Prompte*, to consult
with the captain about what was best to be done, and we
saw no more of him till next day afternoon, as it had

fallen a calm, and the ship had drifted away to the north. As we had been at quarters all day, and no victuals cooked, we were of course all hungry enough; and we began to look out for something to eat. In the galley we found several pots of stewed meat and fowls, which we supposed had been cooked for the captain's dinner; but as they tasted high seasoned and looked yellow, perhaps by curry, we would not venture upon them, for fear the Spaniards had put poison therein.

However, there were in the coops plenty of good fowls, and without leave or license we made free to take them, and (without being very nice in gutting or picking) soon had them grilled on the galley fire, and had a famous blow-out. In the cabin locker there was plenty of wine, and porter in bottles; and, without leave of signor her captain, we made free, and drank sufficient without any one getting the worse for it. All this time we kept our arms by our side, and the guns pointed to the shore, as we did not know how soon we might be attacked, as we heard the drums beating along shore, and not far from us.

We lay under arms at our quarters the rest of the night, that we might not be taken by surprise; and when daylight appeared, to our regret we beheld the *Prompte* far off, and nearly hull down, having drifted away in a calm by the current, and moreover a multitude of Spaniards, some on horseback, were collected abreast of the ship. I therefore ordered a shot to be fired from one of the great guns over their heads, to know their intentions, and before they had time to smell the gunpowder off they all started, and we saw no more of them. One of our people having gone below for a cartridge to load the gun again, came hastily up and said the hold was full of water, and all the powder spoiled; this concerned us greatly, as our chief hope of defence was in the great guns, in case they had brought any field-pieces down to attack us, and which we expected.

We were now in a most critical situation, having beside one discharge of the great guns only some musketry with us. Luckily for us they made no attempt to retake the ship, and glad were we at noon to see the *Prompte* with a staggering sea breeze coming rapidly toward us; and soon after Lieutenant Barnes came on board, highly pleased that we were safe, and told me that we were to get all the stores out of her we could, and then set her on fire.

Therefore, with all the *Prompte's* boats and the large launch we had got out, we were employed all the afternoon till sunset in sending from the prize cordage, canvas, and other useful things, and even unbent the best of her sails from the yard and sent them on board, and when all this was done liberty was given to plunder.

Mr. Barnes and I searched the captain's cabin, and under his bed I found a bag containing a thousand dollars, and many boxes of cigars in the pantry; we found many tablespoons and forks (all solid silver), and in the priest's berth a crucifix, some pots and spoons, all silver, with other valuables. All these were taken out of the cabin and placed under a sentry on the quarterdeck, where all was to be collected and kept together; when we went below, her 'tween-decks was like a fair, the chests being broken open and the clothes strewn about, and among them many laced coats, cocked hats, and other valuable clothing, fine shirts, and trousers, etc., that had belonged to the Spanish officers. No doubt but many of our men got a supply of dollars there, and had concealed them about their clothes, as they brought very little to the stock on the quarterdeck and there was no time to search them.

At dusk, having got all we could, we in the last boat hoisted her colours and then set her on fire in three places, which soon set her in a blaze. We had hardly got a musket-shot from her, when to our surprise we heard a volley of musketry fired at us from the shore from people we had not seen since the morning, but without doing any injury. When we got alongside our ship there was fine fun and laughing : the reason was, our people in the boat had dressed themselves in Spanish uniform, some with lace clothes, and dressed much like our artillery officers, some had large cocked hats, some lace jackets, and white frilled shirts, and so metamorphosed that their messmates hardly knew them again.

After seeing the prize burnt to the water's edge we took her launch in tow, as she would be very convenient for watering His Majesty's ships, and arrived with her at New Providence. Here we sold the silver plate, which, together with the dollars found, gave me as my share 17 dollars. The canvas and cordage got out of the prize we left with the agents, Munro & Forbes, to sell at vendue or auction, but I have never had a penny for them to this day.

We only stopped to water our ships, and then took our departure to Jamaica ; and a few days after we detained two Americans with contraband goods on board, and saw them safe into New Providence ; after that we chased and captured a fast-sailing American schooner that had often escaped our cruisers by her superior sailing : she was entirely laden with naval stores for the enemy at Havanna, and her we saw safe into New Providence ; and, as I have never returned to that place since, I never got a penny for her, nor for the cables, cordage, and canvas taken out of the *Cargadora* store ship nor vouchers nor anything else. My agent, Mr. Kane of Gosport, and I have sent several letters to New Providence concerning them, but never could get an answer ; those salutary laws for making agents responsible for unclaimed prize money were not enforced then—they could keep it as long as they pleased.

We arrived at Port Royal in Jamaica on March 17, 1799, and in passing along shore saw many of the *Hermione's* men hanging in chains. Here I found that I had been appointed to the *Yacht* (64 guns), but being absent another gunner got her, as she was ordered to England. Fortunately for me I never joined her, for not long after she was lost and all hands.

CHAPTER VIII

1799–1802

AT MARTINIQUE IN H.M.S. "TROMP"

Joins H.M.S. *Regulus* at Port Royal—Convoys 125 merchantmen to Spithead—Docked at Woolwich—Visits the Navy Agent in Downing Street—Sees Mr. Pitt riding in the Park—Escapes from swindlers—Transferred to H.M.S. *Tromp*—Ordered to Martinique—His wife determines to go with him—Madeira—Fort Royal, Martinique—Great sickness breaks out—The *Tromp* becomes a prison ship—Rear-Admiral Duckworth (*alias* "Old Tommy")—Prisoners arrive—New Union Jack received (Jan. 12, 1801)—Sir Robert Calder arrives in pursuit of Admiral Ganteaume —Five hundred prisoners sent to England—Marine eaten by shark—"Old Tommy" orders a court-martial for Christmas Day —French proceedings at St. Domingo—Dominican insurrection put down—Treaty of peace between Great Britain and France ratified (Peace of Amiens)—Commodore Stopford succeeds to command—The blacks plot an insurrection—Baffled by Gen. Maitland and the Commodore—Thanks of Parliament received— *Tromp* leaves Martinique homeward bound (July 1802)—Takes the 64th Regt. to St. Kitts—and part of the 3rd Buffs home— Reaches the Needles Sept. 1802.

WHILE at Port Royal I was much gratified in finding myself appointed to the *Regulus* (44 guns), commanded by my old friend Captain George Eyre, who commanded the *Prompte* when we came from England; so I left the "happy *Prompte*," a ship where there was none of your browbeating allowed, nor that austere authority where two men durst hardly be seen speaking together (as I have seen since in the service). The *Prompte's* crew were like a family united, and would, both officers and men, risk their lives to assist each other. This I knew well, having belonged to her more than five years in continual active service, and on many trying occasions too.

When I joined the *Regulus* she was getting in a new mainmast, and, to add to my comfort, our captain got orders to convoy the homeward-bound Indiamen to England, and Richard Rodney Bligh, Vice-admiral of the White and lately second in command here, hoisted his flag on board the *Regulus* for a passage home. On June 20, 1799, we weighed anchor and went round the east end of Jamaica to Port Antonio, where the convoy was collecting, and saluted the Governor with fifteen guns.

The *Serpent*, sloop-of-war, and *Recovery*, schooner, joined us here, and on July 2 we set sail with 125 merchantmen under the convoy, but owing to light winds and a lee-current were twenty-six days in getting as far as St. Domingo—a distance we could have run in a day with a fair wind and good breeze. Here we sent the *Recovery* in chase after a couple of small Spanish vessels, which she captured, and we sent her with them to Jamaica.

We had had a tedious passage of thirteen weeks from Port Royal, and had many invalids on board, whom we now sent on shore to Deal Hospital; received fresh provisions and new sheet-anchor and cable, in lieu of the other left at Jamaica, as is usual with ships returning to England.

The Admiral struck his flag, and left us for London, and we were ordered to Spithead to land his luggage, he being a resident of Gosport. Off Folkestone a gale came on from the westward and drove us into the Downs again, where we moored the ship and struck lower yards and topmasts. It coming to blow harder, both our cables broke, the ship ran her gun-room ports under water, and when she came broadside to the wind, lay on her beam-ends, and was driving fast towards the Goodwin Sands before the sheet-anchor was let go; but (thank God) that brought her up, which was more than we expected.

Fortunately for us, the cable was a new one, and not like our old worn-out cables we had brought from the West Indies. But when it brought the ship up I never saw such a strain on a rope before—it absolutely shrank to near half its size.

We all expected that we should be ordered from here to Woolwich to be paid off, but an order came for us to proceed to Holland to assist in bringing over to England the Duke of York's army. But our rudder being in a bad state the captain had a survey held on it, and, the bearding being found defective and reported to the Board, another order came for us to proceed to Woolwich.

In going out of the Downs, and near the North Foreland, in hazy weather, we saw a laden collier close under our bows, who hailed and said there was a French privateer near, which had endeavoured to board him; the haze clearing away at the time, we soon saw the rascal. Seeing us, he immediately set off and ran over the sands, where there was not water deep enough for us to follow; so we made a signal to Admiral Lutwidge, who sent a cutter after her, but whether she took her or not we never heard.

We came to anchor in Long Reach, and sent out powder, guns, and stores in lighters to Woolwich, and after this we got under way; but so many other ships were working their way up to London that we often got foul of each other and carried away one of their bowsprits. At Gallions, where we came to anchor (the flood tide being done), a heavy squall came on and drove the ship on shore; we shored her up with the square topmasts, and when the flood tide rose again we got her off. In entering Woolwich Reach we got so entangled among a number of merchant vessels that we carried away the mizzenmast of one, the jibboom of another, a sloop had her mast carried away, and we all drove on shore together; assistance came from Woolwich Dockyard, and our ship was soon hove off and taken alongside of the old *Rainbow* hulk, and there secured.

But the *Rainbow* was in such a miserable condition that the wind and rain blew through her sides into the cabins that were allotted to us, so we applied and got leave to live on shore while the *Regulus* was in dock; and I got a furnished room at a Mrs. Loupe's, near the churchyard, at four shillings a week.

One of these days, while the *Regulus* was in dock, I went to London to inquire of Mr. Maude, a navy agent, about my Surinam prize money, which Desbro', the agent at Martinique, had told us of. This Mr. Maude had the paying of it in London, as the money had been remitted to England; and when I arrived at Charing Cross I inquired of a person the way to Downing Street, and he told me. Immediately a genteel-looking man dressed in black came up, and in a whispering manner, as if afraid to be heard, said, " Sir, you should not ask information from any one in the street, or they may lead you wrong; it's best to inquire at a shop; but as you were asking the way to Downing Street, I am going that way and will be very glad to accompany you if you have no objections."

I thought this very kind, and thanked him, and accepted the offer, and in going along he was very talkative and told me he had been a purser in the navy. However, I thought him too inquisitive, and as he knew I was a naval officer by my uniform, I gave him indifferent answers; and when we came to Downing Street he pointed out the house of Mr. Maude, so I thanked him, went in, and was not sorry in getting rid of so inquisitive a stranger.

Mr. Maude told me that he never had received orders

from Desbro' at Martinique to pay prize-money, therefore it must, he said, be a mistake; so I, being in want of money, asked him to let me have £10 on my agent's account, Mr. James Hane, of Gosport, which he very kindly did. Finding nothing more to be done, I took my leave, but no sooner had I got into the street than whom should I see but Mr. Purser again waiting for me; and his first question was to know what success I had got, as no doubt he knew very well that I had come after money, so I again gave him an indifferent answer. He was not to be put off so easy, and entreated me to take a step into the Park, as it was close at hand, and I would see the King, as the carriage was waiting for him at Buckingham House; so as I had never seen his Majesty I agreed to go with him, but was determined to be on my guard, for I had been in London often enough to know that there were plenty of sharpers in it.

In going through the Park we met the celebrated Mr. Pitt, our Prime Minister, coming from Buckingham House on horseback. "Well," thinks I, "this is something: if I see nothing else I can say I have seen Mr. Pitt, and that is a small feather in my hat." But we did not see the King, though the carriage was waiting for him. After waiting some time I proposed taking my leave of Mr. Purser, but he said I must go and see Chelsea first. I told him I would not, as it was getting late, and I had to go to Woolwich.

"Then," said he, "we must have a glass of grog together before we part;" and he took me into a low public-house of no creditable appearance, and into a back room, and called for two glasses of warm grog. But we had hardly sat down before a tall, sallow, thin-looking chap, dressed in shabby black clothes, came in, and without any ceremony began in a countrified tone to tell us that he had just come to "Lunnon," had been to the Bank and made a poor bank of it, for he had got all the money, and then spread a handful of bank-notes on the table.

Mr. Purser laughed, and said he could show bank-notes too, and he put some on the table, and whispering to me, said, "Show him that you have got some too." I saw into their scheme, and this gave me more suspicion that I was among sharpers, for if I had put my ten-pound-note on the table they would soon have shuffled it among theirs, which no doubt were counterfeits. I should have been cheated out of mine and got a bad one in lieu of it; so I said, "Take no notice of him, and let him go his own way."

Finding the bait would not take, Mr. Purser proposed having a game of cards and pulled a pack out of his pocket, and this immediately let me know what company I was in; so up I got, wished them a good evening, without stopping to hear what they had to say, hurried out of the house, and glad was I when I got into the street again. I took a coach, it being now dark, to Greenwich, then went to Woolwich; and glad was I to get home safe with my ten-pound note, being nearly all the money I had.

In the latter end of January 1800 the *Regulus* came out of dock, having been fitted up for a troopship and a poop put on her. Our noble commander, Captain Eyre, left us soon after, with three hearty cheers from the ship's company, and was succeeded by Thomas Presland, Esq., a master and commander, and our crew of three hundred men was reduced to one hundred and fifty-five.

On March 23 we, the *Dromedary*, *Serapis*, and *Inconstant* all set sail together from Woolwich, and went to Long Reach, where we came to anchor, and got on board the guns, powder, and other stores; then proceeded to the Nore, where we came to anchor and moored ship;

and soon after I received a letter from the Admiralty appointing me to a higher rate. Her name was the *Tromp*, an old 54-gun ship, but now in dock at Chatham getting repaired. Although I had to acknowledge the receipt of this letter and thanks for my promotion, I took the liberty to inform their Lordships that I was a young man, and humbly solicited their Lordships to give me a ship or more active service; and their answer was that when their arrangements permitted they would be glad to give me a more active ship.

I was succeeded in the *Regulus* by a Mr. Emerson, gunner of the *Arrow* sloop-of-war, and got my things in our boat landed at Sheerness; and when I got my things on the jetty I sent the boat on board again as desired; and now came trouble after trouble.

This was on a Saturday afternoon, and raining, and such a miserable place was Sheerness at this time that I could not get a cart to carry my things up to the Marlborough Inn, and had to leave my poor wife on the jetty in the rain watching our things during the time I was in search of one. At last, late in the evening, a brewer's dray came along, and by rewarding the man we got our things taken to the inn—if it deserved that name—got a supper there, and a bed.

Early next morning we were roused up, as the passage vessel was ready to start for Chatham, and being still raining, had all my luggage and cabin furniture and culinary utensils to lug through the wet to the passage vessel. When at noon we arrived at Chatham I had to hire a wherry to carry them to the *Tromp*, she having come out of dock the day before; and when I got alongside of her could hardly find a piece of rope long enough to reach from the lower deck port into the wherry to haul my things up, and there was only one man on board (a ship-keeper) and he a cripple, and all this on a good Sunday.

No officer in shifting from ship to ship has more bother than a warrant officer; he has not only his chests and bedding to lug about but also his cabin furniture, cooking utensils, and if he has his wife with him so much the worse; when I had got all on board there was no provision or water, and the cabins being just painted there was no living in them, so I waited till I saw a wherry come along, and called her alongside, then went on shore (my wife and I) and put up at the Red Lion public-house, where we got refreshment. This cost me no small expense, and Government allowed nothing for it.

Early in June Commander Terence O'Neil came on board and commissioned the ship, and (what was rather strange) after reading his commission he directly read the articles of war to the people, which gave us a suspicious opinion of him: however he proved to be a very good man and officer. Soon after Lieutenants Pine and Franklin joined the ship. Then Mr. Macgra the master, and Allen the purser; and then we began to take in naval stores for that miserable sickly place Martinique, in the West Indies.

When we got the hold full of stores the lower deck ports were barred and caulked and the deck filled with wet spars, leaving just room enough to work the cables; her main deck was sparred over, and we then got the upper deck guns in and bent the sails, and went to the Nore, where we moored ship. I again wrote to the Admiralty for a more active ship, and received for answer that they could add nothing to their former letter, so I was obliged to submit, but thought it hard that I should be sent out again to the West Indies.

We returned the dockyard people to the flagship here (all except 155 we were ordered to keep, and of course we kept the best, little thinking nearly all these brave fellows were so soon to die in the West Indies). Beside a master's mate and four midshipmen being allowed us, several others, fine young men, who most of them had passed for lieutenants, went out with us in hopes of soon getting commissions, as so many death vacancies occurred there; but almost every one of them lost their lives by the yellow fever.

On July 10 got under way for Spithead, and spoke the *Dart* sloop of war (Captain Campbell), with her prize, the *Désirée*, a French frigate of 40 guns, which she had cut out of Calais last night by boarding, and with very little loss.

On the 15th came to anchor at Spithead and moored the ship, hoping we should remain here some time, as a convoy was to collect and go out with us; but only two days after, as I was on the platform at Portsmouth, had the mortification to see the signal for sailing at our ship's masthead, which vexed me greatly: I would rather have seen the *Tromp* on the top of Portsdown Hill. So I hastened to Portsea to bid my wife and friends adieu, but found that she had fixed her mind to go with me, as it was reported the voyage would be short and the ship would return when she had delivered her stores; so (after some entreaty) I gave my consent, especially as the captain's, the master's, the purser's, and boatswain's wives were going with them; the serjeant of marines and six other men's wives had leave to go; a person would have thought they were all insane wishing to go to such a sickly country!

As there was no time to be lost, we took a hasty leave of our friends; my wife in parting from her parents almost fainted, but was still determined to go with me. This was a most trying occasion, and I was so moved I hardly knew how to act; however, we soon overcame it. We got our linen all wet from the washerwoman, who had no time to finish, and returned on board very much mortified at being hurried off in such a manner.

The *Venus* frigate (Captain Graves—as commodore), together with the *Circe* (28 guns, Captain Wolley), *Asp* gun brig (Lieutenant Farrier), and we, with nineteen sail of merchantmen, got under way together next morning and proceeded to sea with a fair wind and fine weather, little thinking how few of us would return again! On August 1, 1800, we got sight of Madeira, and well it was for the convoy that we had not the charge of them, for Mr. Macgra, our master, was near eighty miles out of his reckoning, but whether it was his fault (for he was not one of the best navigators in the world) or the iron rails round the after hatchway that attracted the compass, we could not tell, but the latter was blamed for it.

On the following morning, at half-past one, the captain's wife was delivered of a fine boy; and at ten we came to anchor in fifty-two fathoms in Funchal Roads, Madeira, about a mile from the land, and soon had plenty of shore boats alongside with pineapples, grapes, pears, oranges, cucumbers, and onions to sell, and several friars and others came on board to see the ship. I took my wife on shore to see the place, but there is nothing particular to be seen in the town, which has narrow dirty streets and swarms of beggars, who stick close to the English, knowing them to be more charitable than their own people. We dined with some of our shipmates at the Royal George Inn, and although we had some of the worst Madeira wine I ever drank we were charged ten shillings each of us for our dinner.

Madeira rises pleasantly from the shore to a considerable height, so after having a peep into a church not very grand, my wife and I went up the hill to have a look at a white nunnery about half a mile distant, and we found the nuns very communicative, but could not understand them very well; only a few wooden banisters separated them from us. They wished very much for my wife to go inside, but she, being afraid they would not let her out again, would not venture; they presented us through the banisters with some little baskets of artificial flowers, and we gave them a small knife and a pair of scissors, which pleased them very well; but there were no Venuses among them!

Here we watered our ship and laid in a good stock of fresh beef, fruit, and vegetables, and on the 9th we got under way with the convoy, but left our anchor behind, it being foul of a rock. We had a fine large breeze in our favour, and after having got a good distance from Madeira two Portuguese boys discovered themselves, they having hid themselves below to stay in the ship. As the boatswain and I had no servants, the captain gave one named Pizarro to the boatswain and the other to me; my boy's proper name was Jehoikin, but the clerk thought he said Joe King, and his name was put on the books as such, and he went by it all the time he was in the ship.

I got a few clothes made, and a canvas cap with *Tromp* on the front of it, and a little box to keep them in, and so careful was he of them that he would take them out two or three times a day, smooth them down and then put them in again. He turned out to be a worthy little fellow, and got as much attached to me and my wife as if we had been his parents; but, poor little fellow, he could not understand English, yet he soon learnt his duty and was very diligent and cleanly.

Eight days after leaving Madeira we crossed the line, with the usual ceremony of Neptune and his crew, shaving and ducking, and on September 2 came to anchor at Barbados, after a pleasant passage from Spithead of six weeks and four days, and out of that time stopped a week at Madeira.

Next morning we got under way, left the convoy, and steered N.N.W. instead of N.W., which showed what a navigator old Macgra the master was. Next morning we ought to have been near Martinique, but saw nothing of it, so altered our course seven points, namely to W. by S., and at noon saw it; but were too late to get into Fort Royal Bay before sunset, so hove-to for the night, and next morning bore away, passed Diamond Rock at eleven, and came to anchor at two in Fort Royal Bay in nineteen fathoms.

Fort Royal Town is neatly built, with lofty stone-built houses; in front towards the bay is high rocky ground, now strongly fortified, and called Fort Edward. Around the town is a large creek called by the inhabitants the Carnash, and both ends come into Fort Royal Bay; the north-west end is shallow, and only fit for boats to go in; but the south-east end is deep enough for a ship-of-the-line to enter, and a little way up it is a fine dockyard and gun wharf. Here we took our ship, and moored her with her head towards the Cabaretta Point, and her stern close under the ramparts of Fort Edward, to be convenient for sending the stores to the dockyard; but we had little benefit from the sea breeze.

Rear-Admiral Duckworth was Commander-in-Chief here at this time, but on our arrival was absent in his ship the *Leviathan*; when he returned his chaplain came on board, and baptized our captain's son by the name of Charles, there being no Protestant minister at this place. He then hurried away on shore to Fort Royal to marry and baptize those that had been waiting for him, then to St. Pierre and other parts of the island to do the same; and no doubt but he got his pockets well filled before he returned on board again.

There was an agent of transports here named Whittaker, who always took care to be first on board to tell the Admiral the news; and being asked how the *Tromp* got on in delivering her stores, he told him rather slowly;

and when our captain went on board the *Leviathan* to pay his respects to the Admiral (who was none of the best-tempered men) he told our Captain that we were dilatory in getting the stores out, which hurt our captain's feelings much, as the story was untrue.

The consequence was (and let this be known to tale-bearers) the death of many brave men; for after this reprimand, when a boat-load of stores or raft of spars were ready to put off from the ship, they were ordered away directly, rain or shine, and the people getting wet with rain and letting their clothes dry on their back with the hot sun when the shower was over, brought a dangerous fever on them which affected the whole ship, and we thought one time that no one would survive it.

Every day for some time we were sending people to the hospital, and few returned. The captain and purser with their wives left the ship to live on shore; the doctor went to the hospital and got invalided; the first lieutenant, Mr. Pine, and the clerk, his brother (whom by-the-bye he had much neglected, though a very decent man), both died; next the master with his wife (large in a family way) both died; then the marine officer; and the wardroom was cleared of all its officers except the sick second lieutenant, Mr. Frankland.

Next died Mr. Campbell, the boatswain, leaving a wife and son and daughter on board; next went Mr. Hogan, the surgeon-assistant, a funny little fellow who pretended to tell by their constitutions who would die and who would not, little thinking he was to go so soon himself; next followed near all our fine young midshipmen who had come out for promotion; then the master-at-arms, the armourer, gunner's mate (a fine stout fellow), the captain's steward, cook and tailor, then the captain's lady's maid, and many brave men. Mr. Jury, the carpenter, got the fever too, but would not go to the hospital, as so many were dying there every day; he went on shore to sick quarters at his own expense, and partially recovered.

What few of us were left endeavoured to heave the ship's stern round to the wind, that the sea breeze might blow through her, but found ourselves unequal to the task. And now, worse than all, I found that my poor wife had got the fever, which troubled me very much; I would have given all the world to have had her home again.

She found that nothing would stay on her stomach, and was falling away so much that I immediately took her on shore to Fort Royal, and put her under the care of a French black woman named Madame Janet, and who was said to be an excellent nurse, and I got a French doctor named Dash, a man near eighty years of age and said to be very skilful, who had dwelt long on the island, and understood the nature of the West India fevers well.

Now instead of trying to eat this and that, and force the stomach, as my wife had been advised to do, Doctor Dash would not allow her to eat anything; she was put to bed in an airy room, and the only thing she was to take was tezan [*tisane*] to drink. What the French call tezan is made thus: Take a vegetable something like lettuce, put it into a pot, then pour boiling water on it, and when cool it is ready for use. This my wife had to drink as often as she pleased, but nothing of any kind to eat, and by these means in a few days the fever, thank God, was starved out of her. When her appetite came, she was at first permitted to eat only little at a time, and by degrees recovered, but very weak; the skin on her hands and feet came off like peelings of onions.

Dr. Galispie [? Gillespie], head surgeon of the hospital, came on board to see what could be done with the ship; but as we had already smoked the 'tween-decks and sprinkled them with vinegar, together with airing stoves and pumping clean water in and out of the hold, all he could advise us was to wear flannel next our skins.

Some negroes were sent off from the shore to assist in delivering the stores, but they soon got so frightened that they would not come again on any account; so the Admiral ordered the seamen from the transports to assist us, and on October 21 we got all the stores delivered from the ship. They consisted chiefly of anchors, cables, cordage, canvas, spars, elm and oak planks, and after all this was done we got the ship warped from the Carnash into the bay, and anchored her stern to the wind on a bank about a mile outside of Port Edward, where we lay open to the sea breeze.

The few hands left were now set to work to wash their blankets and bed-ticks, and the flocks sent on shore by the Admiral's order to be dried in ovens. A Mr. Hearn from the *Leviathan* came on board as acting master, and promised to do great things in bringing the ship into a healthy state. In two or three days he caught the fever, but would not believe it, and when requested to go to the hospital refused; however, he was soon compelled to go, but not before his hands and feet were dead, and he died that night, having been only a week on board.

By the ship lying with her stern to the wind, and the sea breeze blowing through her fore and aft, she began to be more healthy, and some black mechanics came off from the dockyard and cut scuttle-holes through her sides on the orlop deck for the admission of air, which made her more so.

Our chief hopes were that we should soon be ordered home again, but we were grievously disappointed, for the Admiral came on board to muster the ship's company or plan her out for a prison ship. When the purser's name was called over in mustering, he was put down invalided, and Old Tommy (as the sailors called the

Admiral) got foul of him, told him if he went to England he never would get a ship again, and as for the fever, "I have had it," said he, "aye, and a relapse too, have I not, Mr. Hedlam?" said he to his secretary; and of course Mr. Hedlam said "Yes," so the purser was compelled to give it up and remain. My name being called over next, "Well," says Old Tommy to me, "you have not been (Mr. Richardson) on the sick list?" "No, sir," I replied. "I thought so," said he; "I can see that you are a good man, and I will do something for you. Mr. Hedlam, put Mr. Richardson's name down in your book for fear I should forget"; and thus he palavered me over with promises he never intended to fulfil.

When Mr. Jury, the carpenter, was called, he too was down to be invalided, and got a lecture from Old Tommy, as how he ought to be ashamed, being a young man, to think of such a thing; and though very weak and poorly, he was compelled to remain. He then left us with the marines and men enough to man two boats, took all the rest on board the *Leviathan*, and my little boy Joe King with them.

Old Tommy intended to keep him for a servant, but could get no good out of him, as the poor boy fretted so, and was crying every day to be sent back to the *Tromp*. When I heard this I wrote to the Admiral requesting the favour of having the boy returned to me again, but never received any answer.

Captain O'Neil was succeeded by Mr. Frankland, our second lieutenant, and took a passage, he and his lady, to England in a transport. Men from the ships in the bay came on board and assisted in unrigging the ship, and nothing left standing but the three lower masts, bowsprit, and rigging appertaining to them; the rest were sent to the dockyard, and guns with the ammunition to the gun wharf—all except one carronade, which we kept on board; the ground tier of casks were to be kept full of fresh water in case of emergency, but not for present use, and one month's bread and salt provisions.

On November 4, I got my wife on board, tolerably well, thank God, from her sickness, but had a heavy bill to pay out of my small income (which was 3s. a day); so I drew a bill on my agent at Gosport for £20, and got $78 for it. $48 of these I paid Madame Janet for board and lodging, and $18 to Doctor Dash, all which was thought reasonable; so I had only $12 left out of my $78. However, to bring up the leeway, I received $42 for assisting in delivering the stores, being $1 a day for six weeks.

Mr. Steward, the master attendant, came on board with a party of black fellows from the dockyard, and laid out two anchors with chain cables astern to secure the ship, and a stream anchor and cable ahead to prevent her from swinging round by the land beeeze at night; and a party of black artificers came on board to fit her up for a prison ship.

These were the most dilatory set of artificers I ever saw set to work. When they came on board in the morning it took them till breakfast time to grind their tools, then they slowly went to work till eleven, when they left off to cook their dinners; after dinner a nap, and so on till the evening, when they left off and went on shore. They made our lieutenant a dripstone stand of fir, which might be worth about $2, and we calculated that it cost Government £24; their pay was $2 a day and provisions, but they being slaves and lent to Government, their masters got the money, and only allowed them a small pittance, so no wonder they were so dilatory.

Our small crew were victualled from the shore, and every morning the jolly-boat went for our day's stock of fresh beef, bread, and a turn of fresh water. The beef was like carrion; a man could bring up the side a whole quarter in his hand, it was so small and thin.

Our lower deck was kept wholly for prisoners, and the main deck (from the bows to a strong bulkhead across by the mainmast) likewise; abaft that for our people, and abaft them cabins for our officers; but the wardroom was kept for the prisoners that were officers. They had their provision brought off daily in a large boat, sent by Mr. Parker, their agent, and cartels were permitted at this time between here and Guadeloupe for exchanging prisoners.

On December 1 we received on board 491 prisoners, and next day 309 more, of different colours, but most of them blacks. The few marines we had left, and who had recovered from the fever, were so weak and looked so sickly, that we were obliged to apply for more assistance to guard and watch the prisoners, and a serjeant's guard of the 14th Regiment was sent on board for that purpose, to be relieved every month; the cutter and jolly-boat lay alongside each night with their gear ready to pursue any of the prisoners who might get out to swim on shore, and many attempts were made for that purpose by them, as will be seen hereafter; our fine copper-bottomed launch was kept at the dockyard to be ready whenever we wanted her.

January 4, 1801.—A Lieutenant Byam joined us, and succeeded Lieutenant Franklin (a good officer) in charge of the ship. He was a complete rough knot, and said once that he would not give a damn for a fellow that did not like grog; he seldom went to bed sober, and sometimes when he had been on shore and come off in the evening he staggered so that the quarterdeck was hardly large enough to hold him, and sometimes would tumble down on the cabin floor when he reached it, and lie there. Old Tommy, hearing that he belonged to a great family (the Byams in the West of England), took him into the *Leviathan*, and soon after made him a Commander: so much for Old Tommy's making officers of merit.

Received on board a black French colonel named

Johnny Conner, to be kept under close confinement for endeavouring to raise an insurrection on shore among the black French inhabitants ; to look at him one would suppose that he would hardly say bo' to a goose.

The other prisoners now on board had found means to get some of their port bars loose and get overboard ; the ship's side was so decayed that some of the bolts of the bars could be pulled out with very little force, and the artificers who fitted them being French blacks, no doubt put many slack bolts in ; every dark night some of the prisoners were getting out and swimming to the shore. There were two more prison ships here besides ours (which lay nearer the shore)—both merchant ships hired into the service, one named the *Superbe* and the other the *Thomas*—and they were much in the same state as ourselves in regard to casualties.

Our prisoners had only been five days on board when three of them got the bars of a port loose and slipped into the water, intending to swim on shore : but our sentinels saw them and fired, and the cutter and jolly-boat being sent immediately after them, they were taken and brought on board. The punishment we were allowed to give was to put them in irons on the poop and keep them there ten days and nights on half allowance of provisions, and to be the last exchanged in cartels.

Soon after this twelve prisoners escaped from the *Thomas* at night, swam to an American schooner, boarded, got her under way, and arrived safe at Guadeloupe with her.

One of these days a boat alongside of us, belonging to a prize just arrived, was boarded by three of our prisoners, who slipped down the ship's side and got into her. They instantly put off, set the sails, and would have escaped had not the agent's ship, which they had to pass, fired into her and shot away the main sheet ; this so frightened them that they surrendered.

In June (1800), when the dark nights came on, fourteen prisoners got out of our ship and were swimming to the shore ; the alarm being given, we pursued them with our boats and caught thirteen : one of them said a shark was going to seize him ; he let go his bundle he had with him and the shark left him to follow it, and was supposed to have caught the one prisoner we had not taken.

One morning at two o'clock the master of a schooner came on board and told us that about twenty prisoners had boarded his vessel, driven him and his crew into the boat, and set off with her ; the *Garland* cutter (a tender to the flag ship) was sent in pursuit, but never caught them ; on mustering our prisoners we found eighteen missing.

This day, January 12, 1801, were displayed for the first time here the new Union Jack, in reference to the Union between Great Britain and Ireland, and royal salutes fired from the ships and batteries on the occasion. Arrived a cartel with English prisoners from Guadeloupe, and we sent on board her nineteen men, ten women, and ten children who had been prisoners here. On handing their bedding up the cartel's side the feet of a boy were seen sticking out of one of them, and he was soon taken out and brought back as a deserter.

February 24, 1801.—This day " Old Tommy," our Admiral, received instructions from England to capture all Swedes and Danes and their islands in these parts. An expedition was soon got ready, and sailed under the command of Tommy, the troops being under General Maitland. They, with little resistance, soon captured St. Martin's, St. Thomas, St. Bartholomew, and Santa Cruz, all islands. For this business Tommy got knighted, and when the expedition sailed from here, and Old Tommy was out of sight, our commander gave us liberty to go on shore.

Surely some men have not the feeling of brutes. Who

would ever think that we, amongst so much sickness and death, should be deprived of our liberty from going on shore for a little recreation, and the ship so near to it, and for no fault of ours? Ah, Tommy, Tommy, if you are not paid off for it in this world, you may be in the next!

When the expedition sailed there was not a King's ship left here but ours, therefore the prisoners on board made up their minds to take the ship from us and escape, which they might easily have done by taking us by surprise, as sometimes there were eight hundred of them on deck together, and seldom more than twenty of us at a time to guard them. But, fortunately for us, one of the prisoners, a white man (and a Frenchman), gave us timely notice, as he was afraid there would be too much bloodshed, and we immediately prepared to defend ourselves by double shotting the carronade and pointing it to them, it being mounted on a travelling carriage on the quarterdeck for the purpose; we likewise armed ourselves with swords and pistols, and kept continually on our guard night and day until the expedition returned.

The prisoners, seeing this, suspected the very person who had informed against them, and swore vengeance against him; but we prevented that by permitting him to live among our people, and when the cartel arrived he was the first that was exchanged.

March 25.—Arrived and anchored here, being in pursuit of a French squadron under the command of Monsieur Ganteaume, the following British ships-of-war under Rear-Admiral Sir Robert Calder:

Prince of Wales (flag ship)	98 guns.
Pompée	80 „
La Juste	80 „
Cumberland	74 „
Courageux	74 „
Spencer	74 „
Thames (frigate)	32 „

They went to Cas de Navire to water, and then sailed again to the westward. We received on board our ship a great many Danes and Swedes captured with their islands; and (what is very remarkable) the trade winds have ceased these last six days, and we have had light winds from the westward.

There were so many prisoners now (on board and on shore) as to endanger the safety of the island, therefore Old Tommy ordered five hundred to be sent on board transports bound to England, and the *Montague* (74 guns), touching here at this time, a great many were sent on board her for England likewise. What a contrast this is in worldly affairs! The prisoners, most of them being natives or settlers on these islands, lamented much on being sent to England, while we would have given all we were worth to have been sent there!

In searching the prisoners' berths below we found they had got some of the bars loose ready for a start the first dark night that came, and, worse than that, we found that they had emptied the whole ground tier of casks of fresh water, which we had kept as a reserve in case the ship had been blown out to sea by a hurricane. However, had that been the case, salt water instead of fresh would have been our portion, as the ship would soon have gone to the bottom. The lower deck ports had been hanging so long on the hinges that few of them would drop when the rope was let go, neither had we port bars to bar them in; moreover the two chain cables were let out at the gunroom ports, and there was no security there for keeping the sea out had a hurricane come on. A forlorn hope indeed for us Englishmen, cooped up in an old prison ship where the prisoners were continually plotting to rise upon us! I often secretly wished she would sink where she was, for then we had some hopes of saving ourselves, as her poop would be out of water.

The *Calcutta* (50 guns and the same rate as the *Tromp*) called here on her way to England, and she being short of a gunner, the agent of transports, unknown to me, recommended me to Old Tommy for the vacancy. But what was Old Tommy's answer? Why, because I was married: "a married man," said he, "was a loss to the service." So he broke his word, for he had promised before that he would do something for me. Now Old Tommy himself was not only a married man, but had been twice married, and his second wife was some years younger than his daughter by the first wife; so you may see what an old rip we had to deal with. How could any one put confidence in such a man?

One evening, not late, the captain of the *Highland Lass* transport, lying near, hailed and said there was a mutiny on board his ship, so we sent a boat and brought from her the boatswain and four men and put them in irons. Next day, by Old Tommy's orders, we gave the boatswain two dozen lashes and the others eighteen each, and then sent them on board their ship again.

One of these evenings, it being very dark, as the doctor and I were talking together, we heard a file at work close under his cabin, so I took one of my pistols, which I always kept by me, but now only loaded with powder and no shot. I went on deck, then over the side silently, and down on the port lid, where they were at work, and peeping under saw one of them filing away at one of the port bars and many looking on. So I held the pistol under and fired right amongst them, which frightened them so that they gave a shout and fled in all directions. The guard was sent below instantly to see and discover who they were, as we thought they would be marked by the gunpowder; but they being black and so numerous, we gave it up.

The number of prisoners on board at this time were:

on board the *Tromp*, 687; on board the *Superb*, 224; on board the *Thomas*, 110: total 1022; besides a thousand more in the gaol and some at the hospital.

One Sunday evening, as some marines were enjoying themselves on the forecastle, one of them being groggy fell overboard and was seen to swim to the stream cable, it being then dark. The boat was without delay pushed ahead to pick him up, but could see nothing of him. Next day, when the people were at dinner, his body floated up to the surface of the water. A boat was sent, which took him up and brought him alongside, but such a sight I hope I shall never see again. The head was clean off, the left arm and leg gone, with a piece of thigh hanging with a gash, several gashes were across his belly—all done by a shark. All his clothes were torn off except a part of his trousers, and the name, Samuel Hayley, on the inside of the waistband, was the only thing by which we knew it was he.

I went in the boat to get him interred at the hospital burying-ground; but Dr. Gillespie refused it, saying none were buried there but such as died in the hospital: those that die on board were buried in the sea. (I have been informed that he got two pounds a head for those that he buried. If that is true, he must have got a good sum, as so many were dying day and night of the yellow fever.) When I told him the state the man's body was in, he came down with me to the boat to see it, and declared he had never seen such a sight before. He then altered his mind, and gave consent to inter him in the hospital ground, which was only digging a hole and putting the corpse in without any coffin.

When I returned on board I was told that a shark had been seen swimming about the ship, no doubt in search of the remains of poor Hayley; and we had many of us reason to be thankful to a merciful God that we had escaped those ravenous creatures, for we had several times gone overboard in the evenings to have a swim and refresh ourselves, not thinking any sharks near— as the prisoners had so often got overboard to swim on shore, and no shark came near them except one, and that was a good distance off. I have been told that when several people are swimming together a shark is afraid to come near them, and I believe that it is true.

On November 11, 1801, arrived the *Wilmington* schooner from England with the happy and joyful news of preliminaries of peace being signed between Great Britain and France. She soon sailed again to convey the happy news to the other islands. The *Pelican* arrived soon after with duplicates, and royal salutes were fired from the ships and batteries on this joyful occasion.

In the early part of the French Revolution there were a number of priests who refused to take the national oath, and five hundred of them were banished to Cayenne (a place to the windward of Surinam); but now Bonaparte has sent out and given them liberty to return to France again. They shipped on board a vessel at Cayenne to return; but she soon sprang a leak, and they bore up and ran into Surinam, which now belongs to the English. From there they were sent here, and put on board our ship; but only thirty-four now remained. As they were objects of pity, they were allowed to go on shore and be at liberty to go where they pleased. Our master and I bought each of us a parrot from them. Mine could say nothing but "Tom Toddy," and his nothing but "Byewood"; and there was nothing but "Tom Toddy" and "Byewood" all day long from them. He soon taught his to stand on his shoulder to eat, and kiss him; and one day, when he was bragging of the parrot, and showing how it would kiss him, it got hold of his nose and almost bit a piece out, which caused fine laughing among us.

As my agent had mentioned in his letter to me that he could get no account of any Surinam prize-money, I went on shore to old Desbro', the agent, who still remained here, and asked him the reason of it. He gave me a tedious account about a Mr. Brymer, who, he said, had been co-agent with him. "But," said he, "this island is to be given up to the French; your ship is going to England, and perhaps I may go with her, and then I will soon see it all settled." "But," I answered, "suppose you do not go to England in our ship, where am I to find you?" "Oh," says he, "I will give you my address," and wrote down No. 2, Biliter Square, London.

I then asked him for some money, and think he would have given me some, as he asked how much I wanted; but Captain Western, of the *Tamar* frigate, came in at the time and drew his attention to something else, so I returned on board. But the little hump-backed fellow did not return to England after all; when the island was given up he went to America, and cheated us all.

December 25.—This being Christmas Day, and a day above all other days in the year to be kept holy and joyful, what would our good people in England have thought had they known that Old Tommy had ordered a court-martial to be held on four men belonging to the *Castor* frigate for seditious speeches and leaving their duty? The case was as follows:

The *Castor* being at sea, the hands were turned up to reef the top sails; but the captain made the maintop men reef the sail over again so many times that the men got out of patience, came down and ran below, and gave three cheers. The marines, being quickly armed, were sent below before the men had time to arm themselves. Four of the ringleaders were secured, and the rest dispersed themselves and returned to their duty.

Daniel Colvet was sentenced to receive five hundred

lashes round the fleet ; John Long and Barthow Reardon, three hundred each ; and William Lenfield to be hung at the yard-arm on board his own ship. A boat from each ship, with two marines armed in each, was ordered to attend the execution, and I was sent in our boat. A few minutes after he was run up to the yard-arm he began to groan, and soon after so loud that he was heard some distance off. He then struggled and drew up his legs and arms ; but as the latter were only fastened above the elbows, he made a shift with his hands to reach the noose of the halter, and, pulling it closer, soon expired. Thus it may be said that the poor fellow finished his own existence. The knot of the halter had been placed under his chin instead of being under the ear ; it was a great shame that the poor fellow was not lowered down again to put the halter aright. When his body had hung the usual time, it was lowered down and committed to the deep. The following day the other three poor fellows were punished round the fleet without any mitigation of their punishment by that old rip, Old Tommy.

To show how much Old Tommy was inclined to justice was, that one day at sea a pig fell overboard, and thinking it was one of his, he ordered the boat to be got out immediately to save it ; but when his steward told him that the pig belonged to the wardroom, he called out, " Never mind the boat : poor piggy must die !"

January 7, 1802.—Arrived here from England the *Saturn* (74 guns), bearing the flag of Rear-Admiral Totty, to succeed Old Tommy in the command on this station. Tommy is appointed to have the command on the Jamaica station, vacant by the death of Lord Hugh Seymour. Mr. Allen, our purser, being so oft on board the *Leviathan* in assisting the secretary, has got into the good graces of Tommy, who is going to take him to Jamaica with him, and I have heard since he got him made contractor for fresh beef for the ship on that station—a lucrative office, I suppose. But he did not live long to enjoy it: the yellow fever took both him and his wife off from this world.

Now Tommy here committed himself again by saying a married man was a loss to the service: if so, why did he take our purser with him? Before the latter left our ship he wished me much to take his situation as purser to the *Tromp*, and said he had sufficient interest with the Admiral to get me appointed; but, as the war was over and little chance of my getting confirmed by the Admiralty, I declined it, and the clerk of the *Saturn* got the situation.

Although peace has seemingly taken place, a black general named Belguard has been brought on board to be detained as a prisoner, but for what reason I don't know; he was second in command at this place, when the English took it. He is a short, dull-looking fellow, but we soon found him to be a deep, cunning chap.

On March 27, 1802, arrived the following ships-of-war from England, viz.:

Téméraire (Rear-Admiral Campbell) . . .	98 guns.
Formidable (Captain Grindal)	98 „
Resolution (Captain Mitchell)	74 „
Orion (Captain Mitchell)	74 „
Majestic (Captain Gould)	74 „
Hector (Captain Skipsey)	74 „
Vengeance (Captain Gould)	74 „
Morgiana	a brig.

and next day arrived another squadron, viz.:

Excellent (Commodore Stopford)	74 guns.
Theseus (Captain J. Bligh)	74 „
Robust (Captain Countess)	74 „
Bellerophon (Captain J. Loring) . . .	74 „
Audacious (Captain S. Peard) . . .	74 „
Magnificent (Captain J. Gifford) . . .	74 „

Great was our surprise at seeing so many line-of-battle ships arrive here, when we thought the war was over. We were sadly afraid that it was going to begin again, and those that wished it said it was, that Lord Cornwallis, our ambassador, had been treated by the French with disrespect and had returned to England; but these rascals soon found themselves disappointed, for we found that these ships had come out as a fleet of observation to watch the motions of a French fleet and army sent out by Bonaparte to recover St. Domingo from the blacks, who were at present masters of it.

These ships soon sailed again for Jamaica, with the exception of the *Saturn*, *Excellent*, and *Magnificent*, which remained here under the command of Rear-Admiral Totty. At this time an insurrection broke out among the English slaves at Dominica; ships and troops were immediately sent from here to assist in quelling them. It was soon done, the 68th Regiment having killed nearly three hundred of them. Some of the ringleaders were brought here and shot.

On April 3 arrived the *Delft*, *Alkmaar*, and *Ceres*, all troopships with troops from England, and brought out the happy and welcome news of the definite treaty of peace having been signed between Great Britain and France, which put our fortune-hunters at this place down in the mouth; the above troopships soon sailed again with their troops for Jamaica.

Surgeon Vetch of the *Saturn*, and acting-physician of the ships here, visited our ship, and I was agreeably surprised to see him again, he being surgeon of the *Regulus* when I belonged to her, and a worthy gentleman he was. My wife was still weak, and he sent her some strengthening medicines. I had often given her a sailing in the jolly-boat about the bay for a change of air, and one of these times we landed on the gravelly beach a little above Monsieur river, where the four marines who formed the jolly-boat's crew soon found out a fine bed of cockles; we took some on board with us, and afterwards sent a bucketful to Admiral Totty, who was as surprised as we were to find such things here. I doubt if the French inhabitants knew anything of them, or surely we should have seen some on shore before this time.

Rear-Admiral Totty, being in a precarious state of health, sailed from here on May 24 in the *Saturn* for England, but died on the passage, and the command devolved on Captain Stopford of the *Excellent*. And now, amidst our glowing hopes of soon returning to England again, we were all at once thrown aback by a general insurrection which threatened to take place on board and all over the island. The case was as follows :—

In the early part of the French Revolution all the French slaves had been emancipated in the West Indies, and had enjoyed that liberty up to this time ; but now a decree had come out from Bonaparte stating that they were all to return to their former masters and become subject to slavery again. This infamous decree spread abroad like wildfire, and the blacks swore that they would rather die than submit to it.

They therefore entered into a conspiracy to put all the white men, of whatever nation, to death, wherever they could find them ; but the white prisoners on board our ship got notice of it, and as they were to be involved in the general destruction they gave us secretly to understand that when they were all on deck they were to make a rush aft and get possession of the ship, which they might easily have done, there being between eight and nine hundred of them against only about twenty of us ; the other two prison ships were to watch their proceedings and rise at the same time, and the other blacks on shore were to do the same.

We soon prepared for our defence and kept on our guard, well armed. Commodore Stopford sent the

Tamar, a 36-gun frigate, to anchor close to us, which eased our minds very much and kept the villains from rising. Three or four days after we got stronger information of their rising, which was as follows. It was our usual custom, when we let the prisoners come up on deck in the morning, to send the guard below to examine their berths, and see there were no port bars loose. This morning, as the guard were doing this, the corporal observed a book lying on one of their little tables, and took it up to look at it. Finding the printing was in French he put it down again, but in doing so a letter dropped out of it, which he took up. He found it was addressed to the "Citoyen de Liberté"; it looked suspicious, and he brought it on the quarterdeck to the officer of the watch. Our surgeon, who understood French, read it, and found it was written by the black general Belguard, who was sent here the other day (for his signature was to it and he did not deny it); and his advice to the prisoners was that they should not be so soon discouraged, but rise boldly at once and get possession of the ship if they wished to regain their liberty, and that he held a correspondence with those on shore, who would rise at the same time and get possession of the island.

We sent this letter to Commodore Stopford, and he ordered the black general to be put on board the *Castor* frigate and sent away; but where they took him to I don't know. Notice of this business was sent on shore to General Maitland, who at first made light of the matter; but he soon received information from another quarter that astonished him.

It was that on June 4, close at hand (being the King's birthday, on which he had to give a dinner to his chief officers and the heads of departments, as is customary on that day), the blacks were to rise. One part of them was to attack the General's house in the evening, when it was supposed he would be off his guard, and put him and every other white man to death; another party was to get possession of the forts, and do the same; and the rest take possession of the town, and do the same. No white man was to be spared; and this plan of theirs extended to St. Pierre and all over the island, and those on board the prison ships were to follow their example.

The General was not slack in preventing their design; the troops all over the island were ordered under arms, the white militia was called out, the guards doubled everywhere, patrols to parade in the streets and examine every suspicious place. In looking into the prison, where there were generally between ten and fourteen hundred prisoners kept, it was found that a partition had been taken down to make more room for a sally out, and a black commissary was arrested.

These were most perilous times, especially to us cooped up in the *Tromp* among so many black fellows, and all of them our enemies; and, to make the matter worse, the guns at Fort Edward were pointed at our ship to sink her if the prisoners got possession of her. My poor wife was very uneasy at this, and wanted much that a boat should be sent to the Fort to tell them not to fire at the after part of the ship, where the officers and crew were, but at the fore part, where the blacks resided, little thinking that if the fore part of the ship sank the after part would soon follow! I was a thousand times more concerned for her than myself, and would have given all the world, had it been in my power, to have had her safe home among her friends in Portsea.

After a storm comes a calm, for by the judicious management of the General and others their plans were, thank God, prevented; and Commodore Stopford hastened to get us clear of the prisoners. One hundred and thirty-one Spaniards were sent away, and all the black fellows put on board the *Thalia* frigate, now a troopship, and sent to those barren islands (the Saints), where they must either starve or submit to their former masters; and the white French prisoners on board were soon liberated and the ship cleared, much to our satisfaction.

A packet from England arrived, and a letter of thanks from both Houses of Parliament was read to the ship's crew for their meritorious conduct during the war.

On July 1, 1802, we got under way, and, blessed be God, we left our dreary station, where we had lain nearly two years. At noon we came to anchor at Cas de Navire to water the ship, but our anchor being too light, we nearly drove off the bank into deep water, and by letting go the best bower in time brought her up. We had to weigh anchor again to get near the watering-place, which gave us much trouble, being poorly manned and the decks encumbered with empty casks; when our water was completed we received on board the 64th Regiment, under the command of Colonel Pakenham, who, with their wives and children and our crew, made nearly a thousand souls on board.

We took the troops to St. Kitts and came to anchor in Old Roads, and at midnight broke adrift, our cable having been chafed through against a rock; got the sails to work her in again, but finding the current too strong and a strong swell against us, we bore up, ran farther to leeward, and came to anchor at Sandy Point.

Here several sloops brought us more fresh water; and several invalids, and Colonel Blunt, officers, etc., with 430 privates of the 3rd Regiment, or Buffs, with their wives and children, embarked on board for a passage to England. The remainder of the regiment stayed behind, and would not embark in our old ship, thinking she would never reach home.

July 17.—We got under way (with the *Hornet* in company), and put all hands on an allowance of fresh water; on the 19th took our departure from the island of St. Martin's, and bid a welcome adieu to the West Indies. The *Hornet* then left us to proceed to her former station, and we proceeded on in the old *Tromp* much better than we expected, for although her bottom was so foul, that the grass from it streamed a yard or two behind her, we sometimes got nine knots out of her; but she was light on the water, not having her guns on board, and few or no stores.

One of these days, in setting up the main topmast shrouds, the iron top-maul fell down from the top among a circle of soldiers, stove in a plank of the quarterdeck, and never hurt one of them. For this the man that let it fall got two dozen, and the captain of the top two dozen for not having a lanyard fast to it.

After being three weeks on our passage a strong gale of wind came on against us, then in the latitude of 36°14′ N., which brought the ship under close-reefed maintopsail and foresail, and as the sea began to rise the old ship began to leak, which kept our two pumps agoing; a leak broke out near the bread-room, which we got stopped. One of the pumps got choked; hoisted it up and cleared it, and wore ship to head the sea better. The soldier officers got afraid, and wanted our commander to bear away for Halifax, but we (the ship's officers) were against it, and fortunately we were, for the wind changed next day in our favour.

An artilleryman fell overboard, and a boat was sent, which took him up, but he was so exhausted that he died in half an hour after. Also departed this life Captain Gardner, of the Buffs, aged sixty; he was beloved in the regiment, and we committed his body to the deep with the usual ceremony, and fired off three volleys of musketry.

August 25.—Passed a corpse floating on the water rolled up in a red flag. Reduced all hands to two quarts of water each for twenty-four hours, and as we were now by our reckoning about 188 miles to the westward of Scilly, I had the last of my pigs killed. It was a fine one, and the serjeant of the soldier officers' mess begged hard of me to let him have a quarter, as they were now living on the ship's allowance, and offered me any price for it, so I let him have one at the West India price—viz. three bits at eighteenpence a pound, which greatly satisfied him. When his officers went to dinner they were much surprised to see a fine loin of roast pork on the table, and, on inquiring of the serjeant where he got it, were so well pleased that they sent me their thanks and three bottles of Burton ale. Some I gave to my brother officers and the poor women, but not a morsel to the captain's mess, although he was on salt provisions : the reason was that I thought him an arbitrary fellow, and did not like him. He soon began to show that he felt it by some insignificant airs, but I cared little about him now, being so near home.

September 5, 1802.—Saw the Lizard, and next day got a pilot off Portland, who took the ship through the Needles, and at midnight came to anchor once more (blessed be God for it) on English ground at Spithead, after a passage of sixty-eight days from Fort Royal, Martinique, and two years and seven weeks' absence from England. We lost by death on the passage home four seamen, two artillerymen, two soldiers, and four children ; and of those who left England in the ship, *only my wife and I, with two others, returned in her.*

Here we got information that orders had been sent out to Commodore Stopford to send our ship to Halifax, to remain there as a hulk or receiving ship ; but (thank God) the order had not arrived when we sailed, or I should have despaired of ever seeing Old England again. Well may we say with the Psalmist, "Our souls have escaped even as a bird out of the snare of the fowler; the snare is broken, and we are delivered."

Early next morning my wife went on shore to her friends, who received her as one risen from the dead, as they had often heard that we both had died in the West Indies. Our ship was soon after ordered into Portsmouth Harbour to be paid off, and in unrigging her I was nearly losing my life after all; for in lowering the maintopsail yard over the side it went by the run, a rope or something from it struck me on the face, cut my cheek open, and knocked me down senseless in the main chains. Thank God, I soon recovered, and the surgeon offered me for the hurt a smart ticket, but knowing I should soon be well I would not accept it.

Our ship was taken to the upper part of Porchester Lake, and there moored head and stern, and we hoped now to have had time to recover ourselves and recruit, our bodies being brought very low, the skin and sinews of my hands being like those of an old man, by poor diet and sickly hot climates. And having a little leisure to reflect, I made out a petition and sent it to the Admiralty, to endeavour to get the compensation for the other servant's pay that had been stopped from me, and wrote as follows:

"*To the Right Honourable the Lord Commissioners of the Admiralty.*

" The humble petition of William Richardson, gunner of H.M.S. *Tromp*, humbly showeth that your petitioner was promoted in April 1800 to H.M.S. *Tromp*, on the establishment of a fourth rate, and received his pay as such for her annually, with the compensation for two servants when in commission; but since June 8, 1801, the ship being still in commission and employed as a prison ship at Martinico, where everything was excessively dear, your petitioner has been allowed only compensation for one servant to

October 6, 1802, and, having a wife and family, reduces him to great distress.

"Your petitioner begs leave to acquaint your Lordships that the deduction for agency and fees of office for passing his accounts reduces his pay considerably less than if the ship had been in a state of ordinary.

"I therefore humbly implore and trust that your Lordships will take my case into consideration and allow me compensation for the other servant, and your petitioner, as in duty bound, will ever pray.

"WM. RICHARDSON."

"*October* 12, 1802."

This petition had the desired effect, and their Lordships complied with my request, for about a month after, when my accounts had passed at the Board of Ordnance, I received all my pay and compensation for two servants, which amounted to upwards of £80, a sum greater by double than I ever had been possessed of before, and for the first time set up housekeeping, bought goods, took part of a house (No. 24, Hawk Street), and paid my agent what I owed him—about £15.

The old *Tromp* had hitherto been much infested with rats, and now, since the provisions had been sent out of her, and they had nothing to eat, they were like to take possession of the ship from us by their fighting and noise night and day; and our wooden-legged cook killed many of them by throwing a broom-stick at them when they got many together near the galley, and he, with the boys, were almost continually at war with them, and enjoyed the fun; so we reported the rats to the master-attendant, and he sent off Hammond, the rat-catcher, who soon poisoned them all except one.

Mr. Oades, our carpenter, who had exchanged from the *Magnanime* with Mr. Jury, our carpenter, at Martinique (the *Tromp* being a higher rate than the former), was a chubby little fellow, and very fond of firing at the gulls, and when he went below always left the musket ready and his boy to call him when any gulls came near; and often was the cry to Mr. Oades, and often he fired, but never hit anything, because he said the powder was bad; but the boatswain said the barrel was crooked, and no wonder he could not hit anything; but this was only quizzing him. At last there was a cry out for Mr. Oades to make haste, for there was a large rat in the dirt-tub, and down he came as quick as possible, crept quietly along to the dirt-tub, fired, and killed the rat, the only one that was remaining, and which highly delighted him; but the old boatswain said that he almost touched it with the muzzle of the piece before he fired. To conclude, little did poor Lewis Oades think at this time that it would be his fate to be shot, and which actually happened three years after, on board the *Téméraire* at the Battle of Trafalgar.

CHAPTER IX

1803–06

SIR RICHARD STRACHAN'S VICTORY

War with France renewed—H.M.S. *Prompte* commissioned for harbour service at Falmouth—False alarm at Spithead—Trouble with the first lieutenant—Gets appointed to H.M.S. *Cæsar* as gunner—Sir Richard Strachan becomes captain—Join the Channel Fleet under Cornwallis—Just miss the French and Spanish Fleet—Sir Robert Calder's action—Brush with the French off Brest—Search for the Rochefort Squadron—Pursuit of four line-of-battle ships—Sir Richard Strachan's victory—Return home with the prizes—Reception at Plymouth—Sir Richard's piety—His queer temper—Captain Richardson appointed to the *Cæsar*—His character—Mad Dick fires into H.M.S. *Montagu*.

WHEN the war was over and peace proclaimed, and the old *Tromp* laid up in Porchester Lake, we little expected that she would so soon have been brought forward again. For on March 8 of the following year (1803), after being only six months in ordinary, a general press broke out all over England, and the seamen and marines belonging to the commissioned ships here landed, and this day pressed three hundred men.

The *Dreadnought, Royal Sovereign, Britannia, Windsor Castle, Prince of Wales, Venerable, Russell, Grampus, Loire, Diamond, Aigle, Endymion, Topaze, Galatea, Phœnix, Seahorse, Orpheus,* and *Puissant* were put into commission; and soon after our old ship was brought forward and put into the dockyard basin, to be repaired and fitted up as a guard and hospital ship, to lie at Falmouth.

And in such a hurry were they to get all these ships ready, that the master carpenters of the ships in ordinary were ordered to the dockyard to assist as working hands. A party of them was set to work on our old ship, and received extra wages for it, as well as being exempted from attending duty on board their own ships at the time; and soon they got the old ship patched up in a kind of manner to serve for harbour duty.

In June, Commander J. A. Norway commissioned the ship, while the riggers at the yard rigged her, then got some men from the ships in ordinary, to get her out of the basin to the mooring off Common Hard, and there took in our guns and what few stores were allowed us. We had twelve 24-pounders for our lower deck, and twelve 12-pounders for the main deck, and a carronade for the launch, all of which we could fight on one side if required, as we had portholes enough, Our complement of men was only to be eighty-one, but in case of an invasion by the French, which was daily expected, the sea fencibles at Falmouth were to come on board and assist.

One Sunday morning, as we lay here off Common Hard, guns were heard firing seaward, and a report was soon spread that the French had landed 50,000 men on the Isle of Wight. The alarm guns were fired, the soldiers marched out to Southsea Common, the flat-bottomed boats launched and soon filled with sea fencibles, who rowed out of the harbour, cheering as they went, to Spithead. All things were got ready for a bold defence, and full of animation, except the women, who hid themselves in closets, and one actually died through fright.

The few men we had were taken from us, and, with many others, put on board the *Windsor Castle*, to assist in bending her sails and getting her out of the harbour to Spithead as quickly as possible. I for my part was chiefly concerned at our not having our powder on board (for there is none allowed to be taken in until the ships get to Spithead), for though there was only about half a dozen of us on board, yet we could have loaded the guns and given the enemy a few shots had they attempted to enter into the harbour.

The Port Admiral (Hallowel) went to sea in a frigate to reconnoitre, and kept us all in great suspense until late next day, when he returned and reported that the fleet which had been supposed to be an enemy's, was an English convoy from the West Indies, and they not understanding the signals made to them from the Isle of Wight, caused the alarm; but some said it was only a hoax to try how the people would behave in case of actual invasion.

We soon after had our ship ready for sea, and got her out to Spithead ; but very few hands on board belonged to her, so the *Galatea* frigate was ordered to accompany us, and sent a good many of her hands on board to assist us to Falmouth. We had only one lieutenant, no master, and few petty officers ; I had no mate or armourer or yeoman, and only one man for my crew, and yet I was ordered to take charge of a watch. We set sail with a fresh gale from the eastward, and got outside of the Isle of Wight before we got our guns secured.

We had a short and fine passage to Falmouth, and moored the ship in Carrick Roads, where the *Galatea* took her men from us and departed. One of our midshipmen, a young sailor named Dalgleish, new rigged with uniform from top to toe, had been so seasick during the last night that he lay down on the deck between two of the guns, and when trying to get up in the morning could not ; for the deck had been new caulked and the pitch not scraped off, and he stuck fast to it from head to foot. It was laughable to see how foolish he looked when extricated, and with a line of pitch sticking to his clothes from top to bottom.

The Lords of the Admiralty had at this time formed an opinion that an establishment might be made here for the convenience of the Channel Fleet, and we received orders to supply a Mr. Lockwood, master in the Navy (who had come to survey the harbour), with buoys, buoy-ropes, and compasses to take bearings by; and I was ordered to assist him during the survey, which I did. During this time the *Kitty* (Captain Musgrave), an outward-bound South Seaman or whaler, arrived with a Spanish privateer of superior force, which he captured in the skirts of the Bay of Biscay after an hour's action. The prisoners were brought on board our ship, and I asked one of them who spoke English how they came to let an English merchant ship capture them. "Oh," replied he, " I did not come to sea to fight—I only came to get money." I told him he ought to have fought for the honour of his king and country. " My king and country !" replied he, turning up his eyes : "suppose I get a leg shot off, will my king and country put on another ? "

We had on board here at one time 150 convicts waiting until the *Inconstant* frigate was fitted up to take them to Sierra Leone, and during the three months they were on board I never saw a steadier set of men, or any behave better than they did. Some of them laboured at the forge, and made many things for the officers and ship's use, and that with as much goodwill as if they had been hired and paid for it.

Here Mr. Willis, in 1804, one of the oldest masters in the Navy, joined us; and Mr. Oades, our carpenter, left us, being appointed to a higher rate, and was succeeded by an old grey-headed gentleman named Town. In the evening the captain's clerk and I asked him (being a stranger), to take a glass of grog with us, little thinking he had been inclined too much to the bottle, and we soon found him to be a well informed man. After the second glass began to operate, he began to weep, which surprised us a good deal; and asking him the reason, he said he was confined to his cabin, and did not know what for. We told him he was not, and could hardly reconcile him, and glad were we to see him to his own cabin and into bed. But I must confess it lowered him much in our esteem, as we supposed he had been accustomed to be confined to his cabin for misconduct.

There was an 18-gun brig named the *Dispatch*, building by contract at Mr. Simmonds' yard, near Falmouth, and as the contractor was doubtful of getting her ready for launching at the time appointed for want of men, he applied to our captain, with whom he was acquainted, for the loan of our carpenter's crew (which was only four) to assist, and he would pay them wages for it.

As soon as our captain mentioned this to Mr. Town, he agreed to it immediately, and offered his services to go with them. So off the five set to Mr. Simmonds' yard, about two miles or more from the ship, and were to remain on shore until the brig was launched.

Old Town took lodgings at the Seven Stars public-house in Flushing, a small town near the yard, spent his wages as soon as he got them, and seldom went to bed sober. In the middle of one night he alarmed the whole house by roaring out with his strong voice, " The *Tromp* ahoy! the *Tromp* ahoy!" The landlord, wondering what was the matter, got up, and getting a light went up to old Town's room, and there found him on his face flat on the floor, and striking out with his arms and legs as in the act of swimming. He told me afterwards that he thought he was landing from the ship in the jolly-boat, that the boat got among the rocks, stove herself, and filled with water, and that then he cried out " The *Tromp* ahoy!" But more of him presently.

Our lieutenant, whose name was Macarty, an Irishman, was an officer well enough, but had a practice of washing the interior of the ship so much that her decks were getting green by being hardly ever dry, which made her damp and uncomfortable. So the master and we warrant officers, who had our wives on board, sent them on shore to lodgings at Flushing.

When any of us had leave on shore, we had to land on a rocky shore abreast of the ship (where old Town thought the jolly-boat had swamped with him), and then walk round Trefusis Hill and then to Flushing, a distance of full two miles. When we returned we had to come the same way, and stand at the foot of a damp hill, and there wait until the boat came for us, as the distance was too great to hail the ship.

Now, our lieutenant was a thoughtless fellow, and often kept us waiting, man or woman, for hours before he would send the boat, which caused much grumbling on board, and the master and old Town had frequently said that they would complain to the captain of it, but never did. One morning, on my returning after leave on shore, I was kept waiting as usual on the bottom of the damp hill, although the quartermaster had seen me and told the lieutenant that I was there waiting. So when I got on board I sent my compliments to the captain desiring to speak to him, and was desired to walk into the cabin.

When I entered in I was rather surprised to see the lieutenant and captain at breakfast together; however, I had formed my resolution to speak my mind, which, when I do on any important occasion, I strictly adhere to. So I told the captain how we had been kept so many hours waiting for a boat to get on board on damp ground, prejudicial to our health, and where not a house was near for shelter, and hoped he would redress it for the future.

The lieutenant was much surprised at this, and looked rather silly, and said that he always sent a boat when one could be spared (which was false), and the captain seemed inclined of course to side with him ; so, finding it useless to contend with such powerful adversaries, I requested of the captain to allow me to change into another ship.

His answer was that I might if I wished to ; and so I retired from the cabin. But as soon as the lieutenant had finished breakfast and gone, the captain sent for me, and desired that I would not think of changing, and that everything should be settled to my satisfaction in regard to sending the boat. But it was now too late : I knew that I had committed myself with Macarty ; moreover, a friend told me that he intended to bring me to a court-martial if ever it came into his power to do so. I thanked the captain, retired to my cabin, and began to ponder on what manner I had best to proceed.

I had frequently written to the Admiralty for a more active ship, and received each time the general answer— viz. that I should be considered when an opportunity offered, or that my name was on the list of candidates for promotion ; but every one knows what a long list theirs is.

So at last I ventured to write to Mr. Smith, the secretary to Admiral Young, Commander-in-Chief at Plymouth. Mr. Smith had been purser of the *Prompte*, but I only knew him by sight, as he was seldom on board of her on account of this secretaryship ; and that good man sent me a very obliging answer, and desired that I would send my certificates to him, and he would endeavour to do something for me ; and not long after I received a letter from the Admiralty stating that I should soon be provided for, which gave me some small hopes.

On April 16, 1805, I had the pleasure of receiving a letter from the Admiralty stating that I was appointed gunner of the *Cæsar* at Plymouth, and to repair to that place and receive my warrant ; but I had to wait eleven tedious days before my successor, a Mr. Taylor, from the

Alarm frigate, was appointed. At last he came, and I got my things on board a trading sloop bound to Plymouth, and had to pay fifteen shillings for the passage; so I took my leave of the old *Tromp*, and parted from her feeling I was leaving an old acquaintance with whom I had encountered many dangers, as I had belonged to her five years.

I left her in good time, for soon after contentions broke out among her officers, and old Town among the rest who, though he had often said that the captain was a good man (he could see it by his countenance), now changed his tune because the captain had ordered him to be confined to his cabin for some misdemeanour; indeed, he could have brought him to a court-martial, which might have broke him, but would not, as old Town had a wife and two children.

So old Town, finding he was not altogether safe, took the desperate resolution of bringing the captain to a court-martial, and laid several things to his charge, all of which the captain was acquitted of except one, and that was for having a gentleman's son on the ship's books who had never been on board to do any duty: this was brought in as a false muster, and the captain was dismissed the service. He afterwards got command of a Falmouth packet, beat off a French privateer of superior force, but died of his wounds.

Although old Town had triumphed thus far, yet he did not sleep on beds of roses, for the other officers waited to trepan him. An opportunity soon offered, as he was very open and forward with his tongue, as well as being fond of the bottle. The purser brought him to a court-martial for abusive language, and old Town in his turn was dismissed H.M. service; but his wife, who was a decent woman, and had some acquaintance with Mr. Tucker's family (the builder at Plymouth dockyard), related the business to them in so pathetic a manner, and proved it to be only spite for breaking his captain, and that her husband, being an old man and unable to earn his bread, must starve after his long and faithful services. This had its desired effect, for Mr. Tucker had then a brother, who was secretary at the Admiralty, and to him he wrote explaining the circumstances, and the result was that old Town was reinstated, not in his old ship the *Tromp*, but in a higher rate—a new 74-gun ship building at Chatham. He lived to get superannuated on the highest pension for a warrant officer, and died in old age twenty years or more after this business at Southsea, near Portsmouth.

I left the *Tromp* on April 27, 1805, and next day arrived in the sloop at Plymouth and landed on the Barbican, got my things on shore, and put up at the "West Country" public-house, then went to dock (now Devonport), called at Mr. Rowe's, a distant relation on the wife's side, in Catherine Street, and then took lodgings at No. 20, on Windmill Hill.

Next morning I returned to Plymouth, and went to the Commissioner's Office, where I had to pay £2 8s. for my warrant, then put my accounts for the *Tromp* into the Ordnance Office, to be sent thence to the Board of Ordnance, London, for inspection; and then I returned to my lodgings weary and tired to take some rest.

In the evening of this day the *Cæsar* came out of dock, having got her top sides doubled with thick fir plank and eight diagonal shores on each side in her hold, reaching from the kelson to the ends of the lower deck beams, by the way of strengthening her top sides when rolling. Soon after this we got in her masts and rigged her (being all of the dimensions of a first-rate), and on May 9 Captain J. T. Rodd came on board and commissioned her, and soon after the following officers joined: viz., Mr.

Benjamin Crispin, first lieutenant; Mr. Frizel, second lieutenant; Mr. Macdonald, third lieutenant; Mr. Clark, fourth lieutenant; Mr. Cumby, fifth lieutenant; Mr. Greenway, sixth lieutenant; Mr. Duncan, seventh lieutenant; Mr. Lee, master; Mr. Nutt, surgeon; Mr. Somerville, purser.

On the 31st the *Renown* (74 guns) was paid off here, and we got all the men of her starboard watch, and soon after got our thundering guns on board, amounting to eighty-nine, including the launch's carronade (and the least of them was a 24-pounder). I was now in my element, having got just such a ship as I had long wished for; and when we got her to her moorings (then near the West mud) and had rigged and painted her she was pronounced to be one of the finest and handsomest ships in his Majesty's service, and every one that saw her admired her. The only casualty that occurred during this time was that a man named Hardy fell from the fore-topmast headlong to the deck; the mainstay had broken his fall, or otherwise he would have been knocked to pieces. His thigh was broken by the stay; but he soon got well, and did his duty as captain of the after-guard several years after.

June 25 (1805).—Being all ready, we slipped the moorings, and with a fine breeze went out of Hamoaze in fine style, and came to anchor in Cawsand Bay, where we moored ship. A few days after Captain Rodd was appointed to the *Indefatigable*, a 44-gun frigate, and was succeeded in the command of the *Cæsar* by Sir Richard John Strachan, Bart. Having got our powder on board and crew completed to 719 men and boys, I saw my wife safe off for Portsea, and having got on board twenty live bullocks for the Channel Fleet we got under way on July 7 and proceeded to sea to join them.

Soon after we spoke the *Moucheron* brig, who informed

us that the combined French and Spanish Fleet which had eluded Lord Nelson were on their return from the West Indies for Europe. Shortly after we joined the Channel Fleet off Ushant (under the command of my old shipmate Admiral Cornwallis) and got clear of our live lumber—the bullocks.

July 17.—Admiral Cornwallis having an idea that the enemies' fleet might be intercepted, made a signal, and we all bore away with a fresh easterly wind, and steered away to the westward in hopes of getting sight of them. As we bore away so suddenly, and without previous notice, several men belonging to a Torbay sloop were on board selling their groceries and were taken away with us. The sloop followed to get the men, but was soon run out of sight, and returned to Torbay without them. So we put them into a mess and stationed them to the guns, and they soon got reconciled to their situation.

We searched the Bay of Biscay for eleven days, but could not get sight of the enemy. So we returned to our station off Ushant, where we found the Brest fleet lying quiet in the harbour, but ready for sea apparently. Soon after we heard that Sir Robert Calder had met with the combined fleet we had been looking after, and had had an action with them, but not decisive. He had captured two sail of the line (Spanish), and by comparing accounts we had not been far from them, and had to regret we missed that opportunity, as our fleet was superior to Sir Robert's. Had we been so fortunate, there was not the least doubt but Blue Billy would have captured most of them.

The only fault the *Cæsar* had was that she rolled much, and some four or five shot got loose in the main-deck guns and rolled overboard, and of course I put them down as "lost" in my expense book. But when it was returned to me after being sent to Sir Richard for approval he had erased that part out with his pen, so I went to him on the quarterdeck to know the reason why he had done so. "Oh," replied he, "never mind them few shot, for I mean to get the ship under the enemy's batteries some of these days, and then you may expend as many shot as you like." And every one who knew Sir Richard's character had not the least doubt but that he meant to fulfil his word.

August 21.—Early this morning a signal was made from our inshore squadron that the enemy's fleet in Brest Roads were in motion. We immediately stood in with our fleet to meet them, and in passing the point at St. Matthew's the enemy fired at us from their batteries, but without doing us any harm. Soon after we saw the enemy's fleet in the outer roads at anchor, all ready for a start to sea; and it falling little wind we in the evening brought our fleet to anchor. As an engagement was expected to take place next morning, every ship prepared for battle, the ocean was soon covered with tubs, stools, and other lumber thrown overboard to be clear of the guns; and it was reported among us that if the enemy did not come out next morning the Admiral intended to attack them at their anchorage.

However, early next morning we had the pleasure of seeing them all under way, twenty-two sail of the line, and fine-looking ships, and with a fresh breeze coming towards us. And although our noble fleet was only seventeen sail of the line, we soon got under way and hastened to meet them, hoping to have a glorious day's battle for the honour of old England. But when the enemy got about a gunshot from our van ships their hearts failed them, for they turned tail and made the best of their way to the anchorage again.

The *Cæsar* and *Montague* being nearest to them, our signals were made to harass their rear, and nothing could be more pleasing to Mad Dick (as the sailors called our captain) on such an occasion. We soon opened our fire in fine style, but most particularly on the *Alexander*, an 80-gun ship (bearing the flag of Rear-Admiral Willaumez, which we soon shot away), and would soon have captured her had we been allowed to follow her a little farther; but our French pilot refused to take charge of the ship any longer unless we ceased firing, that he might see the landmarks, which he could not see now for the smoke. So orders were given to cease firing, and luckily we did so, for we soon saw a rock on our lee bow with a white flag flying on it, and at the same time a signal for our recall on board the *Ville de Paris*, Admiral Cornwallis's flag ship. At this time the west point of Bertheaume bore N.½E., only a mile and a half from us, and we had got closer in than prudence required, so we put our ship about, and on returning had to run the gauntlet again, for the batteries along shore kept a constant fire on us. But, thank God, our loss was not so much as might have been expected. Although several shot struck the ship, we had only three men killed and six wounded. Many shells fell around us, and some so near as to make the water splash against the ship. This was the first time I ever saw human blood run out of the scuppers.

Thousands of the French people were on the land looking at us, but what must have been their feelings to see their fine fleet running away from ours of inferior force! Admiral Ganteaume must be a clever fellow if he can trump up a story to satisfy Bonaparte; he may say that we ran, and so we did, but it was after them.

We steered our course to join the British fleet, and glad we had escaped with no more loss. In passing the *Barfleur* Captain Martin hailed and asked our loss. He was much surprised it was no more; he said that we fired so quick that he thought twice our ship was on fire; Sir Richard told him that we had two hundred men on board who never had fired a gun before.

Several occurrences took place this day that may be worth

mentioning. The *Indefatigable* frigate (Captain Rodd) got so near a French three-decker that the gallant Frenchmen fired a whole broadside at her without doing her any injury. I rather think their guns must have been overloaded with shot, or they must have hit her.

A small English sloop or cutter had ventured too near the shore, not considering there was a battery on the heights above her; the enemy let her alone until she began to steer off, and then they opened their fire at her. The shot dropped about her like hail, and the eyes of the whole British fleet were on her, expecting soon to see her go to the bottom. She came off like a little fly swimming on the water, and joined the fleet, fortunately without a shot hitting her.

A shell from the enemy struck the sheet anchor of the *Ville de Paris* and broke it to pieces without doing any injury ; a piece of it fell on the gangway close to where the Admiral was standing. He took it up with the greatest indifference, and put it in his pocket.

A shot struck one of our signalmen on the head, and scattered his brains over a French chart lying on the poop. After his body was thrown overboard his messmates said there was £20 in his pocket, which he had received when the *Renown* was paid off. What a pity so much money should be lost on these occasions !

One of these days, as our fleet was sailing on a wind, two lines abreast, the hands were turned up and sent aft to attend punishing a man. The keen eye of our captain soon saw how our ship started ahead while the hands were aft, and he told the first lieutenant that it showed plainly the ship ought to be trimmed more by the stern. All hands were set about it immediately, until we got her down to 3½ feet deeper than she drew forward, and by doing this she beat everything we had in company with us ; moreover, she did not plunge so much as she had done formerly.

September 20.—We left the fleet cruising off Ushant, and took the command of the inshore squadron to watch the motions of the enemy's ships in Brest Harbour. Our squadron consisted as follows, viz. :

Cæsar (Captain Sir R. J. Strachan) . . .	80 guns.
Namur (Captain Halsted)	74 „
Bellona (Captain Pater)	74 „
Hero (Captain Gardner)	74 „
Captain	74 „

also the *Acasta, Révolutionnaire* and *Santa Margarita* frigates. Three days later the *Diligence*, a navy transport, came into the squadron, and informed us that they had been chased by the Rochefort Squadron, and that the *Calcutta* (50 guns, Captain Woodriff) was taken, and his convoy dispersed. We were at anchor when we received this intelligence, but immediately got the squadron under way and joined Admiral Cornwallis off Ushant with the intelligence ; he instantly ordered us off with the following ships to go in pursuit of them, viz. :

Cæsar (Sir J. R. Strachan, Commodore) . .	80 guns.
Namur (Captain Halsted)	74 „
Bellona (Captain Pater)	74 „
Hero (Captain Gardner)	74 „
Courageux (Captain Lee)	74 „

The Rochefort Squadron were of the same number, but one of them was a three-decker of 120 guns ; so off we set with a flowing sheet and joyful hearts in hopes of soon overtaking them. The *Santa Margarita* frigate was ordered to follow us ; and next day we spoke the *Indefatigable*, who informed us they had been chased by the Rochefort Squadron ten days ago. After this we spoke several neutrals, but got no satisfactory information.

October 12.—We got off Vigo, and sent the *Santa Margarita* in to reconnoitre. She brought us information that a Spanish three-decker, two French 74's, and a Dutch frigate were fitting there. These we knew were not the Rochefort Squadron; however, we kept cruising off there to prevent them forming a junction with these ships (which the sequel proved that they wished to do), for our advance ships saw them several times coming this way, and chase was immediately given; but the weather continued so rough and gloomy that they eluded us in the night by altering their course, and at last, finding they could not get into Vigo without risking an action, they set off for Teneriffe, but this we did not hear of till some time after.

On the last day of October a heavy gale of wind drove our squadron to the northward of Cape Finistère, and on November 2, towards evening, as we were beating to windward to get off Vigo again, we saw a frigate to the N.W. bearing down toward us with signals flying from her mast-head, but could not make them out. Being so gloomy, we thought she had come to recall us, as our provisions were getting short. But at 11 p.m. she came within hail, and proved to be the *Phœnix* (Captain Baker), who soon set our hearts aglow by informing us that he had been chased by the Rochefort Squadron, and that they were then close to leeward of us.

At this news we were all delighted, and instantly bore away before the wind, and soon got sight of six large ships steering before the wind to the eastward. Hammocks were piped up and guns got ready in a few minutes, as we always kept everything ready for action. It being very dark, signals were made with blue lights, false fires, and flashes of gunpowder to denote our movements to the rest of our squadron, and the *Phœnix* was hailed to drop astern to inform the other ships to make every exertion to get up, as we meant to bring the enemy to action immediately.

At midnight it began to rain, and the horizon got so thick that we lost sight of the enemy. This gave us great concern, for fear they should alter their course and run for Ferrol. However, we continued steering to the eastward, and all hands at quarters. At daylight next morning the weather cleared away, and we saw the *Hero*, *Namur*, and *Courageux* and three frigates a long way astern, with all sail set to get up with us, but saw nothing of the *Bellona*. Our ship had all sails set, even to royal steerings, but saw nothing of the enemy. However, we continued the same course in the direction for Rochefort, and at nine this morning had the pleasure of getting sight of them again right ahead, and steering as before with all the sails they could set; but instead of six there were now only four, and they line-of-battle ships.

The weather now became beautiful and the sea smooth, and we came fast up with them. In the evening we were between seven and eight miles from them, but the other ships of our squadron were a long way astern, and at daybreak on November 4 we got within gunshot of the enemy, and then shortened sail to keep pace with them until our squadron got up. The enemy's ships looked all to be two-deckers, but one larger than the rest bore a rear-admiral's flag. At 10 p.m. the *Santa Margarita* came up, and Sir Richard told her captain to get under the enemy's stern and rake them in order to cut away some of their rigging to retard their sailing. They did so for a short time, but the rearmost ship of the enemy, supposed to be the *Scipion* (74 guns), luffed up, and getting some of her after guns to bear, soon almost sank the poor *Santa Margarita*, for she was obliged to bear up as quick as possible with four feet of water in her hold. The first shot she received was on the forecastle, and took the boatswain's head off; another hit her near the water's edge, and the gunner of her told me afterwards that he was over the shoe tops in water in the magazine.

Some of the shots went over our ship, but we did not return any, as our ships were fast coming up.

At 11 a.m. the *Hero* came within hail, and soon after the *Courageux*, but the *Namur* was hull down nearly astern, and as for the *Bellona* we had seen nothing of her since the chase began. The enemy, now finding an action to be unavoidable, took in their steering sails, hauled their wind, formed their line on the starboard tack, and we did the same.

Our captain, being impatient to begin the battle, hailed the *Hero*, and told them to hail the *Courageux* and inform them that he would begin the action immediately without waiting for the *Namur* to come up, and their answer was three hearty British cheers. The enemy, I suppose, thought it in defiance of them, and returned the compliment, but in my humble opinion not in so hearty a manner as ours.

We then edged down towards them, we being to windward, and at ten minutes before twelve at noon began the battle : the *Cæsar* first, *Hero* next, and *Courageux* in the rear, all pretty close to each other, continued firing away with great vigour for nearly an hour and going at the rate of near five knots through the water, by which time the *Cæsar* was nearly up with their van ship, when she, luffing up too much in the wind to rake us, came about on the other tack, which put them in great confusion, and we peppered them well during the time.

The French Admiral, seeing this, was under the necessity of ordering his other ships to put about to support, and formed his line on the larboard tack, apparently very much cut up. We then put our ships about, and soon closed with them again, with this advantage on our side, that we were meeting the *Namur*. She soon joined, which made us of equal numbers, the battle going on as vigorously as ever; and soon after we saw the enemy's masts and yards tumbling fast overboard.

At a quarter past three their Admiral and another, being reduced to mere wrecks, struck their colours; but the other two continued to fight most valiantly, until the *Cæsar*, followed by the *Hero*, ran between them. For nearly twenty minutes the battle continued as hot as ever, and then they surrendered. One of them (the *Mont Blanc*) was dreadfully cut up; whether by accident or design I know not, her jibboom came up to our main rigging, and we thought she meant to board us. But we raked her at the time so severely that, when she struck, she had seven feet of water in her hold, with several of her port lids shot away and guns mismounted.

When her captain (a plain sailor-looking man) came on board to deliver up his sword, Sir Richard told him he was a brave fellow for defending his ship so well. He shrugged up his shoulders and replied that he had done the best he could; but his soldiers and marines, who were a part of Bonaparte's sharpshooters, when they came on board strutted about the deck more like conquerors than prisoners, and said if they had got such a general (meaning admiral) as ours the case might have been different. Vain wretches! what more could they have done, if even Bonaparte had been with them, when their ships were dismasted and unmanageable?

Thus, after a long chase in the Bay of Biscay from Saturday night to Monday noon, we came up with and captured this whole squadron of French line-of-battle ships after as gallant an action [1] as any ever fought during the war. Our masts and rigging were much cut up, and sails shot all to pieces. Our hull did not suffer so much, by the enemy firing high, yet we had three anchors out of the four disabled; but, thanks to God, the loss of our men was not considerable.

[1] Forty-four years after this silver medals were given for this action.

The enemy suffered severely, as follows :

The *Formidable* (84 guns): Rear-Admiral Dumanoir was severely wounded, with 200 men killed and wounded.

Mont Blanc (74 guns, Capt. Villegris): 180 killed and wounded.

Duguay-Trouin (74 guns): Captain Touffet killed ; second captain wounded, and 150 men killed and wounded.

Scipion (74 guns, Capt. Berenger): 200 killed and wounded.

The *Scipion* and *Duguay-Trouin* were totally dismasted ; the *Formidable* and *Mont Blanc* had only their bare foremasts and mizzen-masts standing. Our losses were as follows :

Cæsar	80 guns ; 4 killed and	24	wounded.
Namur . . .	74 ,, 4 ,,	8	,,
Hero . . .	74 ,, 10 ,,	51	,,
Courageux . .	74 ,, 1 ,,	13	,,
Santa Margarita .	36 ,, 1 ,,	6	,,
Phœnix . .	36 ,, 2 ,,	4	,,
Révolutionnaire . .	— ,, 2 ,,	6	,,
Œolus	— ,, — ,,	3	,,

These two last-named frigates came up at the latter part of the action, and, by venturing too near the enemy, caused their loss. When the action was over we felt much disappointment in finding this was not the Rochefort Squadron we had been in search of. Therefore the signal was again made to prepare for battle, as we did not know but we might soon meet with them ; and all hands were set to work to repair the rigging and bend a new set of sails as speedily as possible. Had we fallen in with them they would have had a hard struggle before they could have taken our prizes from us.

Kind Providence still favoured us by giving fine weather, or some of the prizes must have sunk ; so we took them in tow with a fair wind, and on the evening of November 10 we came to anchor in Cawsand Bay, after a glorious cruise of four months and a few days.

During the action a shot from the enemy struck one of our carronades on the forecastle, and knocked the muzzle of it into many pieces. One of them, about the size of a nut, stuck into the head of a fine young fellow stationed there; but he did not know it at the time. After the battle was over he felt a pain in that part of his head, and, putting his hand to it, felt blood. Some one then advised him to go to the doctor; but he refused, saying it was only a trifle. However, as it got more painful, he went, and the doctor soon took the piece out from his skull; but from that moment his senses departed from him, yet his looks were as animated as ever; and he departed this life just after the ship was anchored.

An anecdote was in the Plymouth papers soon after our arrival, which was a fact. It was of two boys who, during the action, had a quarrel about a cartridge of powder for their guns, and to end the dispute they turned to and had a battle for it between themselves. One of them, who was my servant, named John Redman, gained the victory. This (says the Plymouth editor) shows the intrepidity of our British sailors!

Next morning we got our ships and prizes safe up to Hamoaze. In passing the ships lying there they manned their rigging and gave us several hearty cheers. The military bands on the Hoe and at the Devil's Point played up " Rule Britannia," " Britons strike home," and " God save the King " as we passed them. The shore on each side and at the dockyard swarmed with people cheering us; and it was said in the Plymouth papers that upwards of thirty thousand people were assembled on the Hoe and Mount Wise, and some of them cripples, who had not been out of their houses for years before. This was very gratifying to us, but too good to last long.

"*Cæsar* at Sea,
"*November* 6, 1805."

"Sir,
"Having returned thanks to Almighty God for the victory obtained over the French squadron, I beg to make my grateful acknowledgment for the support I received from the ships of the line and frigates, and request the captains will do me the honour to accept of my thanks, and communicate to their respective officers and ships' companies how much I admired their zealous and gallant conduct.

"R. J. STRACHAN."

As we had not a clergyman on board the *Cæsar*, Sir Richard read the prayers himself to the ship's company out of the Book of Common Prayer, and, I think—as I stood close to him at the time—with a devout mind. When he had done he said he had read them very badly (and not "damned" badly, as some said). However, be that as it may, he soon began his old habit of swearing again; and only one day after the battle he called the ship's company a set of "damned mutinous rascals." Yet the sailors liked him for all that, as they knew he had a kind heart, and thought no more of it when his passion was over. They gave him the name of "Mad Dick," and said that when he swore he meant no harm, and when he prayed he meant no good. However, he was a brave, zealous, and active officer, and was always very lenient to a prisoner when tried by a court-martial.

An anecdote was told of him that, when at breakfast at an inn in Portsmouth, and in an upper room—which room went by the name of "The Bear"—he desired the waiter to bring him some more toast. Accordingly, the waiter called down for "more toast to 'The Bear.'" Sir Richard thought the waiter was alluding to him as "The Bear," got up in a passion, seized him by the collar, and would soon have given him a sound thrashing had not the waiter made haste to explain.

On November 13 Sir Richard hoisted his flag (being made Rear-Admiral of the Blue), and we fired a salute of thirteen guns full allowance of powder, which made the shore near North Corner ring again. T. G. Shortland was appointed his captain, and we made all haste in getting in new masts and rigging, and getting the ship ready for sea. On December 13, after being only a month in doing this and getting repairs from shot-holes, etc., we left Hamoaze (the ship at the time covered with snow) and anchored in Cawsand Bay, after having had but few opportunities of enjoying any comfort after all the glory we had received. Our mates were made lieutenants, and all the first lieutenants of our squadron commanders; but the warrant officers, who had the most duty and responsibility in the action, got not even a higher rate.

24th. We got under way in company with the Channel Fleet, and steered away for Ushant; but next day a gale came on from the westward, and we all put into Falmouth Harbour and moored the fleet, this being Christmas Day. A poor Christmas we had of it on account of the weather. Here I saw my old ship, the Tromp, lying as when I left her, and could not help meditating on the dismal and forlorn times I had on board her when in the West Indies, and hugged myself to think I no longer belonged to her.

On the 27th the fleet got under way, and we steered our course for Ushant; but next day a cutter came with despatches from the Commander-in-chief, and the Cæsar was ordered to return to Cawsand Bay again. We soon arrived there, and received orders to complete the ship with stores for foreign service.

Here Captain Shortland left us, but for what reason I could never learn, and another named Charles Richardson succeeded him, who soon let us know his authority and upset all our little comforts. As we lay near the shore in

Cawsand Bay, two of our lieutenants asked (as customary) his leave in the evening to sleep on shore with their wives at Cawsand, close at hand, and they would come on board again early in the morning, as usual, but this he refused them; they answered, that if Sir Richard was on board they were sure he would not have refused them so small a request, and for saying that he put them both under arrest until next day; he seemed to be a person that wanted every one to crouch at his feet, but he got among the wrong sort to do that. Our new first lieutenant was a fine old man and a good sailor, but he could give no liberty to go on shore or anything else, the captain having reserved that power to himself.

Here Sir Richard got a squadron put under his command, which consisted as follows—

Cæsar (Sir R. J. Strachan, Rear-Admiral) .	.	80 guns.
St. George (Captain Bertie) . . .	.	98 „
Montague (Captain R. W. Otway) . .	.	74 „
Bellona (Captain J. E. Douglas) . .	.	74 „
Triumph (Captain Inman) . . .	.	74 „
Terrible (Captain Lord Henry Poulet) .	.	74 „
Melampus (Captain Lord Poyntz) .	.	36 „
Decade (Captain J. Stewart) . .	.	36 „

On January 27, 1806, we got under way with the squadron, and proceeded to the eastward, and soon after off Start Point we met the outward-bound East and West India Fleets under convoy of the *Canada* (74 guns), *Audacious* (74 guns), and the *Scorpion* brig, and took them all under our care, as the enemy had got another squadron at sea.

Being a fair wind and fresh breeze, we steered away all together to the westward, and soon cleared the British Channel. About a week afterwards, the convoy being too much extended, we fired gun after gun with the signal up for them to close nearer, but without much effect, and we then began to fire shot near them (and kept three guns employed at it until we fired twenty-one shot) and then they closed nearer.

The *Montague* (Captain Otway) was stationed on our weather quarter, and some of the shot went whizzing close ahead of him, at which he was highly offended, and soon after sent a lieutenant to know if the shot were intended for him. The poor fellow could not have been sent on a worse errand : the Admiral got foul of him and drove him into his boat, and bawling after him, told him to tell his captain that if he did not keep his proper station, he would fire at him as soon as any other ship in the fleet.

There was not the least doubt but he would, for shortly after we brought the squadron to for the *St. George* to come up, she being a long way astern. When she came up she stood on about a mile or more without shortening sail, in order to have a start ahead when the squadron filled their sails again, and in doing so there could not be much harm, as she was a bad sailer. But Mad Dick got into a passion, and ordered me to fire a shot right into her. She fortunately hove to just at the moment I was going to fire, and I was ordered to stop ; and glad I was of it, for perhaps some innocent man might have suffered by it.

February 26.—We parted company with the convoy ; the West-Indiamen proceeded on in company with the *Canada* (74 guns) and *Scorpion* (18-gun brig) ; the East-Indiamen, being well armed, proceeded on by themselves, and we with our squadron steered away to the southward in search of Willaumez and his squadron, and likewise were in hopes of falling in with the *Marengo* (80-gun ship) and *Belle Poule* frigate under the command of Admiral Lanois, coming to France from the East Indies, and we had good hopes of meeting one or the other of them.

Soon after, being to the westward of Madeira, we captured a valuable merchantman under American colours with East India goods on board (and yet they said they were bound for the East Indies), and there were several foreigners on board of her ; all the captains agreed to her being sent to England except Lord Henry Poulet, and he was for sending her to Gibraltar under the charge of one of our two frigates.

As soon as Sir Richard heard this, his fiery temper arose, as a frigate could not be spared at this time on such an occasion ; so he ordered a signal to be made for the ships to take their men out of the prize and let her go.

She was soon after captured by the *Arab*, a 20-gun ship, and if report says true, the warrant officers in her received £600 a share each of them.

March 23.—Saw the *Egyptian* frigate (Captain Paget) to windward, and made her signal to come within hail ; in passing under our stern to get to leeward of us, our lofty sails took the wind from hers in such a sudden manner that she rolled to windward instantly, and away went her topmasts overboard on the weather side, and the topmen at the masthead ready to furl the topgallant-sails ; fortunately they were all saved, and only one of them seriously injured. Here our Admiral wisely remarked at the time how necessary it was for ships to have always their lee backstays with runners and tackles attached to them, hauled taut and belayed, instead of hanging loose, as they generally are. The *Terrible*, Lord Henry Poulet, was ordered to take the *Egyptian* in tow until she got up other topmasts and put to rights again.

February 3.—It being stormy weather, about three in the morning, and very dark, we found ourselves in the midst of a fleet and close to a three-decker ; hammocks were piped up, the drummer beat to quarters, and we soon got ready for battle. They did not at first answer our night signal, but just as we got ready they answered it, and well they did, or they would soon have got a broadside poured into them. She proved to be the *Ocean*, a new 98-gun ship, and her first trip to sea; she, with the *Euryalus* frigate and a fleet of merchantmen, were bound to the Mediterranean.

At ten next morning saw a fleet of large ships on our weather bow and gave chase after them, hoping that it was the French squadron that we were in search of; but when we got near found they were outward-bound East-Indiamen under convoy of the *Leopard*, a 50-gun ship.

Early on Easter Sunday morning we saw six sail of line-of-battle ships ahead, and immediately gave chase, making sure it must be Willaumez's squadron, or rather Jerome Bonaparte's, as it was called, as he commanded the *Veteran*, one of their ships of the line; but when we got near found them to be a British squadron under the command of Rear-Admiral E. Hervey, so after saluting each other with thirteen guns we parted.

On May 1st we saw a dismasted vessel, and sent the *Decade* to examine her; she brought information that it was an English brig, quite empty and not a soul on board, and how she came to be in that situation we could not find out. Soon after this it began to blow hard from the westward, so we up helm for Ushant and soon after joined the Channel Fleet under the command of the Earl of St. Vincent. Our Admiral, after firing a salute, went on board to pay his respects to the Earl, and when he returned we bore away with our squadron for England, and the next day anchored in Cawsand Bay and saluted the Commander-in-Chief. We found lying here the *St. Joseph* and *Belle Isle*.

On May 11, 1806, Her Royal Highness Caroline, consort to His Royal Highness George, Prince of Wales, being on a visit to Edgecumbe House, paid our Admiral a visit on board the *Cæsar*, accompanied by Lady Hood and some others of distinction, and were received with a royal salute of twenty-one guns. The ship had been cleaned and prepared for the purpose, and all the girls (some hundreds) on board were ordered to keep below on the orlop deck and out of sight until the visit was over.

As Her Royal Highness was going round the decks and viewing the interior, she cast her eyes down the main hatchway, and there saw a number of the girls peeping up at her. "Sir Richard," she said, "you told me there were no women on board the ship, but I am convinced there are, as I have seen them peeping up from that place, and am inclined to think they are put down there on my account. I therefore request that it may no longer be permitted."

So when Her Royal Highness had got on the quarter-deck again the girls were set at liberty, and up they came like a flock of sheep, and the booms and gangways were soon covered with them, staring at the princess as if she had been a being just dropped from the clouds. After the officers had been introduced to her she took her leave, and lay a little distance off in the boat until another salute of twenty-one guns was fired—which delighted her much.

On the 17th Her Royal Highness came off again to visit the *Superb*, bearing the flag of Sir T. Duckworth, lately arrived from the West Indies after gaining a victory there over a French squadron. Our ships manned their yards as before, and we gave Her Royal Highness another salute of twenty-one guns each time in passing our ship. When the *Superb* on her arrival here came to anchor she was put under quarantine a few days, and as Old Tommy was not permitted to land on that account, some of his friends went off in a shore boat to see him; so in order to speak to them more closely he went down the side and got on one of the port lids to talk to them, but scarcely had he got on it, when the port rope broke, and *suss* went Old Tommy down by the run into the boat.

[During the next two years (1806–1808) Richardson continued to serve in the *Cæsar*, which remained Strachan's flagship during the whole time ; the squadron chased the French to the West Indies, but returned after a fruitless cruise of nine months, in which severe weather was experienced off Martinique and near Halifax. After six weeks' rest the squadron (in March 1806) was sent to watch the French off Rochefort, and afterwards it joined Lord Collingwood's fleet and unsuccessfully chased the Toulon Squadron ; the *Cæsar* returned home in October 1808, and here Sir Richard Strachan left her for good.]

CHAPTER X

1808–09

WITH STOPFORD IN THE BASQUE ROADS

Cæsar joins the Channel Fleet under Lord Gambier—Off Ushant—
Captain Richardson allows six merchantmen to escape—Basque
Roads—Another prize lost—Rear-Admiral Stopford appointed
to command—Hoists his flag in the *Cæsar*—His staff—Divine
service held on board—Less swearing—Brest fleet in sight—
Action with French frigates—Brest fleet anchor in Basque Roads
—Stopford's despatch—Lord Gambier arrives—Attack on the
Buoyard shoal—Arrival of Lord Cochrane—Volunteers called for
to man the fireships—Dismissal of Admiral Harvey—Construction
of the fireships and explosion vessels—Fireships sent in—Destruction of French ships—Punishment of the French captains—*Cæsar*
returns home.

ON October 30, 1808, the *Cæsar* got under way, and
we joined the Channel fleet off Ushant, now under the
command of Lord Gambier, consisting of:

Caledonia (Lord Gambier, Capt. William Bedford) 120 guns.
Royal George . . . . 100 „
St. George . . . . 98 „
Dreadnought . . . . 98 „
Téméraire . . . . 98 „
Cæsar (Capt. Charles Richardson) . . . 80 „
Achilles (Sir Richard King) . . . . . 74 „
Triumph . . . . 74 „
Dragon . . . . 74 „

November 15th.—A strong gale of wind came on from
the westward, which caused us all to bear up for Torbay,

228

and while lying there our crew got afflicted with ophthalmia; it began at the right eye and went out at the left, and continued near a week and then left us.

27th.—The wind having come to the north-east, we got under way with fleet and got off Ushant again, but next day shifted to the westward, blew a storm, and drove us back to Torbay again.

December 8.—The wind got to the north-east again; got under way and got off Ushant, but the wind increasing and continuing for several days drove the fleet a long way to the westward.

On the 22nd our signal was made to proceed to Rochefort and relieve the *Gibraltar*. It blew so hard that we bore away and scudded under our foresail. Next day, in setting the close-reefed maintopsail, it still blowing hard, rain and hail, it blew to pieces; sounded frequently in eighty fathoms. A grampus has been following the ship these last twenty-four hours.

December 25.—Saw Sables d'Olonne lighthouse on the French coast, and, in working up along the shore towards Rochefort, the next day at noon we saw eight sail of the enemy's merchant vessels coming down along the shore before the wind, and we put our ships about to cut them off; and now followed a specimen of our captain's abilities.

As we stood in, with the weather moderate, we fired a great many shot, which caused six of them to bring to; but the other two ran on shore among the breakers and soon went to pieces. We now lowered down the quarter and stern boats to take possession of the remaining six, but in the hurry and confusion the captain hurried them away without any arms or ammunition to defend themselves. As the ship was near the land, we wore her round with her head to the offing and maintopsail aback; as she increased her distance gradually, which a ship will

do although her maintopsail be aback, the enemy perceived it, and one of them being armed with about fifty
soldiers on board took her station so as to prevent our
boats from boarding the others. What was to be done?
Our people had no arms or ammunition, so they adopted
the wisest plan, and that was to return to the ship for
some. The enemy, seeing this, bore away before the wind,
and off they ran, and before our boats had reached the
ship they had run so far to leeward that any idea of
following them was given up, and they made their escape
like birds getting free from the fowler.

I never in all my life saw such confusion as was in our
ship at the time : the captain was driving the people about
from one place to another ; one of my crew, named
Andrew Gilman, in firing one of the guns, was so flurried
that he did not observe a samson post up behind him ;
the gun recoiled and killed him against it.

During the time of wearing the ship a boat had been
hoisted up off the booms to be got out, but was left
hanging in the stay tackles and cut a fine caper during
the time, swinging about from one side to the other, until
some of the people lowered her down of their own accord :
had Sir Richard Strachan been in the ship at the time
he certainly would have gone mad. And thus ended as
lubberly a piece of business as ever was heard of, and to
have six merchantmen almost under the muzzle of our
guns and then let them all escape, beats everything !

Next day we ran into Basque Roads, but our ships
were not there ; saw the French squadron lying at the
Ile d'Aix ; as usual they fired a great many guns, but
whether they were exercising their crews, or for some
victory by land, we could not tell. So we sailed out again,
and met the *Aigle* frigate, who informed us that our
squadron was cruising forty miles to the north-west of this
place.

On the first day of this important year [1809] we joined them, consisting of the *Defiance* (Captain Hotham senior officer), with the *Donegal* and *Gibraltar*, and soon after ran into Basque Roads and there came to anchor ; the *Gibraltar* shared out her provisions among us and then sailed for England. The French ships continue to fire many guns, and we suppose they are exercising their people to fire well.

January 7.—This morning we saw a square-rigged vessel at sea and coming in before the wind right toward us. The *Donegal* lay inside, the *Defiance* in the centre, and ours the outside ship, and we made sure of taking a prize. Our captain (I suppose to make up for his late bad conduct) ordered me to get three of the main-deck guns shotted and pointed as far ahead as possible, and then go into the magazine and be ready to supply him with powder, all which was readily done, as if something extraordinary was to be performed ; but he soon made as great a blunder as before, for before the vessel got within gunshot he began to fire, and the captain of the vessel, judging from this that we were enemies, altered his course and ran her on shore near the town of St. Marie's.

The boats of the squadron, manned and armed, immediately went after her ; but by the time they got near the beach was covered with troops and they had to return without performing anything. Thus we lost another prize ; and she must have been of some value, as we heard afterwards that she was a West-Indiaman. Well might the *Defiance's* people ask ours, when alongside in a boat soon afterwards, if we were friends to the French !

19th.—Foggy weather. Observed a chasse-marée near to us ; hoisted French colours and decoyed her alongside, to the utter surprise of the poor Frenchmen. Thus we got a prize at last, though of little value. In the evening saw a brig coming in, and the boats of our squadron went in pursuit of her. She ran on shore, and our people boarded, but could not get her off. Several shot were fired at them from the shore, but no harm done.

22nd.—Strong wind at south, and rain. Saw another French brig coming in, who, on discovering us, made off. In the afternoon another came in, and in passing fired three shot at her, and brought her to. She hoisted cartel colours, and proved to be the *Elizabeth* of London, with a hundred and forty of Junot's soldiers on board from Lisbon. Let her go to proceed to Rochefort, according to the Articles of Capitulation. They reported to us that the English had obtained a great victory in Spain.[1]

27th.—Got under way with the squadron, stood out to sea, then rounded Baleines Lighthouse and came to anchor in the Breton Passage in $16\frac{1}{2}$ fathoms. Next morning got under way and stood out to sea, where we met the *Indefatigable* frigate with dispatches, and were informed that Rear-Admiral Stopford was coming out to take the command, and would hoist his flag on board the *Cæsar*. This news pleased us much, as we wanted a commander of such gallant abilities and knowledge.

29th and *30th.*—Met a convoy of victuallers, but the weather was so stormy these two days that we could get nothing out of them.

February 1.—Ran into Basque Roads, and there came to anchor. Five of the victuallers came in, and we got two of them alongside and cleared them of 119 tons of water. Then arrived more victuallers, and next day the *Naiad* frigate drove a brig on shore near St. Marie's laden with brandy; but the surf soon destroyed her, and our boats chased a sloop on shore laden with prunes near the Breton batteries.

The enemy's squadron fired a great many guns to-day, and had their shops dressed with colours—the English

[1] Corunna, Jan. 16, 1809.

ensign undermost, and the Union downwards. What daring fellows !

7th.—There was a fine chase this day between the *Aigle*, English frigate, and a French sloop. The wind was off the land, and the sloop kept close to the edge of the breakers off Chasseron, so that the *Aigle* could not close with her. Thus they kept running on tack and tack, and the *Aigle* firing at her each time in passing ; but there was such a rolling swell that she never hit her. At last we sent our boats from the squadron manned and armed, and the gallant Frenchman (for really he was a brave fellow) endeavoured to run them down as they came near, but they soon got hold and boarded him, and then he surrendered after doing all a brave man could do. Her name was the *Angélique*, laden with a hundred tons of coffee and sugar from the West Indies. We sent her to England.

15th.—This morning we saw two men hung at the yard-arm of two of the enemy's line-of-battle ships.

The *Calcutta*, formerly a British 50-gun ship, had the English ensign hung Union downwards under her bowsprit, we supposed to insult us ; yet they durst not venture to meet us, although they were superior in force. However, we paid them well for their audaciousness soon after. In the evening Rear-Admiral Stopford arrived in the *Amethyst* frigate.

Next morning the Rear-Admiral came on board and hoisted his flag on board the *Cæsar*, bringing with him two lieutenants, a captain of marines, a chaplain, a secretary and his clerk, two master's mates, nine midshipmen, his coxswain and a band, and two live bullocks, which were very acceptable, as we have not tasted fresh beef this long time.

19th.—Being Sabbath day, a church was rigged out and divine service performed on board the *Cæsar* for the first time since I had belonged to her. The Rev. Mr. Jones, the chaplain, preached an excellent sermon. The ship's crew were very devout and attentive. The Rear-Admiral was on his knees at prayer time ; but it was funny enough to see our captain, how fidgety he was : he neither sat nor stood, and was as unsteady as a weathercock. Some of our nobs thought that a man could not be a good seaman without swearing, but the Admiral let them know the contrary. In the afternoon we saw some chasse-marées stealing along shore, and sent the boats of the squadron after them ; they captured two, one laden with rye and the other with sardinian, a fish like dried herrings. The whole was shared out to the squadron and the vessels broken up for firewood, as their condemnation in England would have cost more than they were worth.

21st.—The wind having come from the east, we got under way, and anchored outside of Baleines Lighthouse for fear the Brest fleet should slip out and come this way, and which they actually did, as will be seen presently. Among some prisoners taken a young man named Bordo (son of our French pilot of that name) was brought on board, and great was their joy in meeting each other again ; but it did not last long, for in the evening they got drunk and fighting with each other, and the cause was that the father had married an Englishwoman. We had two more French pilots on board (both of them emigrants), one named Le Cam and the other Cameron, and although they had emigrated together they could never agree, and had separate messes. Cameron messed with me at first, but finding him a two-faced fellow I turned him off.

23rd.—Arrived the *Emerald* frigate from England with five live bullocks for the squadron, and exercised great guns and small arms at ten in the evening. Observed the *Amazon*, which was looking out in the north-west direction, letting off rockets, so we got the squadron under way to get near her; on meeting they told us they had seen nine sail of large ships coming along shore from the eastward, and steering for Basque Roads; we ordered her astern to inform the *Defiance* and *Donegal* of it, and to tell them to join us with all speed, and then prepared our ship for battle.

We had previously heard of a French squadron of frigates full of stores and ready to slip out of L'Orient for the West Indies, but they were blockaded by four sail of the line under Commodore Beresford; however, we thought they might have stolen out, and were coming this way to join the Rochefort squadron—we therefore crowded all sail to cut them off, and at midnight got sight of them.

It then fortunately for us fell a calm, which made us uneasy lest they should escape; but at dawn a breeze sprang up, and we steered right for them. But judge of our surprise as the daylight appeared to find they were the Brest fleet, eight sail of the line, and one of them a three-decker of 120 guns, and two of them flagships, with two frigates accompanying them! They were going to Basque Roads thinking to catch us there, but thanks to Heaven they were too late, as we were on different tacks. We continued our course and fetched into their wake, then put about and followed them; if they had begun to chase us we must have been obliged to run, for what could our three sail of the line do against such a force? But strange to say they never seemed to interrupt us; perhaps they thought we were not the ships that had been in Basque Roads this winter and were hastening along to catch them.

We made a signal to the *Naiad*, one of our frigates, to proceed with all haste to our Channel Fleet and inform Lord Gambier of the French fleet being here; but before she got hull down she made the signal that another squadron of the enemy was in sight, and coming toward us, which made some on board think we were now caught at last. However, although we had the Brest fleet, the Rochefort squadron, and the others moving down on us, thus being nearly surrounded by them, yet we kept up our spirits, being determined to fight to the last rather than be taken.

As our Admiral knew we could not cope with the Brest fleet, we altered our course to meet those that were coming, and as we drew near found them to be three large French frigates followed by the *Amelia* English frigate and *Dotterel* brig. We got so near that I thought it impossible for them to escape our clutches, and they, seeing their danger, ran in under the batteries of Sables d'Olonne, and there let go their anchors and prepared for battle.

As the wind was now blowing towards the land Rear-Admiral Stopford thought it very improper to come to anchor on a lee shore to fight, but made the signal to prepare to do it with springs on the cables; but the *Defiance*, mistaking the signal, ran in and came to anchor. As she swung round the frigates and batteries cut her severely, so that she was soon obliged to cut her cable and come out again.

Her fore-topsail yard was shot away, her sails and rigging much cut up, and two men killed and twenty-five wounded; however, all the time she was in she behaved gallantly. Hundreds of French people were seen standing on the quays looking at us as we went in, but as soon as we opened our fire they dispersed in an instant. We and the *Donegal* kept under way and as close in shore as the water would admit, and in passing on each tack fired at the frigates, and soon sent them to the bottom; we had not a man hurt, thank God, but were hit by shot from them several times; one went into the bowsprit and

another through the jibboom. The *Donegal* had one killed
and six wounded.

At four in the afternoon we left and went after the
Brest ships, who had been in sight all this time from
our mast-heads, and followed them until they came to
anchor in Basque Roads; but we kept our squadron
under way near the entrance, as we saw some large ships
in the offing, and coming toward us. Our noble Admiral
is as cool and steady as if no enemy was near, and well
might a good Christian know no fear.

One of our frigates—I don't know which it was, as
they were changed so frequently—was stationed between
us and the enemy to look out; and the latter had one
of theirs for the same purpose, so they had frequently to
pass each other on different tacks. British courage was
severely tried, and the captain of our frigate asked
permission by signal for liberty to engage the enemy;
but our Admiral for wise reasons would not grant it.

Next day, the ships we had seen in the offing joined
us, and proved to be the squadron under the command
of Commodore Beresford, consisting of the—

Theseus (Sir J. Beresford)	.	.	.	.	.	74 guns.
Valiant (Capt. John Bligh)	.	.	.	.	.	74 „
Triumph	.	.	.	.	.	.	74 „
Revenge (Capt. Car, or Ker)	.	.	.	.	.	74 „

They were a welcome addition to our little squadron,
making us now seven sail of the line, and Sir John
informed us that when the Brest fleet drove them away
from blockading L'Orient, they ran close in and furled
their sails, but when it came dark they set sail again,
having never let go their anchors. This was a scheme
to make Sir John believe they were going to remain
there all night, in order to get a night's start of him,
and catch us in Basque Roads before he could come to

our assistance. They succeeded so far as getting the night run and no farther, and when Sir John missed them in the morning he came immediately to our assistance.

Although the enemy have now, in conjunction with the Rochefort squadron, eleven sail of the line and a 50, yet they do not think themselves safe. So they got under way to get under shelter of the batteries on the Ile d'Aix; but one of them carrying a broad pennant and named the *Jean Bart* (of 74 guns) got aground on the Palais shoal; soon after she heeled over, then filled, and became a wreck. During this time we had sent the *Indefatigable* frigate to see into the state of the three frigates we had sunk at Sables d'Olonne, and she brought us information that they were wrecks and the French were getting all the stores out of them they could get at. Their names were the *Italien*, *Calypso*, and *Sybille*, each of 40 guns.

Rear-Admiral Stopford's letter to the Admiralty was as follows :

H.M.S. "CAESAR."
February 27, 1809.
*At anchor Baleine Lighthouse N.E. to N. 4 miles
and Chasseron S.S.E. 10 miles.*

Sir,
You will be pleased to acquaint my Lords Commissioners of the Admiralty that on the 23rd instant, being at anchor N.W. of Chasseron Lighthouse, with the *Cæsar*, *Donegal*, and *Defiance*, *Naiad* and *Emerald* frigates, the *Amazon* looking out to the N.W., wind easterly, about 10 p.m. I observed several rockets in the N.W. quarter, which induced me to get under way and stand towards them ; at 11 observed sails to the eastward and to which I gave chase with our squadron until daylight next morning, at which time the strange ships were standing into the Portuis Antioc (the passage to Rochefort) consisting of eight sail of the line, one of them a three-decker, and two frigates ; they hoisted French colours, and conceiving them to be the squadron from

Brest, I immediately dispatched the *Naiad* by signal to acquaint Lord Gambier.

The *Naiad*, having stood a few miles to the N.W., made signal for three sail appearing suspicious. I immediately chased them with the squadron under my command, leaving the *Emerald* and *Amethyst* to watch the enemy. I soon discovered them to be three French frigates standing in for the Sables d'Olonne. I was at the same time joined by the *Amelia* and *Dotterel*.

The French frigates having anchored in a situation I thought attackable, I stood in with the *Cæsar*, *Donegal*, *Defiance*, and *Amelia*, and opened our fire in passing as near as the depth of water would permit the *Cæsar* and *Donegal* to go into. The *Defiance*, being of much less draught of water, anchored within half a mile of them, and in which situation, so judiciously chosen by Captain Hotham, the fire of the *Defiance* and other ships obliged two of the frigates to cut their cables and run on shore.

The ebb tide making and the water falling fast, obliged the *Defiance* to get under sail and all the ships to stand out, leaving all the frigates on shore. Two of them heeling much, they have been noticed closely by Captain Rodd, and by whose report of yesterday afternoon, they appeared with all their topmasts down, sails unbent and main-yards rigged for getting their guns out, and several boats clearing them. I fancy they will endeavour to get over the bar into a small pier, but I am informed by the pilots that it is scarcely practicable.

The batteries protecting these frigates are strong and numerous ; the *Cæsar* has her bowsprit cut and rigging ; the *Defiance* all her masts badly wounded, two men killed and twenty-five wounded ; the *Donegal* one killed and six wounded. These French frigates had been out from L'Orient but two days, and by Captain Irby's report appear to be the *Italien*, *Furieuse*, and *Calypso*.

I am very confident they will never go to sea again. My chief object in attacking them so near a superior force of the enemy was to endeavour to draw them out and give our squadrons more time to assemble, but in this I was disappointed. I returned to Chasseron at sunset, and observed the enemy anchored in Basque Roads, and on the 25th I was joined by Captain Beresford in the *Theseus*, with the *Triumph*, *Valiant*, and *Revenge* and *Indefatigable* frigate. I therefore resumed the blockade of the enemy's ships in Basque Roads, and shall continue it until further orders. The enemy's forces consist of eleven sail of the line and *Calcutta* 50, and four frigates; the force under my command are eleven sail of the line and five frigates.

I have the honour to be, etc.,

ROBERT STOPFORD.

Here was a noble turn off for Captain Hotham's mistake in anchoring by saying his ship drew less water than the others; so did the *Amelia* but did not anchor. But what seemed strange was that he did not mention any assistance from Captain Richardson, captain of the *Cæsar*; the reason was, in my opinion, that he did not like him.

26th.—Sent the *Dotterel* in chase, which took a French sloop laden with wine and brandy; the Frenchman was much surprised in finding us here, as he had been told their fleet had cleared the coast of the English. In the night a French boat came secretly alongside from the shore, with a French general and his wife in her; he told us he had fled in consequence of a duel with a French officer, whom he shot; we sent them to England in the *Dotterel.*

28th.—Sent in the *Donegal* and *Emerald* to reconnoitre the enemy's ships more closely, and they on their return reported that the *Jean Bart's* masts were all gone and the ship full of water, with a lighter alongside to get out what they could save. Report says that Bonaparte has had the captain, whose name is Lebozec, tried and shot. Here the *King George* cutter arrived from England, to inform us that the Brest fleet had got out, and they were very much surprised to find that we were blockading them here. We got our squadron under way, went into Basque Roads, and anchored nearer the enemy.

March 2.—Examined several galliards laden with brandy under licence to carry to our good citizens of London; they informed us that Austria had again declared war against France.

3rd.—Detained and sent to England, after taking the people out of her, a ship from Rochefort with 400 pipes of wine on board and having no register.

4th.—Saw three strangers in the offing, which we supposed to be some of the L'Orient squadron which escaped lately, and hovering about with the intent of getting in here to join their other ships should an opportunity offer; sent the *Donegal* and *Alcmene* in chase of them.

5th.—*The Hero* (74 guns) joined us from Portsmouth.

7th.—Arrived and took command in chief, Admiral Lord Gambier in the *Caledonia*, with the *Tonnant*, *Bellona*, *Illustrious*, and several other smaller vessels, all from England; and next day arrived the *Mediator*, with a number of victuallers, and sent the *Defiance* to England to refit.

16th.—A court-martial was held on board the *Theseus* on Captain Tremlet, of the *Alcmene*, for not joining the *Naiad* (Captain Dundas) when his signal was made to do so, and he was sentenced to be privately reprimanded.

17th.—This day we all shifted our anchorage and moored the ships in the form of an obtuse angle, reaching from one side the channel to the other, to stop the enemy's ships from getting in or out in the night-time. The *Caledonia* lay in the centre, the *Cæsar* at one end and *Tonnant* at the other; the frigates and brigs lay in front, between us and the enemy, and the victuallers outside of all; two boats from each ship, manned and armed, rowed guard at night. We soon captured several chasse-marées, but gave the prisoners their liberty, and for which they were very thankful.

19th.—Performed divine service, and when done a letter containing the thanks of the Lords Commissioners of the Admiralty to Rear-Admiral Stopford, the captains, officers and ships' companies of the squadron under his

16

command was read, for their judicious and gallant conduct in destroying three of the enemy's frigates, and afterwards blockading their fleet with an inferior force.

21st.—Observed the French very busy and their Admiral visiting his several line-of-battle ships; he hoisted his flag alternately as he went from ship to ship. Lord Gambier, with his two captains, viz. Sir Harry Neale, Captain of the Fleet and William Bedford, captain of the *Caledonia*, paid our Admiral a visit on board the *Cæsar* this day.

April 1st.—Observed the enemy very busy at low water on a rocky shoal named the Boyard, a long mile distant and abreast of the Ile d'Aix; and, supposing they intended to erect a battery there, the *Amelia* frigate and *Conflict* brig were sent in to annoy them; when they got as near as their depth of water would allow, they opened their fire, and soon drove the enemy away in their boats; they then out boats, landed on the shoal, and upset the triangles the enemy had erected; the French fleet fired many shot at them during this gallant operation without hurting any one. Our boats (in number four) on their return saw five boats of the enemy coming after them and tossed up their oars to let them come near, but Monsieur soon altered his mind, and returned to his ships again without firing a shot.

3rd.—Arrived from England, in the *Impérieuse*, Lord Cochrane to command the fire-ships which the Lords of the Admiralty have proposed to be sent in among the enemy's ships; and a letter to that purport was posted up on board each line-of-battle ship for volunteers to man them. Numbers offered themselves on board the *Cæsar*, but Mr. Jones, our flag-lieutenant, Mr. Winthorpe, acting lieutenant, and eight seamen were selected; no one was compelled to go, as the enemy by the laws of war can put any one to death who is taken belonging to a fire-ship.

In the forenoon of this day we observed many large boats, some with guns and full of men, rowing along shore on the Oleron side, and we supposed with intent to capture some of our victuallers, who were lying becalmed outside of the roads ; we therefore sent the launches of our fleet armed with carronades and other boats manned and armed to stop them ; a smart fight soon ensued, and the enemy retreated. Our loss in the boats was one lieutenant and one seaman killed and another seaman wounded.

5th.—In consequence of some reproachful words uttered by Rear-Admiral Harvey against Lord Gambier, because his lordship could not grant him the command of leading in the fire-ships (as Lord Cochrane was sent here expressly by the Admiralty for that purpose), Rear Admiral Harvey was ordered to England, and there he was tried by a court-martial which dismissed him the service. He was, however, after some time reinstated.

Having got the victuallers cleared of the provisions and water, twelve of them were selected for fire-ships, and the *Mediator*, 36-gun frigate, was to be fitted for another, in order to go in ahead of the others and clear away all obstacles ; eight others were expected from England, making in all twenty-one, and besides we fitted up three explosion vessels, to lead in the fire-ships and blow up first, to throw the enemy in consternation : all these ('twas thought) were sufficient to destroy the enemy's fleet. We got alongside one of the victuallers a brig of 350 tons named the *Thomas*, and belonging to a Mr. Cowey of North Shields, and immediately began to fit her up for a fire-ship ; we made narrow troughs and laid them fore and aft on the 'tween-decks and then others to cross them, and on these were laid trains of quickmatch ; in the square openings of these troughs we put barrels full of combustible matter, tarred canvas hung over them fastened to the beams, and tarred shavings made out of brooms, and we cut four port-holes on each side for fire to blaze out and a rope of twisted oakum well tarred led up from each of these ports to the standing rigging and up to the mast-heads ; nothing could be more complete for the purpose.

We had captured lately several chasse-marées laden with resin and turpentine, which answered our purpose well, and which probably had been intended by the enemy for the same purpose against us. We placed Congreve's rockets at the yard-arms, but this was an unwise proceeding, as they were as likely to fly into our boats when escaping, after being set on fire, as into the enemy's. Having got all ready, she was hauled off and anchored near us.

My next job was to fit up a chasse-marée (lately taken) for an explosion vessel ; but she rolled so much alongside as to endanger her masts being carried away against our rigging, so she was dropped astern, and hung on by a rope, and then continued to roll as much as ever ;' so that I had to change first one and then another of the carpenter's crew who were on board cutting the fuses, they being seasick. We stowed thirty-six barrels of gunpowder (90 lb. each) in her hold upright and heads out, on each was placed a 10 inch bomb-shell, with a short fuse in order to burst quickly.

A canvas hose well filled with prime powder was laid for a train from the barrels to a small hole cut in her quarter for the purpose, and the train was led through it to her outside, which was well fastened—a port fire which would burn twelve or fifteen minutes so as to give the people alongside in the boat who set it on fire sufficient time to escape before she exploded.

She, with two others fitted up by some of our other ships, was to go in a little before the fire-ships, run under the batteries, and then blow up, in order to put the enemy into such confusion that they might not attempt to board any of the fire-ships as they were running in. When this vessel was ready, I returned on board, it then being four in the afternoon, not having broke my fast the whole day—I had been so busily employed, and the business being so urgent, as she was expected to go in this night.

Lieutenant Davies took charge of her with the jolly-boat and crew; he and Mr. Jones, who went in with the fire-vessel, got made commanders for this business, and well they deserved it; but I, who had the sole charge of fitting them up, the most trouble, and my clothes spoiled by the stuff, did not so much as get a higher rate, which I applied for, and which from my services I thought myself entitled to: such is the encouragement that warrant officers meet with in the Navy! If an action is fought, though they have the principal duty to do in it, they are seldom mentioned in the captain's letter; whilst the purser, doctor, and boys of midshipmen are greatly applauded, though some of them were no more use in the ship at the time than old women!

The following orders were issued:

All launches and other boats of the fleet to assemble alongside of the *Cæsar* and act under the orders of Rear-Admiral Stopford; ships and other vessels to be stationed as follows:

The *Pallas*, *Aigle* and *Unicorn* to lie near the Boyard shoal and receive the boats as they return from the fire-ships.

The *Whiting* schooner, *King George* and *Nimrod* cutters, at the Boyard to throw Congreve's rockets; the *Indefatigable* and *Foxhound* to lie near Aix to protect the *Etna* while she threw her shells into that place; the *Emerald*, *Dotterel*, *Beagle*, *Insolent*, *Conflict* and *Growler* to make a diversion on the east side of Aix; the *Lyra* to lie with lights near the Boyard side, and the *Redpole* with lights on the Aix side, a mile and a quarter from the enemy, as a direction for the explosion and fire-ships to pass between.

Lord Cochrane in the *Impérieuse* was to act as circumstances would permit, he having superintendence of the explosion and fire vessels.

The French ships of the line lay in two tiers across the passage, rather outside of Aix, as they had not room enough to lie in our line ; the frigates lay to the eastward and a great number of gunboats to the westward across the passage, and without (where the line-of-battle ships lay), they had moored a large boom, well secured with chains and anchors, to stop any vessel from entering in. Admiral Willaumez, who commanded the squadron, that we chased in the West Indies in 1806 (which was separated from us in the hurricane), and who commanded the Brest fleet that we had followed in here, has been superseded by a mighty man, if many names can make him so : he is called " Lacharie Jacques Theodore Allemand." This would have disgusted old Mr. Clark, master of the *Tromp* when I was in her : when mustering any of the people who came to join the ship, if they had two Christian names he would say, " Au, mon, I suppose you have come from some ' great family,' " then turning aside and giving a grin, would say again, " I dinna ken how these people come by twa names—it was as much as my poor father and mother could do to get me christened David."

On April 11, at half-past eight in the evening, it being very dark, and a strong tide setting with blowing weather right towards the enemy's ships, the explosion vessels set off, followed by the *Mediator* and other fire-ships. The former soon blew up with a dreadful explosion. The *Mediator* carried away the boom laid across by the enemy, and the other fire-ships followed her in, and the elements were soon in a blaze by their burning. Shells and rockets were flying about in all directions, which made a grand and most awful appearance. All hands were up that were able on board all our fleet, to behold this spectacle, and the blazing light all around gave us a good view of the enemy, and we really thought we saw some of their ships on fire. But it seems they had been prepared for this business, for as the fire-ships closed on them, they slipped or cut their cables and ran their ships on shore; and the fire-ships, after being abandoned by our people, drove with the wind and tide up mid-channel, and passed them; but we were informed by some of the prisoners taken that the *Ocean* lost near two hundred men in extricating a fire-vessel from her, and that she cut and anchored three different times.

At daybreak the following morning we saw all the enemy's ships, except two, on shore on the Palais shoal. The *Ocean* was lying with her stern on the top of the bank and her bows in the water; but next high water she, with two others, by throwing their guns and heavy stores overboard, got afloat again and ran towards Rochefort, until they stuck on the bar, and there remained until they could get more lightened.

At 2 p.m. the *Imperieuse* and some others of a light draught of water which were inside of our fleet, ran into Aix Roads and opened their fire on the *Calcutta*, and soon made her strike her colours. They then set her on fire, as she was fast aground, but it was thought she might have been got off by lightening her. The two line-of-battle ships that had not been on shore now cut their cables and ran towards Rochefort, until the bar brought them up.

The *Revenge*, *Valiant*, and *Etna* bomb were soon after ordered in, and began firing on the other enemy's ships that lay aground, and at five in the evening the *Varsovie*,

Aquilon, and *Tonnère* surrendered, and three more fire-vessels were ordered to be got ready with all dispatch. We got the *Sisters* transport alongside for one of them, and soon fitted her up in a temporary manner for the purpose, and this same afternoon, between five and six o'clock, we got the *Cæsar* under way, and with the *Theseus* and three fire-vessels ran into Aix Roads.

N.B.—In passing the Aix batteries, where our French pilots had said there were as many guns as days in the year, we could not find above thirteen guns that could be directed against us in passing ; and these we thought so little of that we did not return their fire, although they fired pretty smartly at us too with shot and shells, which made the water splash against the ship's side ; yet (thank God) they never hit, though the passage here is only about a mile wide. Captain Beresford of the *Theseus* had his cow put into the ship's head to be out of the way of the guns ; a shot from the enemy killed it, which was the only loss received.

About seven o'clock, just as we were getting nearly out of the range of their guns, our ship took the ground and stuck fast nearly close to the Boyard. The shot and shells were flying about us at the time from Aix and Oleron, but it soon came dark, and they left off, and we had the prudence to still keep all the sails set to make them believe we were running on. However, after dark we took them all in, and as the tide fell the ship heeled much, so we started thirty tons of water overboard to help to lighten her, and ran the after guns forward to bring her more on an even keel. During this business a light was seen by the enemy through one of our port-holes, and we soon had a shot whistling across our quarterdeck. The light was quickly extinguished, and they fired no more. But this shows what a predicament we should have been in had it been daylight.

At eleven at night, with the rise of the tide, she floated again, and we got her into deeper water, where we anchored her more clear from their shot and more clear from the *Calcutta*, which had been all in a blaze only a short distance from us ; the latter when she blew up made a most dreadful explosion, having a great quantity of gunpowder on board and other stores which were intended for Martinique, had we not prevented her. It was said she was worth half a million sterling.

Fortunately none of her fiery timbers fell on board our ship : everything went upwards, with such a field of red fire as illuminated the whole elements. One of our French pilots was so frightened that he dropped down on the deck, and said afterwards that if anybody had told him that the English had done such things, and he had not seen them, he would say it was "one tam lie."

In the course of this eventful night Captain Bligh of the *Valiant* was sent in with the boats manned and armed to reconnoitre the enemy more closely, and on his return informed us that they had got three lines of boats manned and armed to keep off any more fire-ships, and, it beginning to blow strong at the time, the attempt was given up. So we set fire to the *Varsovie*, a new 90-gun ship (for she carried that number), and to the *Aquilon* (74 guns), as they were waterlogged. They burnt to the water's edge, and then blew up. As for the *Tonnère* (74 guns), the enemy set fire to her themselves, and then escaped in their boats.

In the place where we now had anchored we found our ships to ground at low water. And early in the morning, the wind having become favourable, we got under way with the other line-of-battle ships, and left this place, which may be compared to Portsmouth Harbour, and soon after anchored among our other ships in Basque Roads, which may be compared to Spithead. The enemy fired at us from

Aix in passing their line, but, thanks to Providence, not a man was hurt.

The frigates and small craft we left inside, but the enemy had got their ships lightened so much, and into shoal water, that the shot from our frigates could not reach them.

Our loss on this occasion was as follows :

When our fire-ship had got near the enemy an explosion vessel (which they did not not see) blew up, and a piece of one of the shells, which had burst, struck the boat alongside of the fire-ship which Mr. Winthorpe and his four men had to escape in, and stove in her quarter (they were light four-oared gigs, and selected for the purpose), and wounded the boat-keeper in the hand. When they left the fire-ship, it being rough weather, she soon filled with water, and they clung to the boat for safety.

As the ebb tide was setting out strong they drifted out to one of our brigs, who sent her boat to save them ; but two of them were gone and lost through exhaustion. Mr. Winthorpe was found in the boat quite dead, and Yankee Jack and the other were taken out of the gig nearly so, and when carried alongside the brig, Jack requested to be left in the boat until he recovered and got a little stronger, so the boat was dropped astern, and he in her.

He had not been there long before the rope broke, and being very dark, the boat soon drove out of sight, and the first landfall poor Jack made was on the French shore, where he was soon made a prisoner. We all pitied poor Jack Ellis, a good-tempered fellow, and never expected to see him again. But after the war was over, and Jack released, I met him on the Common Hard at Portsea, and was glad to see poor Jack again: he then belonged to a merchant vessel.

He told me that when he was made a prisoner he was

examined strictly to know whether or not he belonged to one of the fire-ships, as by the laws of war they can put any one to death taken in them. But Jack said he belonged to one of the victuallers. They asked him then how he came to have his hand wounded, and he said it was by the boat's gunwale and ship's side as they rolled together, and by sticking to the same story (after being examined thirteen times at Rochefort and other places) he got clear, but remained a prisoner five years. When peace took place in 1814, Jack got released, returned to England, and received the whole of his pay and prize money up to that time.

Lieutenant Jones, who commanded the fire-ship, had likewise a narrow escape. One of the cabin windows had been opened for him to get into the boat, after the fuse was lighted; but the swell was so high, and the sea so rough, they durst not venture near the stern of the vessel for fear of staving the boat against the counter, and—not having a moment to spare—he jumped overboard. The boat took him up, and they all five arrived safe on board.

Lieutenant Davis, with the jolly-boat and four hands, who went in with the explosion vessel, likewise all safely returned on board.

A singular circumstance happened while we lay inside, as follows. The captain of the *Varsovie*, a prisoner, finding we were going to set his ship on fire, got permission to go on board her to get some charts, which he said he set a high value on. He went with Lord Cochrane, and sat alongside of him in the gig, and, strange to say, but actually true, a shot came from the enemy at Aix and killed the French captain on the spot, without either hurting his lordship or any one in the gig.

Other occurrences happened, but we hardly had time to think of them, being so dangerously situated; for who could ever suppose to see four sail of the line go into

Portsmouth Harbour, passing the batteries, and running up as far as the Hardway and there anchoring, and destroying part of the enemy's fleet, and then running the gauntlet out again amidst shot and shells flying about! Such was the case going into Aix Harbour. Had a gale come on from the north-west and blocked us in we should have been in a poor situation, but kind Providence favoured us in everything.

The killed and wounded in the British fleet are: Two officers and eight men killed; nine officers and twenty-six wounded, and one missing (which was Yankee Jack): total forty-six.

On the evening of April 14th the enemy succeeded in lightening the three-decker so much that with a press of sail and a high tide they got her over the bar, and she went up to Rochefort; the Commodore tried hard to get the *Cassard* over, but failed; the *Etna* bomb kept throwing shells, but without any effect, as the swell made her roll so much.

Next day three more of the enemy's line-of-battle ships got over the bar and went to Rochefort; three more remained, but so far up and in the shallow water that our frigates could get near enough for their shot to reach them: the *Etna's* 13-in. mortar split, and all the shells of her 11-in. mortar were fired away, and apparently without doing any execution. Manned all the launches of the fleet to cover the three remaining fire-ships that are to be sent in to-night; but a gale came on with rain, and it was given up.

Next day, the 16th (still stormy weather), the enemy being afraid of an attack on the *Indiana* frigate, which lay aground, set her on fire, and she soon blew up.

17th.—All the enemy's ships this day got over the bar except the *Regulus* (74 guns), which still remained aground near a place called Fouras, about four miles above the

Isle of Aix ; this day we released several male and female prisoners, gave them a boat, and saw them land safe at Rochelle, and hope they are thankful for their deliverance.

19th.—By order of the Commander-in-chief public thanks were given to Almighty God through the fleet for our success over the enemy.

20th.—The *Thunder* bomb arrived from England, and with the *Etna*, who had got a supply of 10-in. shells, and (with two rocket ships and several gun brigs) began to fire away at the *Regulus*, but could not get near enough to make any impression, so we got the transport that we had fitted up for a fire-vessel alongside, and cleared her of all the combustibles.

21st.—The *Hero, Valiant, Gibraltar,* and *Illustrious*, not being wanted here, were ordered out on a cruise.

22nd.—A letter of thanks from the Commander-in-Chief, Lord Gambier, to the Admiral, captains, officers, seamen, and marines of the fleet was read this day to the ship's company for their gallant zeal and services in the late affair against the enemy.

24th.—This day a desperate attack was made again on the poor *Regulus* by the bombs, gun brigs, and other small craft such as drew little water : the *Contest* gun brig behaved well. The enemy returned their fire with such guns as they could get to bear, and after continuing at it nearly all day we gave the business up without making any impression, as our vessels had too much motion by the roughness of the sea ; and soon after the launches and other boats were ordered to return to their respective ships, and all further attempts given up.

27th.—The *Donegal, Bellona, Resolution,* and *Defiance* were ordered to sea, and the rest of us weighed anchor, ran further out and anchored in the same place we formerly lay.

28th.—The tide being very high the poor *Regulus* got

over the bar and went to Rochefort, exulting, no doubt, in their narrow escape from the lion's paw. Orders arrived for the return of Lord Gambier, and we got four months of excellent provisions from the *Caledonia*, and likewise three dozen of Congreve's rockets from the *Cleveland* transport. Next day Lord Gambier sailed for England in the *Caledonia*, leaving the command to Rear-Admiral Stopford in the *Cæsar*, with the *Tonnant*, *Revenge*, and *Aigle* and *Medusa* frigates, four gun brigs, a schooner, and two cutters to watch the motions of the enemy.

Arrived the *Naiad* frigate from England, with the *Hound* and *Vesuvius* bombs; but being too late they were ordered to England again. The *Naiad* had some people on board taken out of a sinking galiot which had only left Rochefort yesterday; they informed us that Bonaparte had ordered the chief officers of his ships at Rochefort to be put under arrest, and 'twas thought some would suffer death; and that they were building two hundred gunboats with all haste to protect their coast.

A man named Wall, who called himself an American, ran away from the *Cassard*, stole a boat and got off to our squadron; he informed us that the *Tourville*, *Regulus*, and *Patriot* are so much disabled that they are ordered to be cut down for mortar vessels, and that the *Ocean* is in a bad state; the *Cassard* is to be docked, but the others were not very much damaged; that Captain Lacaille of the *Tourville* is to suffer two years' imprisonment, to be erased from the list of officers and degraded from the Legion of Honour, and that Captain Porteau of the *Indiana* is to be confined to his chamber three months for setting fire to his ship without orders. Captain de la Roncière of the *Tonnère* is acquitted; but John Baptist Lafon, captain of the *Calcutta*, is to be hanged at the yard-arm on board the *Ocean* for shamefully quitting his ship when in presence of the enemy. This is the fellow who had the English colours hung Union down last winter to insult us, and moreover they were hung under the bowsprit and near the privy: they generally who act in this manner are cowards.

30th.—Divine service performed, and an excellent sermon was preached by the Rev. Mr. Jones, touching on several remarkable instances of divine favour which happened on several occasions on our behalf, and how the very materials the enemy were collecting to destroy us fell into our hands and acted against themselves; how the winds favoured us in going into Aix Roads, and how they shifted to bring us safe out again; these were such convincing facts that they made a great impression on the ship's company.

Next day a bowsprit with the jibboom spritsail yard and part of the knee of the head hanging to it came floating alongside, and we hoisted them on board, and to our surprise found they had belonged to the *Calcutta* when she blew up, and had come, as it were, to do homage for the insult offered on it two or three months ago, by hanging the English colours under it Union downwards. The rascals little thought at the time it would be so soon in our possession; there surely was something mysterious in this.

May 12.—A play was acted on board the *Revenge* called "All the World's a Stage," and several of us went on board to see it, the Admiral among the rest, which gave much satisfaction. As for the *Cæsar*, we never had diversion of any kind to cheer us up during the many weary dull nights we had passed on this station.

24th.—Three very long and large boats belonging to the enemy came out from Aix Roads, and in a daring manner lay on their oars for some time nearly within gunshot, staring at us. We sent our boats manned and armed, who soon made them run, and chased them close in to Aix Roads. Five other boats came out and joined their other three; a smart fire commenced, and the shot from their batteries fell around our boats likewise. Our Admiral, seeing the enemy were getting too powerful, recalled the boats, and they returned without having a man hurt.

June 5.—This morning a heavy gale of wind and rain came on from the westward, which caused the sea to rise much; struck lower yards and topmasts; at 11 a.m. she drove with two cables out; let go the best bower and veered out another cable, which brought her up. The *Tonnant* parted from both anchors and nearly drove on shore near Rochelle, but her sheet anchor being let go brought her up; she made a signal of distress, but no assistance could be given in such stormy weather; fortunately she rode the storm out.

10*th*.—A cartel came in from Cayenne and anchored near us; three French small craft were sent from Rochelle to take the people out of her. An American and a Maltese who came out in these vessels entered into our service, and would not return to Rochelle again: so much for Bonaparte's popularity! They told us the French ships at Rochefort were getting ready very fast and five of them would soon come down; and sure enough this same afternoon we saw three of the rascals coming down the Charente for Aix Roads. Sent our boats to assist the *Tonnant* in sweeping for her anchors, and found one.

17*th*.—This day arrived Rear-Admiral Sotheby in the *Dreadnought* and relieved us in the command; saluted each other with thirteen guns each, distributing our provision (except one month's) to the other ships of the squadron; gave an anchor to the *Tonnant*, and in the evening got under way with glad hearts for Old England.

23*rd*.—Saw the land near the Lizard, and a strange ship of the line with a brig in tow steering to the westward. As she looked suspicious we cleared away for action and steered toward her, and on closing found her to be the *Algeciras* (a Spanish 74), with a brig three days from Spithead and bound for Cadiz with ammunition and other stores for the Spanish patriots.

24th.—Came to anchor in Cawsand Bay and moored ship, hoping to have a little comfort after so many months' absence and hard duty, but we were disappointed. The Admiral struck his flag, the *Cæsar* became a private ship again, but was ordered to be immediately victualled and got ready for sea; so after being here only five days we put to sea again, but with some comfort on my side, for we were bound for Portsmouth.

CHAPTER XI

1809

THE WALCHEREN EXPEDITION

Cæsar to join an expeditionary force—Gambier court-martialled—68th Regiment embark in the *Cæsar*—"Absent without leave"—*Cæsar* joins Strachan's fleet in the Downs—Army under the Earl of Chatham—Off Walcheren Island—Disembarkation on Bree Sand—Naval Brigade land—Surrender of Middleburg—Assault on Camveer fails—Lands with naval rocket party—Camveer capitulates—Enters Camveer with the troops—Bombardment and surrender of Flushing—Fever breaks out—Visits Flushing and Middleburg—Strachan fails to pass Fort Lillo—Fever rampant—Advance on Antwerp abandoned—Submarine mines built—General Don confers with Lord Dalhousie and Sir Eyre Coote—Evacuation decided on—Troops re-embark—Fleet puts to sea—Arrival at Plymouth (January 1810).

July 1.—Came to anchor at Spithead, and a report came on board that we were going on some grand expedition and will have to take troops on board ; and soon after a lighter came from the gun wharf to take on shore our lower deck guns and carriages, and a great many ships are collecting here for some purpose.

5*th.*—The pay-captain came alongside in the commissioner's boat to pay the ship down to six months ; our captain, who is always prying and peeping about, seeing the boat's crew getting their slops on board (to sell as usual on pay days), ordered them to put their slops into their boat again and lay off from the ship. So they went to Captain Larkin, the pay captain, who was at another

258

ship at the time, and told him Captain Richardson would not allow them to serve their slops on board the *Cæsar*; so he sent a note to the pay clerks to stop paying our ship. A great altercation ensued, the port admiral was very angry, the payment of the ship was ordered to go on, and an order issued from Sir Roger Curtis, the Commander-in-Chief here, stating that whenever the commissioner's boat was attending the payment of any ship, a commissioned officer must attend at the gangway and see that a rope is given ahead and astern to moor the boats to, and that two boat-keepers should remain in her, and the rest be allowed to sell their slops on board.

In consequence of a court-martial going to be held on Lord Gambier at the instigation of Lord Cochrane for something that had displeased the latter about the Basque Roads business (and for which Lord Gambier was most honourably acquitted) our captain was subpœnaed with the others to attend as witness, and was replaced by a Captain Temple for the time.

Hitherto we could get no liberty on shore, but now, with another captain, we got it, and we also got something else. We had several casks of French brandy taken out of a French prize in Basque Roads, which had been stowed away in the hold (for what purpose I don't know), and this our first lieutenant got leave of Captain Temple to share out to the ship's company, and I received more than ten gallons to my share.

July 13.—To our great disappointment Captain Richardson joined us again, and took command of the ship. He, being a deep Yorkshireman, found out that Rear-Admiral Stopford and Mr. Raven, our master, who were to appear at the court-martial, could give all the evidence required on the part of the *Cæsar*, and so got his attendance dispensed with; and now our liberty was stopped again for going on shore.

Two days after this, the captain and first lieutenant being out of the ship, we, having little or nothing to do, gave many anxious looks to the shore, and then went to the second lieutenant to see if he could not give us his leave. His answer was that he had no orders against it, but if we went he would advise us to come on board again in the evening, as the troops were expected to be embarked daily. So on shore we went, more than a dozen of us officers.

The evening soon came, and our leave had vanished like a dream, so I made up my mind to stop on shore all night, and did so, as there was little hope of soon getting on shore again; and, when I returned on board next morning, was surprised to find all the troops on board, the 68th Regiment of Light Infantry under the command of Colonel Johnstone, with the horses and other traps belonging to them.

" Now," thinks I, " what a pretty mess I have got into under a scolding captain ! " and, moreover, I had been sent for by him and found absent. A message soon arrived that I was wanted by the captain, and when I went I found him shaving himself in his cabin. " Well, sir," said he, " where were you when I first sent for you ? " I answered, " On shore, sir." " And who gave you leave to go on shore ? " I told him the second lieutenant. " And when were you to return on board ? " I answered, " In the evening." " And why did you not ? " " Because I had not time to finish my business." " Very well, sir," replied he : " now remember that it is not my orders you have disobeyed, but the orders of the Commander-in-Chief, and to him I will report you ; " and calling his clerk told him to put my name down on the list as absent without leave. So, knowing it was of no use to reason with him, I left him, regardless of the consequences ; for, though I had previously been pretty well satisfied with the Navy, I was now almost disgusted with it, through his unofficer-like conduct.

When I got out of his cabin and on the quarterdeck, one of our lieutenants asked me how I had got off, and I told him my name was put on a list to be sent to the Commander-in-chief as absent without leave. He smiled, and said so was his, and so was so-and-so (more than a dozen altogether), and which made me smile, for "company in distress makes the trouble the less." Whether the affairs on board at the time were too urgent, or whether he *had* reported us to the Commander-in-chief, we have never heard, and so the business dropped.

July 25.—Employed in receiving more horses and their trappings, and in training up eighty seamen for a brigade to land with the army, and emptying all the 32-pr. cartridges and filling more 24-pr. cartridges, intending, if necessary, to put half the main-deck guns (24-prs.) on the lower deck, so that we might fight both tiers, one side or the other, or all on one side, as our lower-deck guns were left on shore to make room for the troops. A Mr. Rouse, master of the *Puissant*, superseded *pro tempore* Mr. Raven, who is to remain behind to attend the court-martial.

26*th.*—Got under way in company with nineteen sail of the line, with frigates, gunboats, and many transports, all the dockyard lighters, and of other small craft a great number, all under the command of Rear-Admiral Otway, and steered our course to the eastward. At noon the next day it fell a calm, and we came to anchor off Beachy Head. At half-past six weighed anchor again with the flood-tide, and drove close past the *Orion*, *Eagle*, and *Bellona*, and nearly got foul of them in the fog.

27*th.*—At half-past four this morning anchored again; saw part of the fleet through the fog. Two hours after the wind came from the westward, and cleared away the fog. Weighed anchor, and at 3 p.m. came to anchor in the

Downs. Here we found a large fleet lying under the command of Sir Richard Strachan, and for the same expedition; his flag was on board the *St. Domingo.*

Our numerous fleet now consisted of :—8 sail of the line complete with all their guns ; 29 with lower-deck guns out ; 2 of 50 guns ; 3 of 44 guns ; 23 frigates ; 1 20-gun ship ; 31 ship and brig sloops of war ; 23 gun brigs ; 5 bomb vessels ; and 120 hired cutters, with gunboats, etc., in all 245 ships and vessels of war, besides 400 sail of transports, which, and the ships of war, had on board 39,219 troops, including 3,000 cavalry ; the naval part under the command of Sir Richard Strachan, and the army under the command of the Earl of Chatham. Such a fleet and army never left the shores of Great Britain together before.

July 28.—Early this morning the first and second divisions, with the Commanders-in-chief on board, got under way, and, with a fresh gale from the westward, steered in the direction for Flushing, and were soon out of sight. Came on board two North Sea pilots, Messrs. Taylor and Reed ; and just after sunset came alongside Mr. Gray, from London, to join us. He was an old and experienced master in the Navy, and much respected ; but our captain ordered him to the shore again, with his chest and cot, according to his punctuality, as the ships were to have no communication with the shore after sunset. Surely the order did not apply to a case like this ! So he was obliged to land again, find lodgings, and, with other expenses, hire a boat in the morning to bring him on board again. This hurt the poor old master's feelings very much.

29th.—At half-past three this morning we all got under way with the third division, and, having a fine wind in our favour, saw the Island of Walcheren at five in the afternoon. Our first and second division were at anchor near the Stone Deep. We soon came to anchor near them in eight fathoms, and about four miles from the land; but it blew so strong towards the shore, and raised such a surf, that no attempt was made to land, and most of the troops were seasick.

Next morning we all got under way, and ran through the Veer Gat, on the north side of the island, and came to anchor in the Roompot, Flushing being on the south side of Walcheren. In going through the Gat our ship took the ground, broached to, and struck so heavily on the sandy bottom that she nearly shook the lower masts out of the steps, and yet for all this she leaked none. The after guns were run forward, and other things had recourse to in order to bring her more on an even keel, and when the tide rose we got her over the Braak or bar, and soon after came to anchor among the others in the Roompot, about two miles from the shore.

It was a beautiful day and the sea smooth, and we soon had our flat-bottomed and other boats filled with troops, and the twenty-one horses we had on board. They soon joined the others, and off they set towards the shore, cheering each other as they went along. It was a grand sight to see so many heroes in boats extending for miles dashing along to meet their enemies on a foreign shore. They landed on a fine sandy beach (the Bree Sand) without opposition, a mile to the westward of Fort Flaak, and some of our cutters kept firing at the fort to draw their attention from the troops that were landing.

A firing of musketry was soon heard between the sand-hills, and in the evening we had fifty-two prisoners brought on board (two of them females). Our naval brigade of eighty seamen under the command of Captain Richardson were landed at this time.

Next day (31st) Middleburg surrendered without firing a gun; but four companies of the 71st, under Colonel Mackenzie, a brave officer, were repulsed last night in an attempt to take Camveer [1]—a place regularly fortified with ramparts, ditches and drawbridges. They had to march along the sea dyke hoping to take the place by surprise; but the enemy were on the watch, and when our troops got close to the drawbridges, drew them up, and at the same time opened such a heavy fire that our troops were obliged to make a hasty retreat. The enemy made a sally, and the Colonel was wounded and made a prisoner; by some means, however, he fought his way clear of them again; at muster next morning eighty-five of them were missing.

Next morning an order came for me to land and bring the Congreve's rockets I had on board along with me for the investment of the place, Camveer. I was soon landed with the assistance of the seamen's brigade, who were my shipmates; we cut off the upper part of a small tree and put the rocket ladder for elevation against it, placed and primed the rockets, and began to blaze away at a fine rate, and I was soon covered with volumes of smoke.

In a short time one part of the town was set on fire by the rockets, and soon after two other parts; some of our gunboats were also firing shot at the town at the time, and two of them got sunk; a shell burst over our heads without hurting a man. However, the rockets terrified them so much (having never seen such things before) that in the evening they sent out a flag of truce to capitulate, and the terms were sent to the Earl of Chatham at headquarters; however we kept under arms all night, some made little straw huts to lie down in, and stowed themselves away very comfortably, and I lay under a cart.

[N.B.—As soon as it was known the four companies of the 71st had been defeated it was proposed to besiege and bombard the town in regular form, but before they had got a single gun near the place we had caused it to surrender.]

[1] Veere.

I could not rest much under the cart, so got up quite early in the morning and went in search of a rocket which I had fired off : it had ascended above my head and then whirled round and round with its accustomed noise of fire and smoke, so that I thought the rascal was going to attack me; it then shot away in a curve and fell to the ground about half a mile from where it was fired off, and as I went along I met some of our advanced pickets who pointed to the place where they had seen it fall, and I soon found it.

It was stuck so far in the ground that with all my strength I could not drag it out, so was compelled to leave it. In so doing I found myself close to a small cottage standing by itself, with both doors and windows shut; wishing to know if any one was inside I knocked several times, and at last an old man came, seemingly much terrified, and opened the door. I made signs to him that I did not understand Dutch, and that I was thirsty ; he soon understood what I wanted and brought a bowl of excellent milk ; after I had taken sufficient I left him, not wishing to disturb the other inmates if there were any ; and if any I could not see, as the windows were all close shut and the cottage dark.

When our brigade left the ship they had brought two days' rations with them, but I landed in such a hurry that I had brought nothing except a little money in hopes of buying something to eat on shore ; in this I was disappointed, for the only town near was in the hands of the enemy, and that was Camveer. So being hungry after fasting near twenty-four hours, I went in search of something, and not far off saw an orchard, and into it I went and got some apples. Here I met with an English gentleman, who was very talkative ; he had come over in a private capacity to see the operations of the army and their sieges, so we walked along together through the orchard, passed a large mansion, and rambled into the fields, where we saw many of our troops lolling on the ground in a careless manner, and their muskets piled up together. Just at the time and near us came up three deserters from the enemy, fully accoutred, and delivered themselves up to the soldiers. We could not help remarking that had these deserters chosen to have placed themselves behind the hedges, they might easily have popped off our loitering troops before they could have got ready to defend themselves.

Going a little farther, we fell in with an advanced guard of the 42nd Regiment, and on mentioning the circumstance to them they told us that some of their men had been popped off yesterday for want of keeping a good look-out; they advised us not to go any farther, as the enemy's pickets were near at hand and skulking about; so we retraced our steps, and returned to the camp.

[An order was soon after issued stating that so many had been cut off lately by the enemy's riflemen in straggling about that any one hereafter being found more than a mile from the camp should be put to death.]

An answer was sent this morning to Camveer. They had requested to deliver up themselves with the honours of war, and to be sent to Holland; this was refused, and though the Governor had said he would be buried in the ruins of the place before he would surrender he now consented to our terms, and surrendered at discretion.

A little before noon a company of Grenadiers came to take possession of Camveer, and I, being anxious to see the form in delivering up the keys, went along with them. In going along the dyke we passed one of the 71st lying dead on the ground; one would have supposed that he was lying only asleep. When the gates were opened, and during the delivery of the keys, I slipped in, and was the first of our people that entered the town.

I then proceeded along a wide, clean, paved street quite delighted, intending to find out the prison, and inform any of my countrymen who might be there that the place was ours.

I soon met a man who spoke English, and he told me he was glad to see the English there again, and that there was not an English prisoner in the town; so we went into a tavern, and the best I could get for money was some hard Dutch cheese and bread, with some gin grog, and this was the first meal I had got since I left the ship.

I next took a ramble round this neat and clean town, which put me in mind of Portsea (only it has a harbour in the middle of the town), and there I saw the *Growler*, gun brig, formerly British, lying and going to decay. Great havoc had been made among the houses by the shot from our gunboats; one had begun at the corner of a house, and ripped its way along the front of eight more before it stopped; at the outside of the gate lay three of the 71st and two horses dead and unburied, and a painter's shop burnt down by one of the rockets. I was told that a rocket entered into one of the embrasures, killed seven men at the gun, and wounded another.

Having nothing more particular to see, I went to headquarters, and told our captain how badly I was off for want of provisions. He said I had better return on board, and so I intended; but in going along I fell in with one of our lieutenants (Martin) sitting on the grass and enjoying a good meal, and he, being a generous fellow, made me sit down and take a part, and I soon had a good blow-out. By this time it was late in the evening, and as a boat was going off I embraced the opportunity, and returned on board very much fatigued.

For this exploit with the rockets one of my mates (Lawson) whom I had taken on shore to assist me was made a gunner, and appointed to the *Serapis* (44 guns), vacant of a gunner at this time here, and I was told that a first-rate was to be my reward; but I have never got one yet, nor a higher rate than the *Cæsar*, while others whom I had known to have never fired a shot at an enemy, and had very little sea service (but through Parliamentary or petticoat interest), have got first-rates and ships a-building, and are milking the cow, as it were, while others are holding it by the horns.

August 3.—The *Courageux*, in going out, got aground on the shoal we had thumped so hard upon. Sent our launches to her assistance and got her off again without damage. Manned two more gunboats from our ship (with a midshipman and twenty men to each), to assist some others in an attack on Fort Rammekens. Soon after we heard a smart firing from that quarter, and in the evening it surrendered, when eight hundred of the enemy, mostly Frenchmen, were made prisoners. One of the gunboats was sunk in that affair, and four or five men killed and wounded.

5th.—Our army have invested Flushing. In the night the enemy made a sally out, but were driven in again with loss. Major Thompson of the 68th, who came over in our ship, has lost his right arm, and is otherwise severely wounded. Between twenty and thirty of his men were killed and wounded.

6th.—Arrived more troops from England. Sent 137 prisoners on board the *York* for a passage to England. Sent a long gun and cannonade (24-prs. each), and fifty rounds of ammunition, to Captain Woodriff at Camveer.

8th.—Sent by the *Jervis* transport (Coats, master) to the *Fortune* transport (which is to be armed immediately, she being convenient for shoal water)—7 long guns, 24 prs.; 2294 filled cartridges for ditto; 2207 shot, and two tons of wads and the necessary implements for working the guns.

Received on board twenty-six prisoners, two of them women.

It is said that our army are slow in their operations, and that the enemy have got a reinforcement thrown into Flushing.

Sunday, August 13.—While the good people in Old England were this day offering up their prayers to the Almighty God of peace, we here were serving the devil by destroying each other as fast as we could; for at half-past one in the afternoon, our batteries being all ready, began to fire on the town of Flushing, and a tremendous roar (such as has seldom been in battle) was kept up with shot, shells, rockets, and musketry, enough to tear the place in pieces. The following ships, with their lower-deck guns in, attacked it at the same time by sea :

St. Domingo (Rear-Admiral Strachen, Capt. Gill)	74 guns.
Blake (Rear-Admiral Gardner, Capt. Codrington)	74 „
Repulse (Capt. Legge)	74 „
Dannemark (Capt. Bisot)	74 „
Venerable (Capt. King)	74 „
Victorious (Capt. Hammond)	74 „
Audacious (Capt. Campbell)	74 „

At midnight saw part of the town on fire, but the enemy soon extinguished it. The bombardment continued more than thirty-four hours (except an interval of three), when on the 15th, at three in the morning, it surrendered, although the commander-in-chief, General Monnet, had declared that he would be buried in its ruins first. However, it was said that he surrendered only at the intercession of the inhabitants, to save the town from destruction.

It has suffered much, many of its noble buildings being in ruins, and nearly four thousand troops and inhabitants slain. A church, said to be built in memory of Bonaparte when he visited this place, was in such a blaze that the very bells were melted, on the day and very near the hour of his nativity.

Our loss was nearly as follows: The Navy, 9 killed and 55 wounded; the Army, 103 killed and 443 wounded.

An old French captain of the army, who was taken prisoner at the Rammekens, and who has been on board here ever since, always held that we would never take Flushing, and now we having taken that place says, "Ah, but you will never take Antwerp." What vanity these Frenchmen have got in them!

17th.—Lieutenant Rolls, with our brigade of seamen, returned on board, and next day we sent our boats to assist in embarking the prisoners on board the following ships for England—viz. :

On board the *Orion* (74 guns)	.	.	.	500 prisoners.
,, ,, ,, *Alfred* (74 guns)	.	.	.	550 ,,
,, ,, ,, *Bellona* (74 guns)	.	.	.	500 ,,
,, ,, ,, *Revenge* (74 guns)	.	.	.	500 ,,
,, ,, ,, *Marlborough* (74 guns)	.	.	600 ,,
,, ,, ,, *Namur* (74 guns)	.	.	.	550 ,,
,, ,, ,, *Hero* (74 guns)	.	.	.	550 ,,
,, ,, ,, *Resolution* (74 guns)	.	.	500 ,,
,, ,, ,, *Monarch* (74 guns)	.	.	500 ,,
,, ,, ,, *Serapis* (44 guns)	.	.	.	400 ,,
,, ,, ,, *Weymouth* (36 guns)	.	.	300 ,,
			Total	5450	,,

besides a good many sent away before in the *York*. They were a mixture of French, Dutch, Germans, and Russians.[1]

Since the surrender of Flushing Sir Richard Strachan,

---

[1] The numbers who surrendered with General Monnet were :

Officers	117 ⎫
Non Commissioned Officers and rank and file	3,773 ⎬ Total 4,379.
Sick	489 ⎭

Before the surrender 1000 sick and wounded had been sent to Cadsand.

with his squadron, has moved up the West Scheldt to co-operate with the army against Antwerp. The enemy have eight sail of the line, several frigates and gunboats. They have retreated up to Fort Lillo, a strong place twelve miles on this side of Antwerp. Sir Richard Keats is up the East Scheldt with a small squadron watching the motions of the enemy there. We have received on board some wounded Russian soldiers who had been in the French service.

30th.—An order came on board for us to leave the Roompot and bring the ship round to Flushing, which was on the other side of the Isle of Walcheren; so we got under way for this difficult shoal-water trip and passed over the Braak Sand we had formerly grounded on, then passed round Oostkapelle into the Stone Deep, and entered the narrows named the Banyard (having then only $28\frac{1}{2}$ feet of water), with a cutter on each bow to sound the depth of water. Our ship when ready for sea, with all her guns and stores on board, drew 27 feet of water, but now she only drew 25; and now we came to anchor to wait for a fair wind. Several of our people who were of the landing party were now affected with fever and ague, or, as it was afterwards called, the " Walcheren fever," and one of them died.

Early next morning, the wind having come fair, and our ship trimmed to near an even keel, we got under way and went through the Durloo Passage (carrying $28\frac{1}{2}$ feet of water). At eight in the evening came to anchor abreast of Flushing, in deeper water, and moored the ship about two cable lengths from the town. We found lying here the *Dannemark*, bearing the flag of Rear-Admiral Otway and the *Victorious* with a great number of transports, five of which had been armed from the fleet. We got alongside and cleared them of their stores; soon after we cleared two more of their guns, 1,466 filled cartridges and 2,130 shot (all 18 pounders), and this day Rear-Admiral Otway shifted his flag to the *Cæsar* and brought his retinue with him.

September 5.—This day, having some time to spare, I went on shore to see the place, and landed where our seamen's battery had been erected, but the ground was now levelled and the trenches filled up. I observed that the moat on the west side of Flushing was not above half leg deep, and might easily have been stormed there without waiting a fortnight in making breaching batteries, and I was not the only one that thought so. I then rambled along a fine road, went through a neat little village named Cowkirk, and saw many of our troops, who were taken by the fever and ague, and billeted here lying lolling on the ground in their great coats and night-caps under a burning sun—enough to give any one a fever, and no wonder so many of them died !

Going along I passed several fine mansions with beautiful gardens, which put me in mind of old England, and then arrived at Middleburg, the capital, situated in the centre of the island. This is supposed to be as fine a place as any belonging to the Dutch ; canals are cut, which bring vessels of burden close to the houses, which are well-built and lofty and the streets wide, clean, and neatly paved ; it is near five miles from Flushing, having a paved road for carriages all the way, over which numbers are continually travelling. The Stadthouse is a very lofty pile and can be seen a long way off at sea ; I did not observe any fortifications about it.

I left Middleburg and travelled towards Flushing, and about half-way I passed East Soberg, where our camp stood during the siege, and where many of our soldiers' huts are still standing ; soon after I got into Flushing, which is a regular strong fortified place ; in taking a walk round the ramparts I counted eighty-three guns (nearly all brass) and twenty-three brass mortars and howitzers.

The town was in a miserable state from the effects of the bombardment, hardly a house escaped injury, and many totally destroyed; their fine Stadthouse is burnt down, and so was a fine elegant church. In looking at the ruins of it I got close to the mouth of a pit, nearly full of both sexes who lost their lives in the siege; the uppermost was a female of a bulky size, and I was told that a number of people of both sexes were in the church when it fell, and were buried under its ruins, and this is very probable, as the bombardment began on a Sunday.

They represent General Monnet as a tyrant, and that when the women solicited him to surrender in order to save the town from destruction, he ordered the soldiers to fire on them; but of the second in command they spoke in high terms.

Flushing has two harbours, the old and the new; in the latter was a line-of-battle ship up in frame named the *Royal Hollander*, a frigate named the *Fidelle*, and a brig nearly finished. I slept at the " Seven Stars "; for eating and drinking the charges were moderate, and next morning I returned on board.

September 6.—Sir Richard Strachan's squadron were not able to pass Fort Lillo, as the enemy have got such strong reinforcements; they returned here again this day, and report says that any further attempts on Antwerp are given up. Had our ships of war and transports pushed up on our first arrival, Antwerp would soon have been taken; but our commanders were misled by the Dutch pilots, who told them that the batteries in Flushing and Cadsand would soon destroy any ships that passed between them; yet our ships did pass between them, and before Flushing surrendered, and received little or no injury.

Our soldiers were at this time very sickly, and report

said that 10,000 were dead and on the sick list, and that many were being sent to England that were not wanted [1]; indeed, so unhealthy is this island, that when the French had possession of it they computed their loss by sickness annually at 1,700 men. We expected soon to have a visit from them, as they have now got possession of South Beveland, there being only a narrow river named the Sloe between them and Walcheren, and we have sent many gunboats there to prevent them getting over.

All the carpenters of our ships of war here, with their crews, have been sent on shore to take the *Royal Hollander* to pieces, that her frame may be sent to England and rebuilt there; [2] the frigate and brig are to be finished as speedily as possible and sent to England.

9th.—A heavy gale came on from the north-west, with rain; the *Bellona's* launch filled astern of us and went adrift with her gear and an 18-pounder carronade in her. The tide was running at a great rate; hove sixty tons of shingle ballast overboard to make room for horses, and laid a platform for them. Sent Mr. Watkins, assistant surgeon, with several sick people to England.

12th.—Received on board six casks of money.

14th.—All hopes of conquering any further are now given up, as the Earl of Chatham, Commander-in-chief of the Army, sailed away this day for England in the *Venerable*. Arrived several transports from England with fresh water, as the Walcheren water is said to be not good. For my part I thought it as good as any I had ever drunk, and had many a good swig of it: how fantastical are some people!

22nd.—Sir Richard Strachan took his departure for

---

[1] On Sept. 19 the "daily state" showed 224 officers and 9,627 other ranks sick.

[2] This was afterwards done, and she was named the *Chatham*.

England, and the command of the Fleet was left to Rear-Admiral Otway, consisting of—

Cæsar (Flagship)	80 guns.
Impétueux (Capt. Lawford)	74 „
Namur (Capt. Jones)	74 „
Revenge (Capt. Paget)	54 „
Theseus (Capt. Beresford)	74 „
Repulse (Capt. Legge)	47 „
Courageux (Capt. Plampin)	74 „
Dannemark (Capt. Bissot)	74 „
Aboukir (Capt. Parker)	74 „
Victorious (Capt. Hammond)	74 „
Hero (Capt. Newnham)	74 „
Resolution (Capt. Burlton).	74 „
Audacious (Capt. Campbel)	74 „
Leyden (Capt. Usher)	64 „
Agincourt (Capt. Kent)	64 „

with the *Impérieuse* and *Aigle* frigates, and a great number of brigs, cutters, gunboats, and transports. After this it came stormy weather for several days, with gales and hail from the north-west blowing right into the harbour, which rose the sea so much that several transports drove and went on shore. One of these nights we heard guns of distress from the seaward, but the weather was so stormy we could send them no assistance. When daylight appeared we saw the *Venerable* coming in before the wind, nearly water-logged, with her main and mizzen-masts gone. She had been too late to see the marks for coming in, and was compelled to anchor outside. She soon drove on a bank, threw some of her after-guns overboard, and struck on them, which damaged her bottom. We towed her into the new harbour and to the dockyard to get repaired— the water was nearly up to her lower deck—and got her lower-deck guns out, and mounted them on board the *Cæsar*.

16th.—Punished several people for absenting themselves

from the dockyard without leave. The *Namur* is taking in the *Royal Hollander's* timbers to carry to England.

20th.—Sir Home Popham and Sir Eyre Cooke paid a visit to our Admiral this day; sent two hundred men on shore to do duty at the dockyard.

October 1.—The captain's steward of the *Pallas* frigate had the temerity to land with the jolly-boat at North Beveland to purchase some stock from the Dutch farmers. A party of the enemy soon captured him and the boat, and what stock was in her; but the crew got to a Dutchman's boat a little distance off, and escaped in her. As soon as this was known the *Pallas* manned her boats, and with the assistance of some of our gunboats landed and pursued the enemy, but could not overtake them. However, they recovered their jolly-boat again.

9th.—The brig being finished at the dockyard, was launched, and named the *Voiture*; she was brought alongside our ship, temporarily rigged, commissioned by Mr. Popplewell, our flag-lieutenant, and sent to England.

Received from the *Berwick* cutter six copper submarine carcasses, some to hold 540 lb. of powder, and others 405 lb.; they were intended to sink a ship, and used as follows. Suppose a light rope about six fathoms long to be stretched across a head of a ship, and one carcasse fastened to one end and another to the other; then lower them down in the water by buoy ropes to each about twenty-one feet for a line-of-battle ship, and then let them hang by cork buoys; and when let go they will drift with the tide towards the ship, suspended in that manner, and when the middle part of the six-fathom rope gets over the ship's cable it brings the carcasses round, and they swing under the ship's bilge-way: there is a piece of clockwork, water-tight, fixed to each, which you must set to the number of minutes you suppose it to require in reaching the ship's bottom. It then blows up, and 'tis said, will blow a hole in a line-of-battle ship's bottom. Johnstone the smuggler laid one down near the gates of the new harbour before Flushing surrendered, but we never heard of any damage being done by it. As for our part we never tried them—indeed, our Admiral said it was not a fair proceeding.

Three of our officers and I landed this day at Flushing, then took a coach and rode a distance of five miles to Middleburg, fare only sixpence-halfpenny each, we dined at the "Domberg" Tavern, had a good dinner, and (with claret included) only paid two shillings each; we then went to have a look at their famous Stadthouse, and went to the top of it, where we had a fine view all over the Island, part of Holland, the Netherlands and the ocean. It has a large gilded cock for a vane; about half way up the stairs we counted forty bells of different sizes, and (what is rather remarkable) there were no tongues to them—they are hit with a hammer. The town appeared extensive and of an oval form, clean and populous. It is reported that Bonaparte is coming here with 200,000 men. In the evening took coach for Flushing, and then returned on board.

21st.—A court-martial was held on the master of the *Venerable*, who was dismissed the service.

23rd.—A court-martial was held on board the *Impétueux* on a master's mate commanding a gunboat, for landing on the enemy's coast, where he had a man killed and another taken prisoner. Sentenced to be reprimanded.

24th.—Arrived the *Daphne* from England with General Don on board to inspect the situation of Walcheren. He paid our Admiral a visit.

26th.—The *Venerable* sailed for England, rigged and accompanied by the *Dannemark* and *Gambier* cutter.

29th.—General Lord Dalhousie came on board, and a council was held in the cabin by the superior officers to consider whether it would be best to keep possession of the island or evacuate it. A deserter from the enemy came on board and brought a newspaper, which reports there are 100,000 men coming to oppose us.

30th.—General Don, the Earl of Dalhousie, and Sir Eyre Coote have been on board to-day, and held another council with our Admiral; the result was, the two latter, Dalhousie and Coote, soon took their departure for England, and we suppose it is settled not to keep the island, for soon after our people on shore began to dismantle the batteries of their copper and brass guns.

November 23.—A hundred men from each line-of-battle ship are employed on shore daily in dismantling the batteries and putting the guns and mortars on board the transports: we received nineteen on board of different calibres, some brass and some copper. Some are employed in breaking up the piers of the new harbour, and filling it up with rubbish, to prevent the enemy's ships from entering in and lying up in the winter (to be clear of the ice coming down the Scheldt); and a great deal of concealed East India produce has been discovered to-day.

December 4.—Lady Don with her maid and a coach were received on board to-day for a passage to England when we sail, which time cannot be long distant. The General went on shore again to forward the preparations for evacuating the place; received stores from the dockyard, as it is to be destroyed.

6th.—A flag of truce has been sent to us this day from Cadsand, and which is to let us know that if we destroy the works they will harass our rear in embarking; the answer from General Don was that if they did he would open the sluices on them.

9th.—General Don and his retinue came on board, and all the troops embarked except the rearguard; the gates of the new harbour undermined and blown up; the dockyard had been cleared of all its stores previously, and now all the storehouses were set on fire and burnt to the ground, which made an awful appearance; Sir Richard Strachan arrived in the *Jason* frigate to command the evacuation on the naval part.

11th.—Fresh gales with a rapid spring tide; the *Revenge* nearly drove foul of us; many of the transports drove as the gale freshened, and damaged each other, as they were so numerous; several drove on shore near Flushing, and three were totally wrecked.

12th.—The south-west gale still continuing several more transports drove on shore near Flushing, with signals of distress flying, and the sea breaking right over them; but in the evening it became moderate, and some of them were got afloat again; a dockyard lighter was sunk laden with copper. We are now all ready for starting, but have to wait for a fair wind; and not only that, but must have it at the top of the spring tides, as there is only nineteen feet water at low water in going through the Durloo Passage, and the pilots will not take charge till then.

15th and 16th.—Heard a great many guns fired towards the Sloe, and found it to be from our gunboats: the enemy had been throwing up batteries in the night to drive off our gunboats and get across to Walcheren; but our gunboats on perceiving them at daylight soon knocked them to pieces; eight midshipmen who had deserted from a French prison came on board. The *Jason* was ordered up to Borslen; the enemy fired shots and shells at her, but without effect.

20th.—The boats of the *Diana* frigate attempted to cut out some of the enemy's gunboats last night, but the latter were too powerful for them, and the boats had to retreat after losing a lieutenant and midshipman, and some seamen wounded.

22nd.—Got under way with the fleet, and got near a mile and a half down, and there anchored again. The inhabitants of Walcheren, poor creatures, are at this time to be pitied, and they may well call themselves unfortunate: about two years ago the sea broke over the dykes, destroyed much property, and many lives were lost; in the late bombardment their ancient town has been nearly destroyed, and two thousand of the inhabitants slain; and the dread of Bonaparte coming (who they expect will lay heavy taxes on them to make good the works we have destroyed) fills them with despondency. Such is the ruin of warfare! As for our part we are tired enough of the place; when we left England it was thought three weeks would finish the business, and now we have been here twenty-one, and not gone yet.

December 23.—At last the wind has come fair, and the tides at the highest; all the ships of war and a great number of transports got under way, and proceeded through the Durloo Channel. Signal was made at the same time to all the frigates and gunboats stationed around the island to get under way and follow us. A great many shot and shells were fired at us by the enemy from Cawsand without hurting anybody; and we all, thank God, got safe to sea. A young man named Harvey, a native of Southampton, piloted us out, and we carried 6½ fathoms at high water over the flats. The marks from the shore were as follows:

The middle mill at Flushing on a line with the highest steeple—or a white wall with the southermost windmill.

The course out by compass was N.W. ½ N. 2½ miles, and after passing the Elboog, W.N.W. 7¾, then N.W. clear out to sea.

24th.—At sunset saw the South Foreland.

25th.—Christmas Day. Off Beachy Head, and beaten to

windward against a strong north-wester under treble-reefed topsails.

27th.—Light winds a little past noon, the tide being against us. We came to anchor four or five miles to the eastward of St. Helen's. Rear-Admiral Otway, General and Lady Don and suite went on board an Isle of Wight vessel and proceeded to Portsmouth, and the Deal pilots went also by the same conveyance.

28th.—We got to Spithead and moored ship; here we found the *Caledonia* and *St. Joseph* lying as we left them in July last.

[The Walcheren expedition cost the country some £835,000: about 4,000 men died, of whom only 106 were killed in action. Out of 35,000 officers and men who returned home 11,500 were in hospital: many of these died, and of those who recovered the greater number suffered with a ruined constitution for the rest of their lives.]

CHAPTER XII

1810–19

LISBON AND THE PENINSULAR WAR

Cæsar ordered to Portugal—Lisbon and its palaces—Capsized in the Tagus—Captain Richardson leaves—Sunday observance by the Portuguese—Flogging in the British Navy—Reflections on the press gang—Lord Wellington's doings—Conspiracy against the British—Victory of Busaco—Wellington falls back on Torres Vedras—Naval brigade to the front—Massena retreats—Lord William Fitzroy court-martialled—*Cæsar* to hand in stores—Execution of a traitor—*Cæsar* ordered home—Paid off and laid up—H.M.S. *Bellerophon* at Portsmouth with Bonaparte on board—Transferred to the *Bedford* and to the *Pitt*—Superannuated. Adieu.

March 9th, 1810.—Received orders to take as much provision on board as we could stow and proceed to Lisbon.

25th.—Saw the Rock of Lisbon, and got a pilot on board about noon ; at half-past three in the afternoon anchored in twenty-three fathoms, and moored ship abreast of the ancient city of Lisbon. Found lying here the *Barfleur*, Admiral Berkeley, Vice of the Red and Commander-in-chief, his captain Sir Thomas Hardy, and the *Impétueux* (74 guns), which had left Cawsand Bay with us ; but on the passage we had kept our ship several hours from her right course in order that the sun might bear so as to dry the paint on her sides, and that was the reason she arrived before us.

A great many transports are lying here, and report says General Massena with a large French army is soon expected to enter Portugal and advance on Lisbon. Lord Wellington has got 60,000 British, Spanish and Portuguese troops to withstand them. A boat came alongside with fruit to sell, and we got twenty fine oranges for sixpence.

This city of Lisbon is said to have been built 278 years after the Flood, by Elisha, the grandson of Noah; the harbour is one of the finest in the world, and abreast of Lisbon it is four miles across. The city is extensive, houses grand and lofty, and like old Rome stands on seven hills; the entrance of the harbour is defended by forts, St. Julian and Baglio.

28th.—About two hundred prisoners have been brought into Lisbon this day; they had been foraging, and dressed in English uniforms, but could not deceive our troops under Lord Wellington, who made them all prisoners.

April 11th.—This morning Mr. Palmer, our carpenter. Mr. Cowling, surgeon's assistant, and I went on shore to have a look at this ancient place, the city of Lisbon, and landed at Buenos Ayres, which is at the west end of the city, and where their East India warehouses stand. Here we found the place, like most Popish countries, swarming with beggars, monks, and friars; and a most disagreeable noise from the numerous carts passing along (something like the noise of a bagpipe and grindstone working together), by the creaking of their wooden axletrees which revolve, the wheels being fastened to them, and drawn or rather pushed along by bullocks, the dragropes over their horns.

We next took a walk of three or four miles to see Belem and the new palace building there, with the Queen's gardens and museum and castle. The latter, which stands near the river's side, is not formidable, having only two brass guns mounted on its top, but a battery of twenty guns has been erected lately near it.

The new palace will be a fine one when finished, and commands a noble prospect of the Tagus and the ocean ; the Queen's gardens were beautiful, having several fountains spouting their water, and a number of gold and silver fish sporting about ; but the greatest curiosity was the museum, and would have been more so had not the French under Junot plundered it of many valuables when they were here.

Here we visited a famous monastery. On our entrance the people were on their knees on the floor at prayers ; one man was kneeling before an image and holding both his arms upright—we supposed he was doing penance. We went upstairs and got into a long, narrow room, where we counted 72 cabins on each side, and said to be for the accommodation of 132 monks. A text from Scripture was over each door.

Here we saw many fine pictures from Scripture, and several others of the Royal Family of Portugal. There seemed to be a great family likeness among them, their noses small and monkey-like. A beautiful garden is attached to this monastery, and the monks were very civil and polite ; on taking our leave we saw the penitent still holding up his arms as before. We had a poor dinner at Belem, and everything dear on account of the disturbed state of the country ; we then hired a Portuguese boat with two men to take us to Lisbon.

It was a beautiful day and the wind with a rapid flood tide in our favour. The surgeon's assistant, being warm with the wine, had taken the helm and insisted on steering the boat, and we let him have his own way, and he was in high glee. We set off under a sprit sail and went rapidly along, but had to caution him several times on his bad steering ; at last he gave her such a yaw that the sail blew over the other way and upset the boat.

I scrambled over the upper quarter of the boat, and when she got keel up I crawled across it and sat there, much wet. The first I saw was Cowling, the surgeon's assistant, who had caught hold of an oar, but it being too light to support him he let it go and began to swim towards the shore, but swam very badly, and had not a boat come speedily from a Falmouth packet and taken him in, he would soon have gone to the bottom. A few seconds after I saw Palmer, the carpenter, come up with his head above water, who gave such a bellow as to be heard near a mile off; not being able to swim, he was nearly going down again, when I pushed one end of the boat's backboard, which I found floating near me, to him, keeping hold of the other end and my seat at the same time; when he got hold of it I drew him toward me, but cautioned him not to bear too heavy on the boat, as she would not bear both, and he had wisdom enough to take my advice; the packet's boat came soon after and took us in. How the two watermen escaped I never could learn; but when the boat landed us at Lisbon, with the watermen's boat in tow, we found them there ready to receive us, and (after satisfying them for their trouble) we repaired to Cairns Hotel, where we got our clothes dried and some refreshment.

We slept on shore that night, and next morning, after breakfast, took a boat near Black Horse Square to carry us on board; but as soon as the watermen began to set their sail, Cowling begged and entreated that it might not be set, or else land him again, such a fright had he got from the recent business; so to satisfy him the sail was not set and we were rowed to the ship.

We had previously agreed to let no one know, when we got on board, what had happened; so after a while we asked the news, and were answered nothing particular, only that a boat was upset yesterday with three mid-shipmen in her, but they understood that they were all saved; so we laughed in our sleeves and left them no wiser.

After this I went on shore again with some of our midshipmen to have a look at the city, with its fine streets, churches and gardens, and found gold and silver streets, the grandest and best having been built since the earthquake in 1755. In one of the churches there had been, we were told, the twelve Apostles in solid silver, but when the French under Junot came, in 1808, they took them; when the priest remonstrated on such sacrilege, they told him to get twelve wooden ones, which would answer the same purpose.

Here were many beautiful gardens, adorned with statues representing the human virtues, and a very ancient citadel situated in the very dirtiest part of the city and almost tumbling down (with the exception of one part which has been lately repaired, whereon are six guns and three mortars mounted). This citadel or tower is very ancient and commanded the city; the streets about it are narrow and dirty, and when Junot was here he made them keep their streets cleaner. Soon after they had a sickness in the place, and said it was caused by that.

There are several noble squares in Lisbon. One is named the Pracada Commercia (or Black Horse Square by the English) situated by the river's side; there is in it a noble equestrian statue larger than life, and said to represent Joseph, the first one of their kings; it stands on a great and high pedestal, whose north side represents the Royal Arms of Portugal with several females, one larger than the rest. On the east side was represented a large elephant led by a female, and trampling over a man lying prostrate on the ground, and his armour scattered about; this we supposed was an emblem of their conquests in the East Indies. The west side was nearly the same as the latter, only it had a horse for an elephant. On the south side was the ocean, and a ship under full sail with the arms of Portugal above her—all exceedingly well executed, and gives pleasure to the beholder. The statue has turned black through time, and that is the reason the English call it Black Horse Square.

After we had dined at Cairns Hotel on roast beef, cold, with some veal and salad, two bottles of wine and two of porter, the bill when brought in amounted to 1,200 reis, which startled us, but inquiring about it found it was very reasonable, 1,200 reis being equal to only three dollars.

One day we went to see a very grand church belonging to the Augustines, richly ornamented with mosaic work and grand pictures; one was our Saviour giving sight to a blind man. The richness of this church is said to be sufficient to support all the numerous maimed, sick, and poor beggars in Lisbon. We next took a look at a nunnery of the first order, which contained nuns of the first families in Portugal, who have liberty to go out occasionally and visit their friends; the door being open, we took the liberty to go in, and walked along a short passage or court to a room where we observed four old and two young nuns, who, on seeing us, seemed much surprised, I suppose at our intrusion; but John Bull had come to assist the Portuguese, and he thought he had a right to go anywhere. However, we were very circumspect in our behaviour; they saw it, and were not displeased; they spoke to us in French, of which we could understand but little; however, they were good tempered and laughed at our mistakes, and we parted with the greatest good-humour on both sides.

We next went to see a famous aqueduct, about two or three miles out of Lisbon, which stands like a bridge across the valley of Alcantara and supplies the whole city of Lisbon with good water, that comes from a considerable distance in the interior. It is supported by thirty-five arches, of different sizes, owing to the inequality of the ground, the tenth being the highest; one of our officers sounded with a line and found its height to be seventy-six yards from top to bottom; on the top it is forty-five feet wide, with a good road on each side for walking over it; on the centre, between the two roads, runs the water under a covered conductor. It being Sunday evening, thousands of the inhabitants (mostly females, and dressed much after the English manner) were walking to and fro over it for recreation. This part of the country looks delightful.

We rambled a little farther to have a look at the villa of the Marquis of Abrantes, who is now in France, being a partisan of Bonaparte. We found it to be a neat building, but not large, its papered walls describing battles and bull-fights; and here we got plenty of fruit in the gardens for nothing. We next visited a little village where wine is sold from the tap, the same as beer is sold in England, and had a pot of it, which was much better and one-fourth cheaper than we get it in Lisbon.

Some days after this we went over to the south side of the Tagus, opposite Lisbon, and landed under a high and steep rocky shore, where the shipping get their water. We then scrambled up a traversing road until we got on the top near the town of Almada, commonly called Old Lisbon by sailors; and here we had a charming view of all the shipping in the river, and Lisbon with its grand churches, etc., and Belem and Fort St. Julian, and a long distance into the ocean.

The town of Almada is pleasantly situated, with good

buildings and a church, where people were counting out dollars in the porchway and boys letting off crackers, and we supposed a wedding was there. We then walked a mile or more higher up the Tagus, to have a look at the Prince Regent's gardens, and found them very extensive. Here were fine ripe grapes lying on the ground, enough to load a small ship, with plenty of apple trees, pears, cherries, and other delicious fruits ready for our acceptance, as there was no one looking after them on account of the disturbed state of the country, and the Prince Regent having emigrated to the Brazils on account of the French, who now threaten to invade the country again.

18th.—Arrived the *Semiramis* frigate (Captain Granger) and report says he is going to exchange with our captain. By a new regulation of the Admiralty, Captain G. is too old a post captain to hold a frigate, and ours too young to hold a line-of-battle ship; and on the 23rd the exchange took place, much to our joy and satisfaction, for Captain Granger was a good captain to sail under, and we soon found it so much to our comfort.

Captain R. had his usual bad luck: after he left us, in convoying some Indiamen home, he ran foul of one of them, and damaged his ship so much that with great difficulty they got her into Plymouth without sinking. In another frigate he was the cause of stopping the China trade, and 'tis thought that he will never be employed again.

May 1.—Lord Wellington has had a battle with the French, who have had a reinforcement of 30,000 men under General Massena. All the troops here that can be spared are ordered to join his lordship.

2nd.—Served out the clothes of the men that deserted from us at Plymouth to those now on board who are in the most need. Sheriff Homer fell overboard in the night, and was lost.

8th.—Report says that the French are advancing and Lord Wellington retreating.

17th.—A foretop man named Tobin, a deserter, returned again on account of the King's proclamation which pardons all deserters who return to their ships again.

May 25.—Having blacked the ship's bins and other places two days ago (and which ought to have been dry now) a shower of rain came on to-day and washed it all off. On examining one of the blacking kegs, found the stuff in it a mixture of soot and vinegar instead of black varnish.

31st.—Lieutenant Thompson has exchanged from our ship with Lieutenant Suckling of the *Talbot*, a nephew of Lord Nelson.

June 4.—This day being the anniversary of the birth of King George III., we hoisted the standard at the main, Union at the fore, and a Portuguese ensign at the mizzen. At 1 p.m. every British ship-of-war manned its yards and fired salutes of twenty-one guns each. More than three hundred transports with merchantmen reaching near five miles along the shore had their colours displayed, and fired their guns, which made a noble appearance. In the evening the Portuguese illuminated their houses all along the shore in grand style.

The mates and midshipmen of our ship gave a general invitation to the mates and midshipmen of the fleet to a dinner, and between thirty and forty came on board, had a good blow-out, drank plenty of grog and stopped all night. Next morning some of them were found asleep in the table tiers with their clothes on, and some in other places, and when awoke wondered how they came there, thinking at the time that they were on board their own ship, which caused fine fun and laughter among them.

12th.—Sailed for England the *Talbot* sloop-of-war, with

a great many transports, having French prisoners on board, under her convoy.

16th.—Arrived the *Cornelia*, a Spanish frigate, and report says that the French have taken a 30-gun battery from the Portuguese, but that a Spanish army had retaken it, and made seven thousand of the French prisoners, and that foreigners are deserting from the French daily.

The Sunday following, the following advertisement was published in English and Portuguese, and gives an idea how the Sabbath is kept here:—

"*June* 24, 1810, Sunday. At the Salitre Bull-feast place the company of tumblers, rope dancers and equilibrium vaulters will display to the respectable spectators, several sorts of their performances at 5 o'clock and a half in the afternoon. At the arrival of the worthy Senator Judge of the Rue de Nova quarter, Inspector of the same place, the scene will open by all the company appearing to pay their homage to the said Inspector and spectators.

The amusement will begin by a famous dancer on the tight rope with and without the balancer.

A Portuguese girl five years old, will perform several equilibriums on the rope, affording much to be admir'd; the second female dancer will dance a minuet on the rope, and will also perform several other evolutions.

John Baptiste will perform great evolutions and droll jumps.

Elizabeth Romano will dance the English turn agreeable to the sound and time of a great band of music, and perform other evolutions which will afford great admiration—in particular that of dancing with chains on her feet.

Felix Antonio will play a skirmish part—the famous harlequin will perform the great difficult equilibrium of going up on a rope from the stage to the second box story.

Little Betty will perform the fire exercise on the rope; the grand collation will be given to five people all in a square on the tape; one of the greatest equilibriums will be executed without any of the performers making use of the balancer.

There is also to take place the great and difficult equilibrium of three dancers appearing together one over the other in a pyramidical form, and the amusement is to finish with jumps and equilibriums perform'd on chairs, candlesticks, and other balanced movements.

All the rest of the company promise to do their utmost abilities to please the publick, to whom they will always feel thankful, and they engage to afford on the said afternoon an amusement worthy of such a respectable circle of spectators.

All convenient measures are taken to maintain tranquillity and good order. The admitting price is at the shady side 240 reis and sunny side 120; boxes as usual."

So much for Sabbath-keeping in Portugal, among so many priests, monks and friars!

June 25.—A transport boat upset near us, but by speedy assistance they were saved. Sent Samuel Morgan, a prisoner for desertion, on board the *Barfleur* to await his trial, and next day he and two men belonging to the *Kent* (likewise for desertion) were tried by a court-martial and each sentenced to three hundred lashes. Poor Morgan was much pitied, being a good and mild creature, and almost fainted when the sentence was pronounced. By the kind interference of the humane Lady Hardy poor Morgan afterwards got reprieved, but the other two poor fellows were punished round the fleet; but did not receive their number of lashes because they could not bear it, so they were sent on board the flag-ship until they recovered to receive the remainder.

Horrid work! could any one bear to see a beast used so, let alone a fellow creature? People may talk of negro slavery and the whip, but let them look nearer home, and see a poor sailor arrived from a long voyage, exulting in the pleasure of soon being among his dearest friends and relations. Behold him just entering the door, when a press gang seizes him like a felon, drags him away and puts him into the tender's hold, and from thence he is sent on board a man-of-war, perhaps ready to sail to some foreign station, without seeing either his wife, friends or relations ; if he complains he is likely to be seized up and flogged with a cat, much more severe than the negro driver's whip, and if he deserts he is flogged round the fleet nearly to death. Surely they had better shoot a man at once : it would be greater lenity ! [1]

It may be said that England cannot do without pressing. Be it so ; but then let it be done in a more equitable manner, and let sailors arriving from long voyages have liberty a month or more to spend their money and enjoy themselves with their friends ; then I will be bound to say they will endure pressing with more patience, be better satisfied, and not so ready to desert.

July 9th.—Our advanced frigates are called in, as an engagement is soon expected, and two of our midshipmen with four seamen are sent to attend a signal station, which communicates between us and Lord Wellington.

August 3.—In consequence of her Royal Highness Princess Maria Theresa of Portugal being united in matrimony to a Spanish Prince, Don Pedro, the British and Portuguese ships saluted, and in the evening Belem, Buenos Ayres, and Lisbon were superbly illuminated, also the Portuguese shipping.

It is said that the 95th Regiment has suffered much in rescuing two Portuguese regiments from being taken by the enemy.

[1] This passage recalls to mind Voltaire's description of the barbarous treatment by the press gang of a Thames boatman who, a few hours before, had been boasting of the superior freedom of English subjects.—*Œuvres Complètes* (Beuchot), vol. xxxviii., p. 22.

7th.—Our Captain (Granger) had a grand ball on board the *Cæsar* to-day, and besides the captains of the fleet, there came near forty Portuguese of both sexes and of the first families; the quarterdeck was grandly decorated, and in the evening dancing began, and was kept up till a late hour, and finished to the satisfaction of all concerned.

September 8, 1810.—A great number of Hanoverian and German soldiers, who had deserted from the enemy, were this day sent to England, and report says our army has met with a defeat.

9th.—Our army has retreated ten or fifteen leagues to a stronger hold, in consequence of the Portuguese Governor of Almeida having gone over to the French and given them Lord Wellington's plans.

12th.—Arrived the *Scylla*, a 20-gun ship; and to my great surprise, I found my brother James to be gunner of her, and of course we were glad to see each other again, this being the third time in twenty-one years (and at seven-year intervals) since we last left Shields; but neither of us knew where our other brothers were (John, Robert, and George).

13th.—A spy has been detected and a most villainous conspiracy discovered among some of the chief families of the Portuguese; a Count and some others that were on board here the other night at the ball are among them, and taken up. Their plan, which was to take place in two days' time, was to blow up the grand magazine and deprive Lord Wellington of ammunition, and then to spread a report that the English had done it, in order to set the inhabitants against them. Eighty were taken in one house consulting about the business, and offered the guard four thousand dollars to allow them to burn their papers and escape; but the honest guard refused to be bribed.

The British Ambassador here, has been very active, and four hundred and fifty more traitors are taken, who were thought to be much attached to the British interest.

But there is no trusting in such treacherous rascals. What a dreadful thing it would have been, and what loss of innocent blood, had their plan succeeded!

A few days after the scoundrels were put on board a large Portuguese frigate and sent to sea, accompanied by the British frigate *Lavinia*. Some say they are going to England, others to the Brazils, and some to Madeira; no matter where they go, so that we are clear of them. A strict search is going on after a Portuguese naval captain who has been forming a plan to send fire-ships down among us.

27th.—Matthew Dun, a remarkably quiet man, fell out of the fore rigging on the forecastle and was killed on the spot. News has just arrived of a famous victory obtained by our troops in Portugal over the French at Busaco. A French general, named Simon, was made a prisoner. He had a dreadful cut on his face by one of our soldiers, and at first he refused to surrender to any one but an officer; it is said that his wife accompanied him in the quality of a page. But notwithstanding this victory our army under Lord Wellington is obliged to retreat, and has taken a strong position at Torres Vedras, about seven leagues from Lisbon, and on a kind of peninsula with the right wing near the Tagus and left wing near the sea; here they are to make their final stand to save Portugal. Our army is 80,000 strong, of English, Spanish, and Portuguese; the enemy, under Massena, 100,000; and 'tis said that if he takes Lisbon, Bonaparte has promised to make him King of Portugal, so there is no doubt but that he will strive to the utmost to gain it. However, every pass between our two wings is very strongly fortified and our troops in good spirits.

All the transports, more than three hundred sail, have dropped down to Belem to be ready to embark the army in case of emergency. Lisbon is full of alarm and fear and the inhabitants of the British interest are preparing to embark, and I have promised my cabin for the convenience of a gentleman's family; but Lord Wellington has caused a proclamation to be read to the public to quiet their fears, and assures them that Lisbon is not in danger, which has in some measure restored tranquillity. The affair, however, must soon be decided, as the French cannot get supplies of provisions for so large an army much longer there. Another spy is taken.

October 10.—In order to strengthen the right wing of our army on the Tagus a flat-bottomed boat, well manned and armed from each line-of-battle ship, and launches with carronades, were sent up to Villa Franca to support that wing which is under the command of Lord Hill; likewise a lieutenant, a midshipman, and fifty seamen from each line-of-battle ship to join that wing and assist in working the artillery. The *Audacious* (74) moved up to succour the boats, and an armed flotilla with the pinnaces and yawls went up to destroy all boats and vessels liable to fall into the hands of the enemy.

The Portuguese are now stirring themselves here, and pressing all the men they can catch to join the army and man a 74, two frigates, and a brig lying here. Lord Wellington has expressed a wish (which is granted) for forming a brigade of seamen and marines, to partake of the glorious achievements of the army, and fifty more seamen from each line-of-battle ship were put into training for that purpose; and forty marines from each line-of-battle ship (armed and accoutred) sent to the British Ambassador's and Admiral's houses, to relieve the guards there, that they might join the army.

The enemy's outposts and ours are frequently within musket-shot of each other. The former is in much want of bread, as the country is drained so; 'tis said ours will advance and put down a loaf of bread in the night and then retreat, then the enemy advances, takes up the loaf and leaves a bottle of wine in return. 'Tis a pity such men should be sent to kill each other. Received on board two brass 3-pounders, and one brass 6-pounder, to be fitted up for our boats.

18th.—This day all the boats of the transports assembled on the south side of the Tagus, and brought over to Lisbon 15,000 Spanish troops, under the command of General Romana; they marched away immediately to join Lord Wellington.

22nd.—Arrived the *Hannibal* (Rear-Admiral Sir Thomas Williams), with the *Elizabeth* (74) and *Mercury* from England with troops. Report says the French must soon retreat for want of provisions.

23rd.—Got the brass guns fitted in the boats; fired several rounds, and found them answer well.

25th.—Arrived the *Dreadnought*, (Captain Linzee), which makes our number as follows:

Barfleur (Admiral Berkely, Commander-in-chief; Capt. Sir Thomas Hardy)	98 guns.
Dreadnought (Capt. Linzee)	98 „
Hannibal (Rear-Admiral, Sir T. Williams)	75 „
Cæsar (Capt. Granger)	84 „
Zealous (Capt. Boys)	74 „
Impetuous (Capt. Lawford)	74 „
Audacious (Capt. Campbel)	74 „
Elizabeth (Capt. Curzon)	74 „
Poictiers (Capt. Beresford)	74 „
Mars (Capt. Katon)	74 „
Tonnant (Capt. Gore)	84 „
Macedonia (Capt. Lord William Fitzroy)	38 „
Saint Fiorenzo (a trooper)	Armed in flute
Melpomene „ „	„ „ „
Mercury „ „	„ „ „

and between three and four hundred transports. The carpenters of the line-of-battle ships are fitting some of them up to carry 6,000 prisoners to England; and amidst this numerous fleet, lying near each other, the *Tonnant* made a signal that she was on fire near the magazine, which alarmed us all in a great degree, as we expected every moment to see her blow up and scatter her burning frame among us. But, thanks to kind Providence, they got it extinguished, and the case was thus: They had been in the habit of acting plays on board her, and the painter being employed in painting some of the screens in the light room (a very wrong place), and in pouring some spirits of turpentine into the paint, and too near the candle, set it on fire.

There has been a great desertion of the German troops from the French army to ours, and 8,000 were shipped off to-day for England. Report says there has been a mutiny among them, and Massena has ordered every fourth man in two German regiments to be shot.

November 20.—The French are obliged to retreat at last; and having taken up a strong hold at Santarem, our armed flotilla, with the seamen and marines that joined the army, have returned to their ships, not being of any further service there. Their only loss was a boat sunk by the enemy's shot, belonging to the *Impétueux*; a midshipman and four seamen are either taken or lost, the others swam to the flotilla and were saved; four men belonging to the *Zealous* are wounded, and one to the *Cæsar* drowned.

One of our men who was with the army told me that one day, in rambling and looking after fruit, he was surprised and made a prisoner by a French picket; when they found he was a sailor they let him go, saying they did not want such as him. Their being short of provisions probably was the cause.

December.—Hardly a night passes in Lisbon without robbery or murder committed. On the 26th, a man supposed to be a captain of a transport was lying in the street dead, with three desperate wounds; but he must have defended himself bravely, as three Portuguese men were lying dead near him.

Lord Wellington, having some apprehension that the enemy might come down on the south side of the Tagus, (and opposite Lisbon), where they might annoy our shipping greatly, a great number of Portuguese people are set to work on these heights to erect batteries, and twenty seamen from each line-of-battle ship are sent to Fort St. Julian, at the entrance of the river, to man it; but in a few weeks these apprehensions ceased and the seamen returned to their ships again, except one of our men whose name was Jerry O'Brien, who was detained to be tried by a court-martial under the following circumstances: He being stationed one night at the gate of the fort as a sentinel, his orders were to let no one enter without giving the parole. An artilleryman, wishing to enter without giving the parole, and forcing his way, was put to death by Jerry by running a bayonet into him. By sentence of the court Jerry was acquitted, as he had only obeyed his orders; but when he returned on board his messmates would not admit him into the mess again, saying he might have secured the man without putting him to death.

January 1, 1811.—Departed this life John Holman, the marine armourer, by a fall only from the forecastle to the main deck. He was a good inoffensive man.

7th.—Report says that we have lost two colonels and five hundred men killed and wounded, in attacking an enemy's battery (and that without success) near to Santarem.

13th.—Lisbon being now out of danger from the enemy, who, it is supposed, will soon be compelled to leave Portugal for want of supplies, the Commander-in-chief has given Sir T. Williams a month's cruise off the Western Islands with a squadron as follows : —

Hannibal (Rear-Admiral Sir T. Williams) . .	74 guns.
Cæsar (Capt. Granger)	80 „
Tonnant (Capt. Sir J. Gore)	80 „
Audacious (Capt. Campbell) . . .	74 „
Macedonian (Capt. Lord William Fitzroy) .	38 „
Zenobia (Capt. Alexander)	18 „

16*th*.—Received orders to get ready for sea, and on the 18th got under way with the squadron, put to sea, and steered away to the westward. We soon left Lisbon behind, where for two months I had enjoyed more leisure than I had ever had before since I came first to sea, and that is more than thirty years since.

February 14.—Saw a ship to windward steering towards us in a very wild manner; when she came within hail, proved to be a homeward-bound English West-Indiaman, having lost her rudder and mizzen topmast. Lord William Fitzroy of the *Macedonia* was ordered to take her in tow and see her safe into Lisbon, and they departed with a fair wind. But when she arrived near the place the wind headed them, and the two ships got foul of each other, and when they got clear his lordship took all the people out of the West-Indiaman and set her on fire, and this valuable ship and cargo were totally destroyed.

We heard afterwards that his lordship had to pay to the underwriters the whole value of the ship and cargo, which served him right. But this was not all, for when the two ships were foul of each other he abused his master and put him in irons, for which he was tried by a court-martial at Lisbon and dismissed the service.

17*th*.—At 10 a.m. saw the Rock of Lisbon, and next

day got a pilot on board, and, being little wind, anchored between St. Julian and Belem.

19th.—Got under way again, but being little wind and such eddies in the tide, neither the *Audacious* nor we could manage our ships, and had to anchor twice to prevent the ships from getting on shore; but in the afternoon a breeze sprang up and carried us up to Lisbon, where we came to anchor and moored ship, being just a month absent and without taking a prize.

20th.—Arrived the *Dannemark* from Portsmouth with troops; a battle is expected between the two armies as soon as the dry weather sets in.

21st.—The master carpenters of the *Dreadnought*, *Impétueux* and *Tonnant*, came on board and held a survey on the defects of the ship; but as their report of survey did not satisfy our captain, he sent a memorial to the Commander-in-chief attested by himself, the first lieutenant, the master and carpenter, stating it to be their opinion that the *Cæsar* was not fit to endure stormy weather at sea.

26th.—When the French under Junot evacuated Lisbon in 1809, a Russian squadron of eight sail of the line was left here; and according to treaty their crews were to be sent to Russia and the ships to England to be restored when peace took place between us and Russia. Seven sail had been sent, but the other not being seaworthy was left here, and in order that her stores might be protected a sergeant's guard from a line-of-battle ship each week took their turns for that purpose. It being the *Zealous's* turn to guard, the sergeant was missing during the week, and it was supposed that he had fallen overboard. A few days after, on board the *Zealous*, a quarrel took place with some of the marines, and from some words that slipped out a suspicion arose that the sergeant had not been lost by accident; a court-martial was the consequence (which lasted two days), and two of the party were found guilty of throwing the sergeant overboard in the night; their sentence was to suffer death, and they were both hung at the yard-arms on board their own ship, and before going off they acknowledged themselves guilty.

March 2. Sent the yawl with her brass 3-pounders manned and armed up the Tagus.

4th.—Arrived the following ships, with troops from England to join Lord Wellington :

Vengeur (Rear-Admiral Sir J. York) . . .	74 guns.
Victory (Capt. Dumaresq)	100 „
Formidable (Capt. Fayerman)	98 „
Orion (Capt. Sir A. C. Dickson) . . .	74 „
Revenge (Capt. Hon. C. Paget)	74 „
Ganges (Capt. Dundas)	74 „
Druid (Capt. Bolton)	32 „
Ethalion (Capt. T. Cochrane)	36 „
Fishguard (Capt. Mason)	36 „

9th.—The squadron under Sir Joseph York sailed again for England.

The French army under Massena (who has these last six months past threatened Lisbon) has at last begun its retreat from Santorem, and is moving toward Spain. To deceive us they left sentinels at their posts as usual, but they were made of straw and covered with regimentals, by which means they got thirty-six hours' start of his lordship; however, he is now pursuing them with all his force, and two days after four thousand of them were taken and brought prisoners to Lisbon, most of them without shoes and in a distressed situation. Yet the enemy conduct their retreat well, and no doubt of it under such a general as Massena; our advanced troops have suffered much for want of provisions, as the enemy destroy all before them. As some of our advance had entered a village they found the skull of a mule clean picked and placed on a dish with a label to it—

"FOR JOHN BULL."

20th.—The *Dreadnought, Hannibal, Tonnant, Mars* and we, are ordered to return to the naval storekeeper a stream cable each, with cordage, canvas, and all the spars that can be spared. This indicates that we shall soon be sent to Old England.

April 2nd.—Returned by order of the Commander-in-chief all the ordnance stores I could spare to the Ordnance department, and, in returning to come on board and coming through Inquisition Square, I soon got amidst thousands of people there. On inquiring of a person near me the cause of such an assembly, he pointed to the left, and on my looking that way, I beheld a criminal whom they were leading to execution.

I fixed my eyes stedfastly on him, and could not help pitying the poor fellow, whose countenance was as pale as death, his eyes fixed on Heaven in mental prayer; and cold must have been the heart that did not pity him. He appeared to be about thirty years of age, tall and with good features; on his head was a white conical cap with the words "Traiture" on it; he walked barefooted, between two monks with several more on each side and in front of him, and a guard of soldiers in the rear.

When the procession arrived in sight of the scaffold they made a stop, then one of the monks held a crucifix to him, which he kissed and hugged to his bosom and prayed fervently for two or three minutes; they then moved on again, and when come to the foot of the scaffold another short prayer was made; he was then led to the top of it, about seven feet high with a platform, and surrounded with friars and monks, and there he made a speech to the audience, which I was sorry I could not understand.

His sentence was to be strangled and burnt to death, so he was placed on a seat with a post behind him, then two of the monks with a rope took two or three turns with it round the culprit's neck and the post; then, putting a stick in between the part of the rope, twisted it round to strangle him; but the rope broke, which caused him to recover a little and struggle much: however, they soon got another and finished the poor fellow's existence; the priests at the time were sprinkling holy water about the place.

His face was then covered for about a quarter of an hour; and finding his heart had ceased to beat, they took away the rope and laid his body down at full length on the scaffold; underneath were a number of faggots, which they set fire to, which soon burnt him to ashes, and these were gathered up and thrown into the river.

Every one seemed much affected, except some of the monks, who treated the poor fellow with the greatest contempt. Just before being strangled, he entreated one of them most piteously for some favour, perhaps absolution, but the monk or priest turned his back on him with the greatest disdain, and shaking his hands behind him seemed to say you may go to the devil for anything I care for you.

The cause of the execution was this: the culprit (whose name was Masquerana, a Portuguese) had been aide-de-camp to the French General Junot; he was detected as a spy, being dressed like a Spanish peasant, and papers from Massena to Bonaparte were found concealed about his body, which proved him to be a traitor. It is said he is the son of a judge who was sent away with the conspirators in September last; his mother is still residing in Lisbon, and the whole family are attached to the French interest.

April 6.—Our captain has received orders to prepare to convoy a number of ships to England.

12th.—Having got all ready for sea at ten this morning, we got under way and bade a final adieu to Lisbon, having the *Cyene* (20-gun ship) and eighty-two transports and merchantmen with us; a Captain Morris, his lady, and several army officers on board, as passengers to England. At midnight a marine was found in the ship's head quite dead; it was supposed he had fallen and struck his temple against something.

17th.—A heavy gale came on from the W.S.W. with rain; down topgallant yards and struck the masts, close-reefed the topsails. At 4 p.m. a heavy squall split the foresail to pieces; bent another, then hove the ship to under close-reefed main topsail and storm staysails; fired several guns for the convoy to close nearer.

20th.—The wind fair but strong, the ship scudding under close-reefed maintopsail and foresail. Saw a strange sail to the eastward that looked large; demanded her number, which she answered with the number of the *Aigle* frigate, then wore round with her head the other way. We then made the private signs to her, to which she answered wrong, and steered more away from us with an English ensign at her peak; yet, strange to say, although she appeared so suspicious, our captain would not follow her. He said she was an English East-Indiaman, but how did he know that?

21st.—Saw the Eddystone lighthouse, and made the signal to the *Cyene* to proceed with the convoy up Channel, and soon after we came to anchor in Cawsand Bay after an absence of fourteen months.

Here we lay during a week, and in that time visited Maker Church and tower, from which is the finest view imaginable of Plymouth Sound, the adjacent country, and the ocean. Here are interred the Edgecumbe family and many other worthies; and, after reading several pathetic and fine inscriptions on the monuments, we returned on board much more satisfied than those who, as soon as they get their foot on shore, steer for a public-house or inn and there remain until they have to return on board.

28*th*. Received orders for the ship to go to Hamoaze; so we sent all the gunpowder to the magazine, got the ship under way and ran her up the river to Hamoaze, where we lashed her alongside of the *Captain*, a receiving-ship. Afterwards got the guns out, stripped the ship of her rigging, sent all the stores on shore and prepared her for docking.

A survey was held on her by the dockyard officers, the report being sent to the Admiralty; and on May 9th an order came down to pay her off and lay her up into a state of ordinary, being six years this very day since she was commissioned, and a persevering time it had been: few ships, I imagine, ever encountered more vicissitudes for the time. We are now no more (thanks be to God) summoned on deck with the cry of "All hands, hoy!" no more does the noise of the drum to quarters announce that an enemy is near, and no more is it "Down chests and up hammocks" to clear away for quarters.

The *Cæsar* never went to sea after this, being completely worn out; of our brave crew fifty able and a hundred ordinary seamen were sent to Spithead to join the *Christian the Seventh*, several others to the *Caledonia*, the rest to the *Salvador* guard-ship here, and the marines to the barracks; she was soon after taken to her moorings near Tor Point, and now we had some leisure to recover and look around us.

In order to amuse myself I bought some elm board, and built myself a little boat about eleven feet long, and rigged her with a mast and sails. Many pleasant excursions I had in her, sometimes fishing in Plymouth Sound and taking a view of the breakwater which they began to build at this time; several times my friend

Mr. Jelly, of Plymouth Dock, and I went up the Tamar in her, and on one occasion visited Tavistock, as he had a daughter at a boarding-school there; at another time visited Cotehele to see a tree thirty-two feet in circumference. At another time there, when the little boat was left alongside a barge at the quay, a countryman came down and went on board the barge to have a look at her; seeing the little boat alongside and knowing no better (thinking I suppose she would bear his weight as well as the lighter), he stepped in, and upset her; fortunately the lightermen were there and caught him up, or otherwise he must assuredly have been drowned.

In October 1813 the *Cæsar* was fitted up for a military store ship for the convenience of receiving transports alongside to take in the military stores for the use of our army in Spain. Mr. Stracey was storekeeper, and resided with his family on board, and we (the three warrant officers) were allowed half a guinea a week each, and the cook 5s. 3d., in order to assist in preserving the stores from embezzlement, and to have the ports and gratings well attended to, to open or shut according to the weather.

We continued very comfortable for five months while Mr. Stracey was on board; but he, being recalled to London to hold a better situation, was succeeded by a half-pay commander in the navy named Price. He soon began to show his quarterdeck airs, and stopped our money, saying it might as well be saved for Government; but he himself did not offer one farthing out of his large emoluments for that purpose. However, he did not enjoy his situation long, for soon after peace took place the *Cæsar* was cleared of all the stores, the establishment at New Passage broken up, and so was the old *Cæsar* broken up soon afterwards.

I had been for some time endeavouring to get a

change to Portsmouth; I now met with an offer from Mr. Walker, gunner of the *Bedford*, and the exchange was soon granted by the Admiralty. So I left the *Cæsar*, after belonging to her ten years and three months. This was on July 27th, 1815; and in passing through the Sound on board a Portsmouth sloop we went close past the stern of the *Bellerophon*, she having Bonaparte a prisoner on board; several French officers were on her poop, but whether Bonaparte was among them or not we could not tell.

We arrived on the 29th at Portsmouth, and I joined the *Bedford*, lying in a state of ordinary in Porchester Lake; and soon after I had the pleasure of saving the life of Mr. Griffiths, boatswain of the *Veteran*. He had been in the ship's boat to the dockyard with only a boy with him; on his return, it then blowing very strong from the westward and a strong tide setting out of the lake, he got foul of the quess warp boom and was thrown overboard. The weather being rainy, no one was on deck to see him, nor did they hear the boy's cries, as the wind was high; but we in our wardroom heard him, and I went on deck not knowing the boatswain was overboard. However, I soon saw him splashing in the water, for he could not swim; and jumped into my little boat, which I had brought from Plymouth with me, and rowed after him with all my might, and caught hold of him just as he was going down; although he had on a great Flushing coat soaked through, as well as his other clothes, I got him dragged into my little boat quite insensible, where he lay like a dead man until his own ship's boat met us and took him in.

In 1817 the *Bedford* was broken up, and I became a supernumerary for six months, and then was appointed to the *Pitt*, a new 74-gun ship at this place, and remained with her until March 1819, at which time so many ships had been broken up, and others sold out of the service, that almost each ship that remained had a double set of warrant officers on board. The Admiralty, therefore, thought proper to make a reduction by superannuation, and being all examined at Haslar Hospital, upwards of a hundred were put down for superannuation, and I among the rest.

As I had not expected this, I could hardly believe it true that I should have my liberty so soon again. I could hardly describe my agreeable feelings, and thought sometimes it was only a dream; but, thanks be to God, it was true, and I hope I shall ever be thankful for such mercies in being delivered from so many dangers and hardships, and hope to pass, please God, the remainder of my days in comfort and peace.

Indeed I had no cause to regret being superannuated, as I considered myself much neglected in promotion, after being so often recommended by my superiors. My name had been more than twelve years on the Admiralty list for promotion. Sir Richard Strachan had written personally to the Admiralty for a warrant to appoint me to a new three-decker building at Plymouth; but another person got her through Parliamentary interest, and one who had seen little sea service during the war. I had followed the sea service up to this time near thirty-nine years in the King's and merchant service, as follows :—

In the Merchant Service from 1780 to 1793 . .	13 years
King's Service, A.B. and Petty Officer . .	2½ ,,
As Gunner	23½ ,,
	39 years

Sea time as Gunner	15 years
Ordinary do.	8½ ,,
	23½ ,,

According to the scale of superannuation, which jumps every five years, this entitled me to £65 per annum, and for which I am satisfied; had I remained twenty-five years I should have got £75. However, thank God, I am contented, and would not change for a commission in the Navy.

Lord of my life, whose gracious power
  Through various scenes my life has led,
And turned aside the fatal hour,
  And lifted up my drooping head,—

Oft has the sea confessed Thy power,
  And brought me back at Thy command,
It could not, Lord, my life devour,
  While in the hollow of Thy hand.

Through all my ways Thy hand I own,
  Thy ruling Providence I see;
Assist me still my course to run,
  And cause me live to come to Thee.

Then will I there fresh anthems raise,
  To Thee, my God and only joy,
And hymns of praise with Love and Grace
  Shall all my future life employ.

I forgot to mention the many excursions I had in my little boat after I was superannuated. She was quite my hobby-horse. I went once to Southampton in her, twice to Netley Abbey, once to Newport in the Isle of Wight, and once to Wootton Bridge; several times to Ryde and other ports adjacent; twice to Fareham and Porchester; and one time I started from Common Hard, sailed past Southsea Castle, then into Langstone Harbour; then struck my mast and went under Post Bridge; then set sail again and touched at Horsey Island, passed Porchester and Tipner, and then arrived at Common Hard again, thus making the compass of Portsea Island in four hours, which island is seventeen miles in circumference. At last, in 1825, having no place convenient for leaving her in the night-time, I broke her up, after having her fourteen years. Several of my acquaintances said that she would some day prove my coffin, but they were quite mistaken.

And now, my good friends, I hope you are satisfied, and thus ends the history of this wandering sailor.

ADIEU

INDEX

THE LIFE AND VOYAGES OF JOSEPH
WIGGINS, F.R.G.S. Modern Discoverer of the Kara Sea
Route to Siberia, based on his Journals and Letters. By
HENRY JOHNSON. With Map and Illustrations. Demy
8vo. 15s. net.

CAPTAIN JAMES COOK, R.N., F.R.S.,
"The Circumnavigator." By ARTHUR KITSON. With Maps
and Illustrations. Demy 8vo. 15s. net.

THE THREE DORSET CAPTAINS AT TRAFALGAR.
THE LIFE AND LETTERS OF THOMAS
MASTERMAN HARDY, with some Account of his
Comrades, CHARLES BULLEN and HENRY DIGBY.
By A. M. BROADLEY and R. G. BARTELOT, M.A. With
Portraits and other Illustrations. Demy 8vo. 15s. net.

OUR NAVAL HEROES. A Series of Bio-
graphies. By various Writers. Edited by G. E. MARINDIN.
With a Preface by Lord CHARLES BERESFORD. With
Portraits. Cheap Edition. Demy 8vo. 5s. net.

A CENTURY OF OUR SEA STORY. By
WALTER JEFFERY. With Illustrations. Crown 8vo. 6s.

THE NAVAL PIONEERS OF AUSTRALIA.
By LOUIS BECKE and WALTER JEFFERY. With Portraits
and Illustrations. Large Crown 8vo. 7s. 6d.

AT SCHOOL AND AT SEA. Sketches of
Life and Character at Harrow in the Forties and sub-
sequently in the Royal Navy. With Experiences and Adventures on the Australian Station, in the South Seas, in
the Black Sea, in the Trenches at Sebastopol, etc., etc. By
"MARTELLO TOWER," a Naval Officer. With Illustrations.
8vo. 16s.

THE VOYAGE OF THE "FOX" IN THE
ARCTIC SEAS IN SEARCH OF FRANKLIN AND
HIS COMPANIONS. By the late Admiral Sir F. LEOPOLD
M'CLINTOCK, R.N. With Portraits and other Illustrations
and Maps. Large Crown 8vo. 2s. 6d. net.

ROUND THE HORN BEFORE THE MAST.

By A. BASIL LUBBOCK. With Illustrations. Large Crown 8vo. 2s. 6d. net.

"Mr. Basil Lubbock has written a book that Clark Russell could hardly have given us in his palmiest days. . . . Not the least remarkable feature of this fascinating 'yarn' is its obvious truthfulness. Who takes up Mr. Lubbock's tale of the sea, and puts it down before finishing it, must be a dull individual."—*Sunday Special.*

THE ROB ROY ON THE JORDAN.

A Canoe Cruise in Palestine, Egypt, and the Waters of Damascus. By JOHN MACGREGOR, M.A., Captain of the Royal Canoe Club. With Maps and Illustrations. Large Crown 8vo. 2s. 6d. net.

"In a handsome form and at a very cheap price Mr. Murray has issued a new edition of Macgregor's 'The Rob Roy on the Jordan.' . . . Mr. Murray is doing good service in issuing such editions."—*Liverpool Courier.*

ROUND ABOUT THE NORTH POLE.

By W. J. GORDON. With Maps and many Woodcuts and other Illustrations by EDWARD WHYMPER. Medium 8vo. 15s. net.

FROM LIBAU TO TSUSHIMA.

A Narrative of the Voyage of Admiral Rojdestvensky's Squadron to the East, including a detailed Account of the Dogger Bank Incident. By the late EUGENE POLITOVSKY, Chief Engineer of the Squadron. Translated by Major F. R. GODFREY, R.M.L.I. Crown 8vo. 6s.

BEFORE PORT ARTHUR IN A DESTROYER.

The Personal Diary of a Japanese Naval Officer. Translated from the Spanish Edition by Captain R. Grant, D.S.O., Rifle Brigade. With Maps and Illustrations. Cheap Edition. Square 8vo. 3s. 6d. net.

WITH THE BORDER RUFFIANS.

Memories of the Far West, 1852—1868. By R. H. WILLIAMS. Edited by E. W. WILLIAMS. With Illustrations. Demy 8vo. 12s. net.

A SOLDIER OF THE LEGION.

An Englishman's Adventures under the French Flag in Algeria and Tonquin. By GEORGE MANINGTON. Edited by WILLIAM B. SLATER and ARTHUR J. SARL. With Maps and Illustrations. Demy 8vo. 10s. 6d. net.

LONDON: JOHN MURRAY, ALBEMARLE STREET

www.ingramcontent.com/pod-product-compliance
Lightning Source LLC
Chambersburg PA
CBHW062034090426

42740CB00016B/2904